PLAY LIKE A
GIRL

A graphic memoir

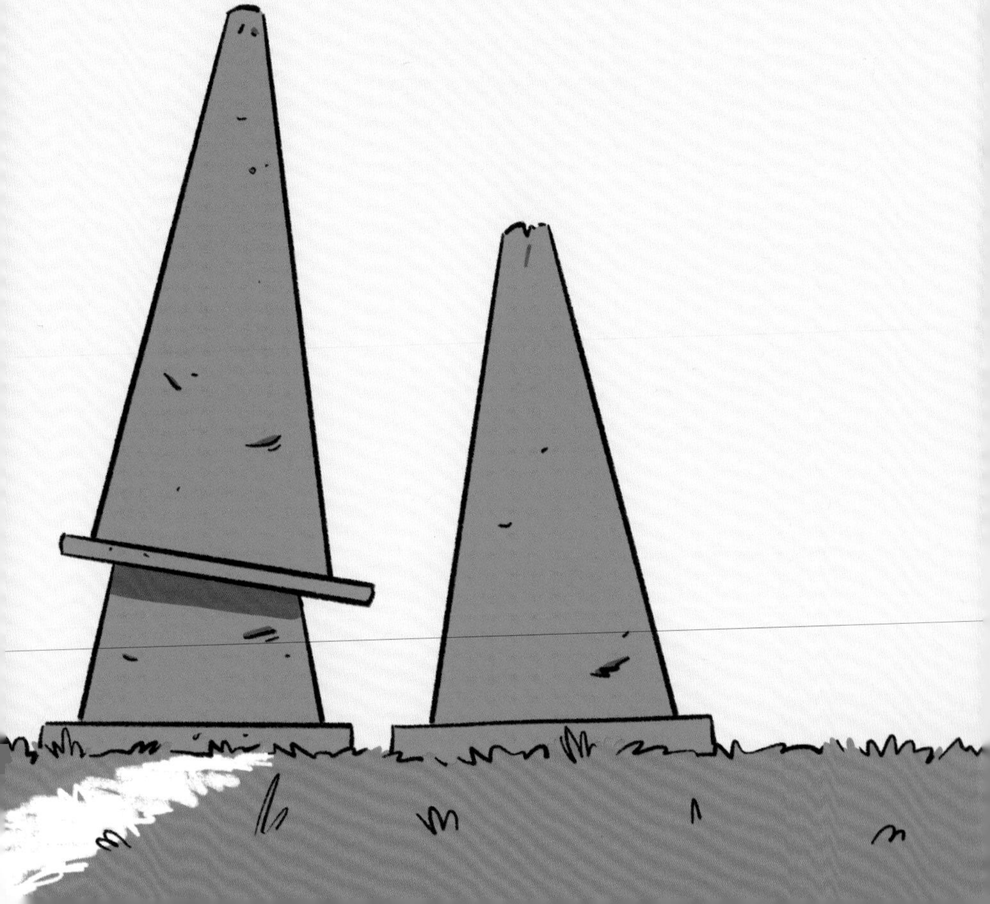

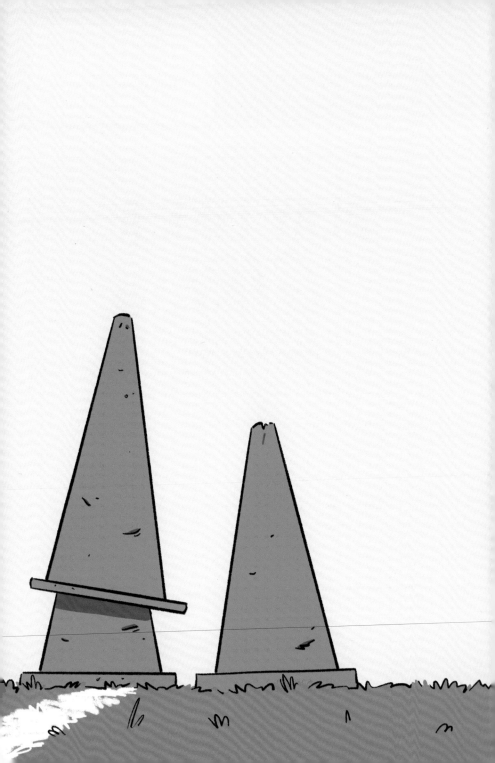

MISTY WILSON

PLAY LIKE A
GIRL

A graphic memoir

ILLUSTRATED BY
DAVID WILSON

BALZER + BRAY
IMPRINTS OF HARPERCOLLINS PUBLISHERS

HARPER
alley

Balzer + Bray is an imprint of HarperCollins Publishers.

HarperAlley is an imprint of HarperCollins Publishers.

Play Like a Girl

Text copyright © 2022 by Misty Wilson

Illustrations copyright © 2022 by David Wilson

Library of Congress Control Number: 2022931778

ISBN 978-0-06-306469-0 (trade bdg.) — ISBN 978-0-06-306468-3 (pbk.)

Typography by David Wilson and Dana Fritts

22 23 24 25 26 RTLO 10 9 8 7 6 5 4 3 2 1

❖

First Edition

FOR ANYONE STRUGGLING TO
FIND THEIR PLACE.
BE UNAPOLOGETICALLY YOU.

CHAPTER 1

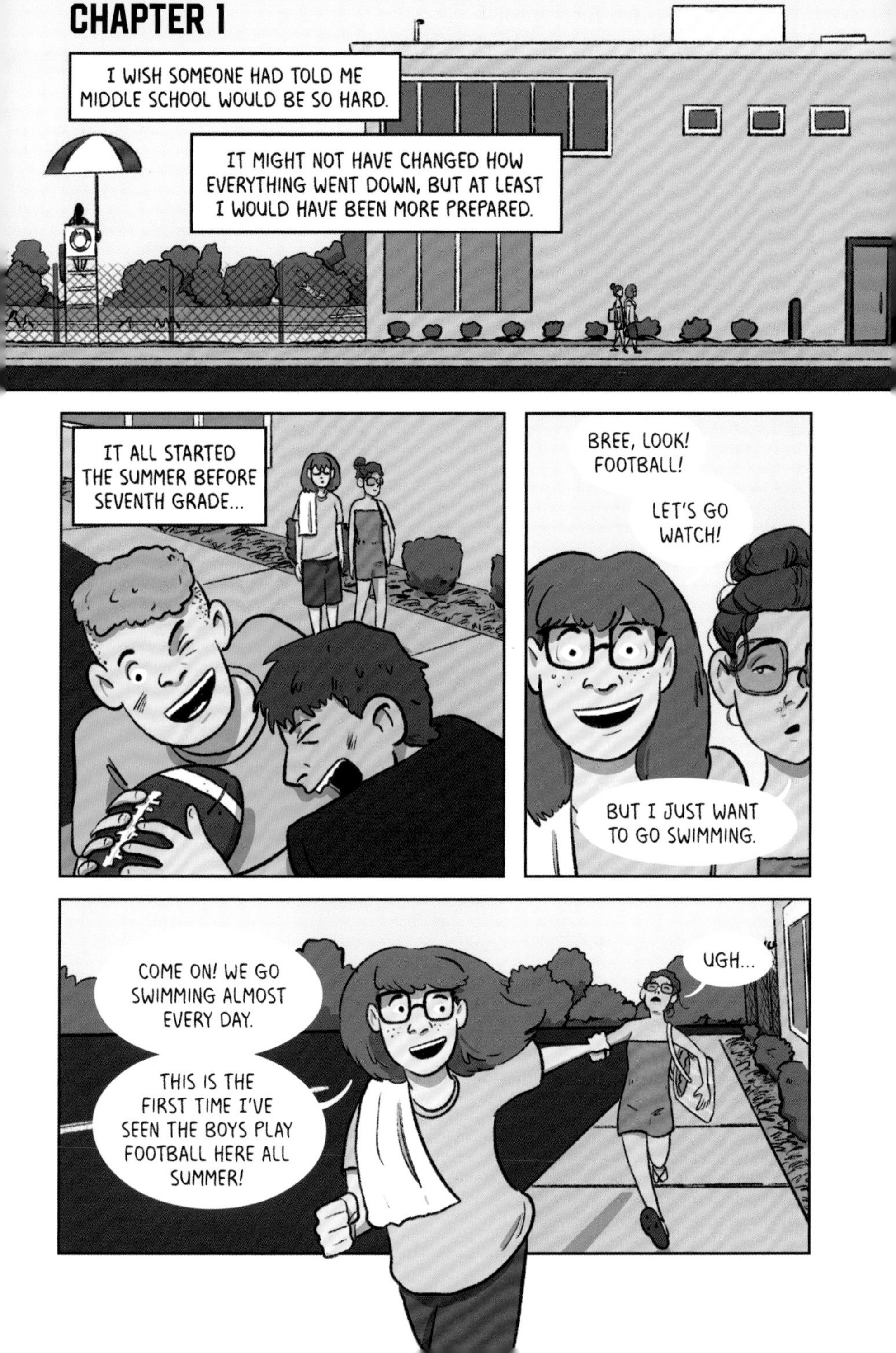
I WISH SOMEONE HAD TOLD ME MIDDLE SCHOOL WOULD BE SO HARD.
IT MIGHT NOT HAVE CHANGED HOW EVERYTHING WENT DOWN, BUT AT LEAST I WOULD HAVE BEEN MORE PREPARED.
IT ALL STARTED THE SUMMER BEFORE SEVENTH GRADE...
BREE, LOOK! FOOTBALL!
LET'S GO WATCH!
BUT I JUST WANT TO GO SWIMMING.
COME ON! WE GO SWIMMING ALMOST EVERY DAY.
THIS IS THE FIRST TIME I'VE SEEN THE BOYS PLAY FOOTBALL HERE ALL SUMMER!
UGH...

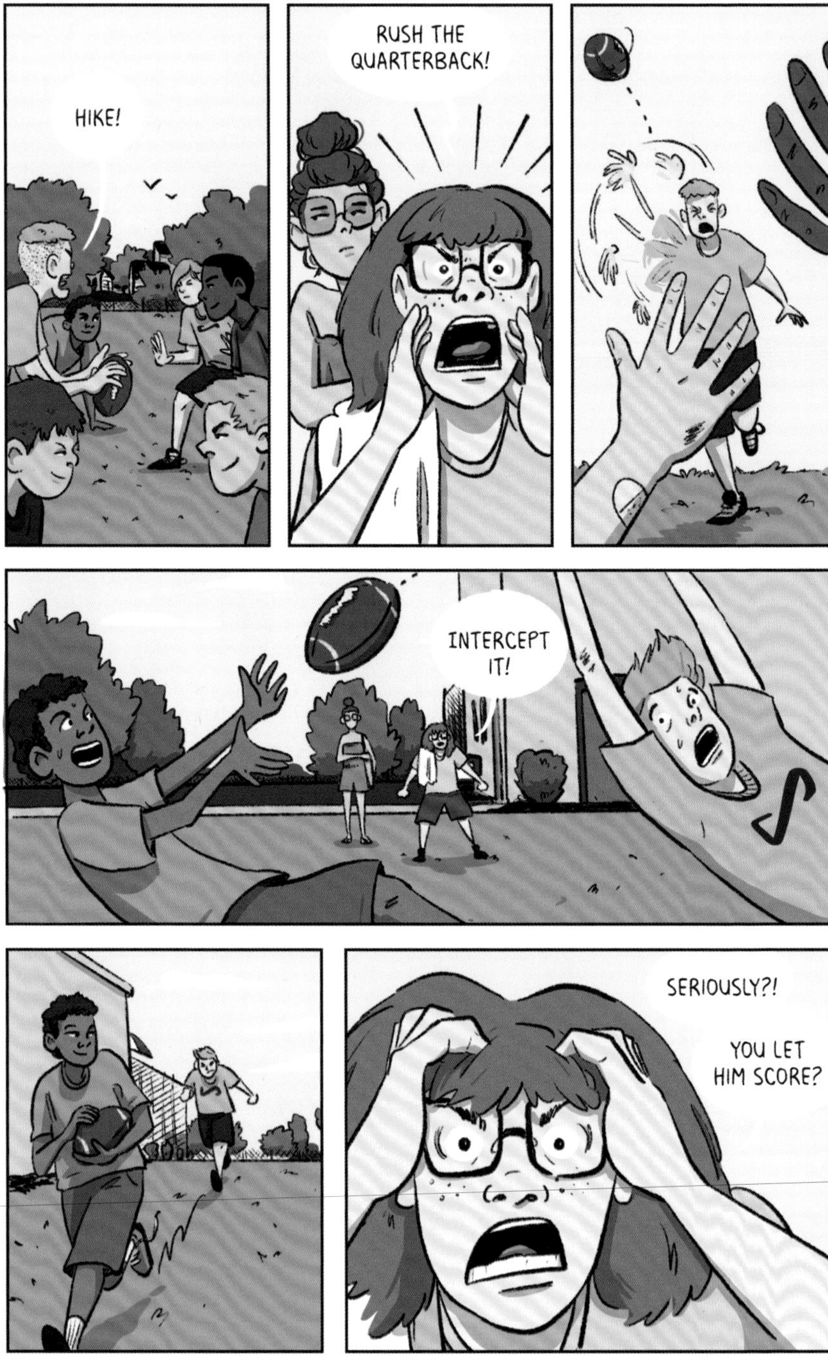
HIKE!
RUSH THE QUARTERBACK!
INTERCEPT IT!
SERIOUSLY?!
YOU LET HIM SCORE?

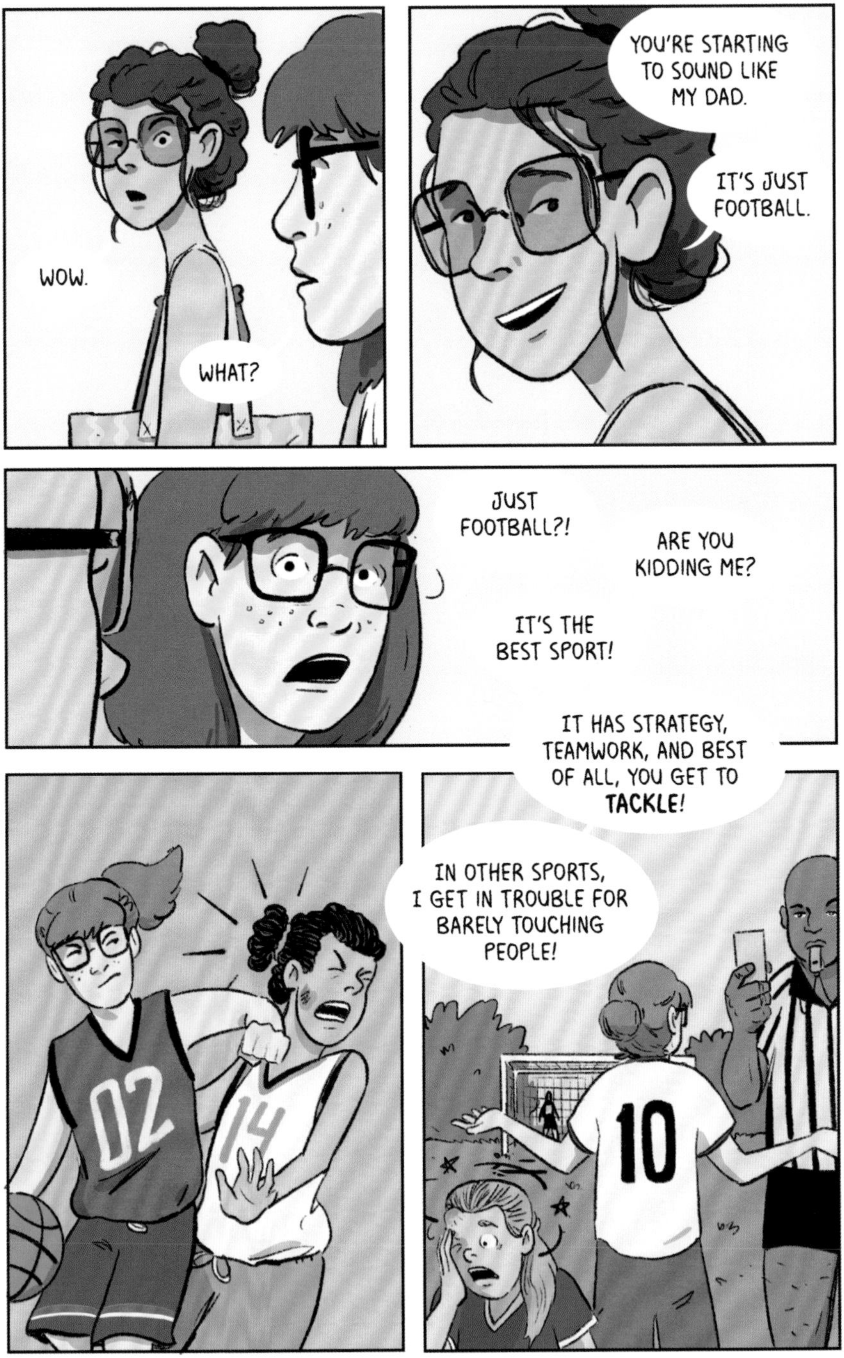
WOW.
WHAT?
YOU'RE STARTING TO SOUND LIKE MY DAD.
IT'S JUST FOOTBALL.
JUST FOOTBALL?!
ARE YOU KIDDING ME?
IT'S THE BEST SPORT!
IT HAS STRATEGY, TEAMWORK, AND BEST OF ALL, YOU GET TO **TACKLE**!
IN OTHER SPORTS, I GET IN TROUBLE FOR BARELY TOUCHING PEOPLE!
02
14
10

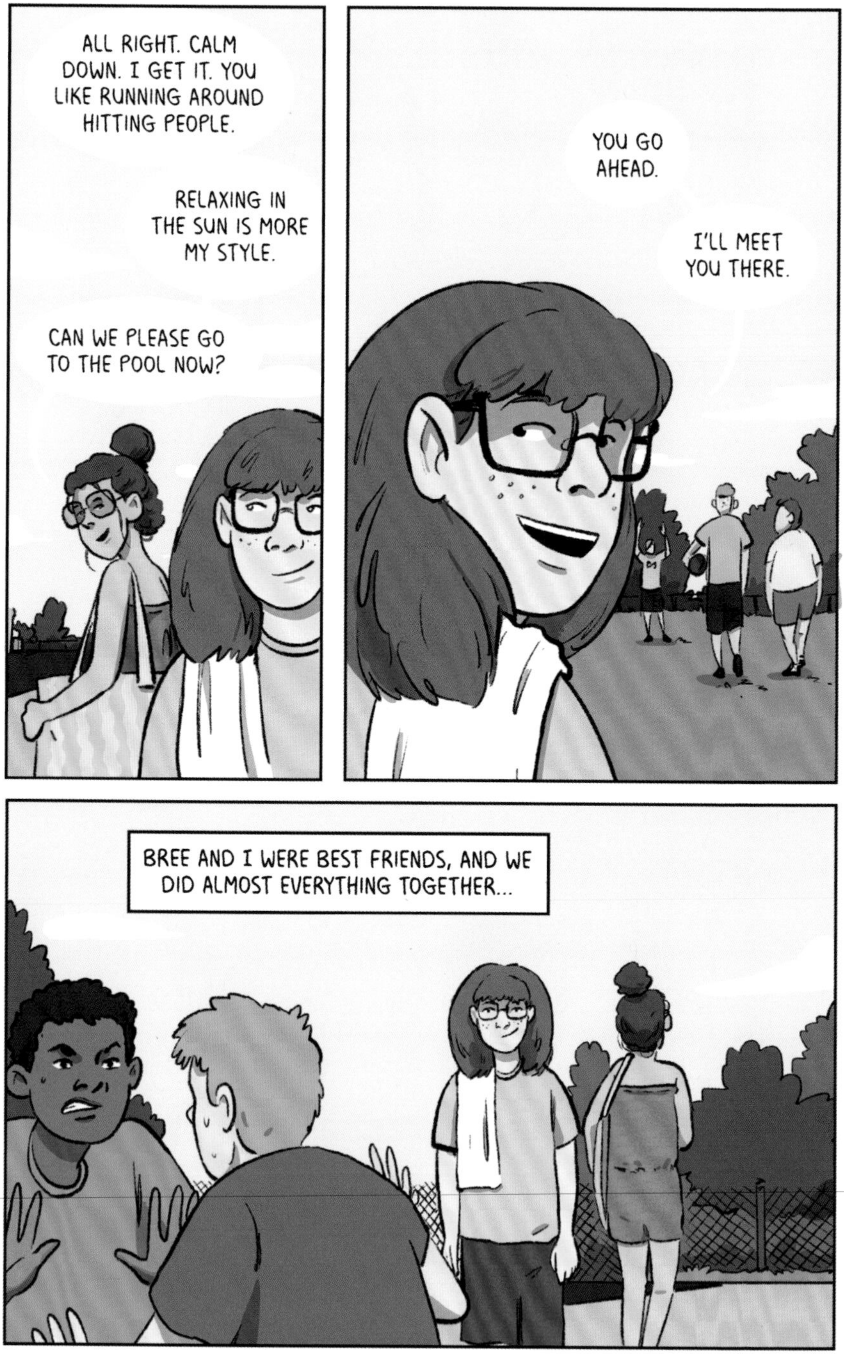
ALL RIGHT. CALM DOWN. I GET IT. YOU LIKE RUNNING AROUND HITTING PEOPLE.
RELAXING IN THE SUN IS MORE MY STYLE.
CAN WE PLEASE GO TO THE POOL NOW?
YOU GO AHEAD.
I'LL MEET YOU THERE.
BREE AND I WERE BEST FRIENDS, AND WE DID ALMOST EVERYTHING TOGETHER...

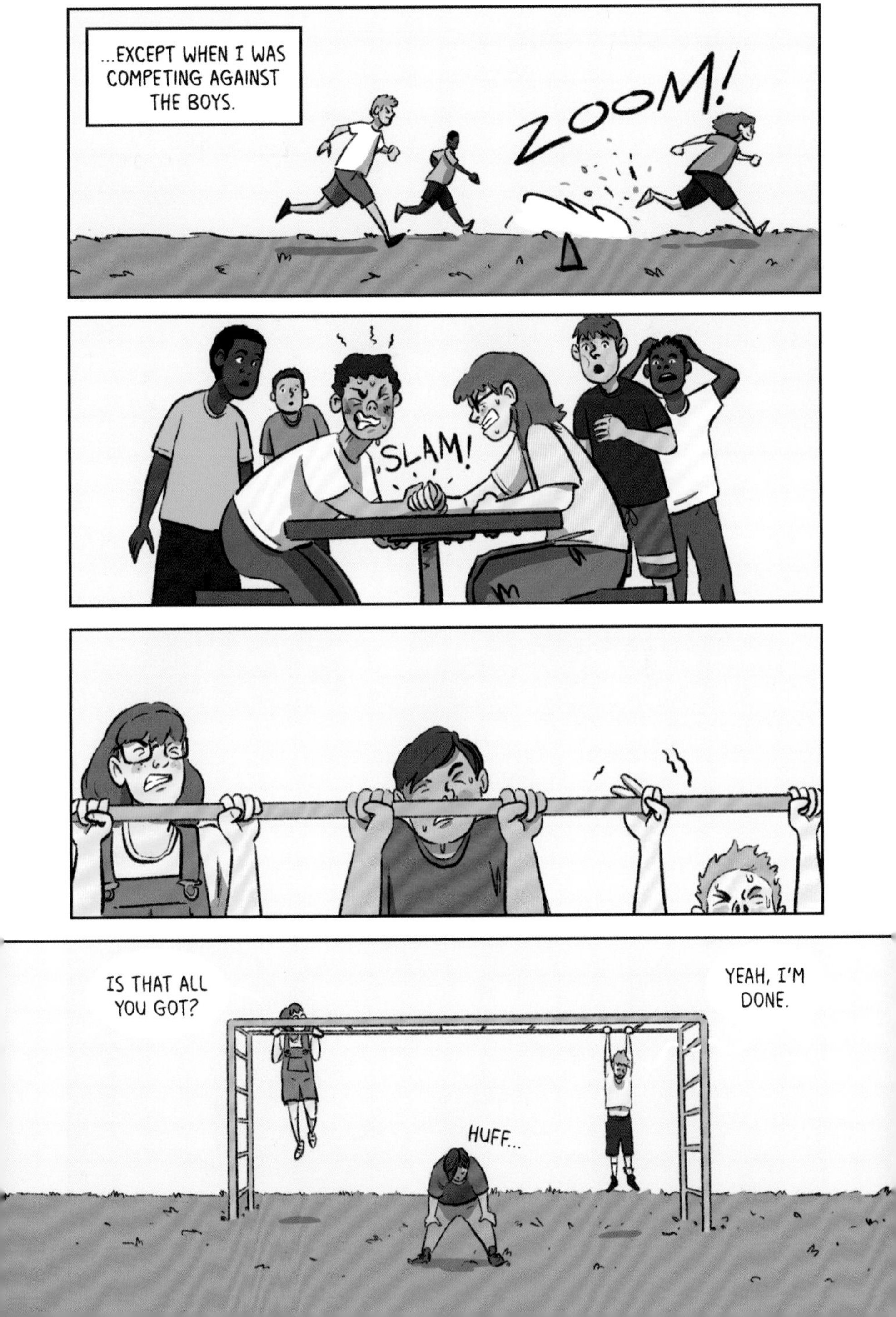
...EXCEPT WHEN I WAS COMPETING AGAINST THE BOYS.
ZOOM!
SLAM!
IS THAT ALL YOU GOT?
YEAH, I'M DONE.
HUFF...

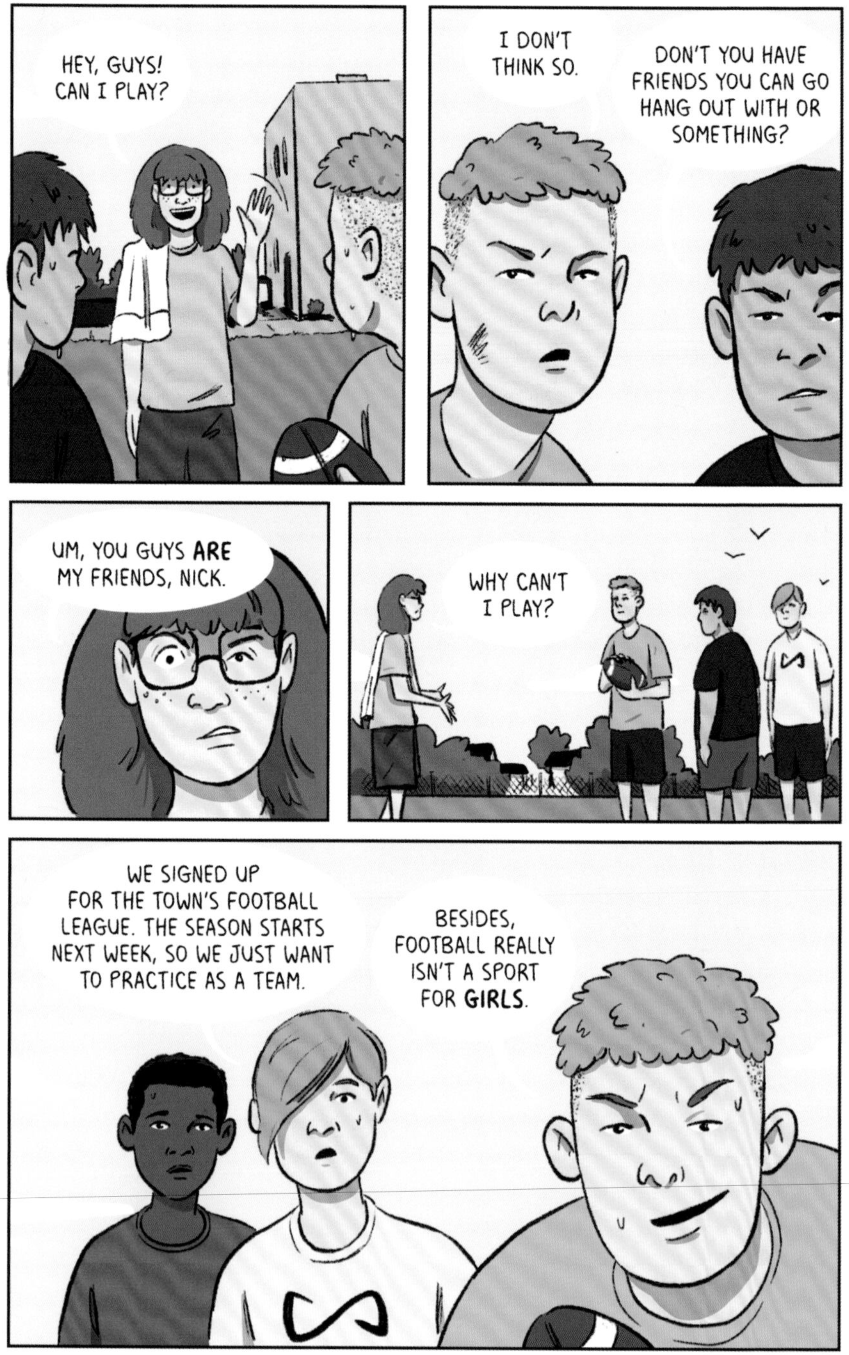
HEY, GUYS!
CAN I PLAY?
I DON'T THINK SO.
DON'T YOU HAVE FRIENDS YOU CAN GO HANG OUT WITH OR SOMETHING?
UM, YOU GUYS **ARE** MY FRIENDS, NICK.
WHY CAN'T I PLAY?
WE SIGNED UP FOR THE TOWN'S FOOTBALL LEAGUE. THE SEASON STARTS NEXT WEEK, SO WE JUST WANT TO PRACTICE AS A TEAM.
BESIDES, FOOTBALL REALLY ISN'T A SPORT FOR **GIRLS**.

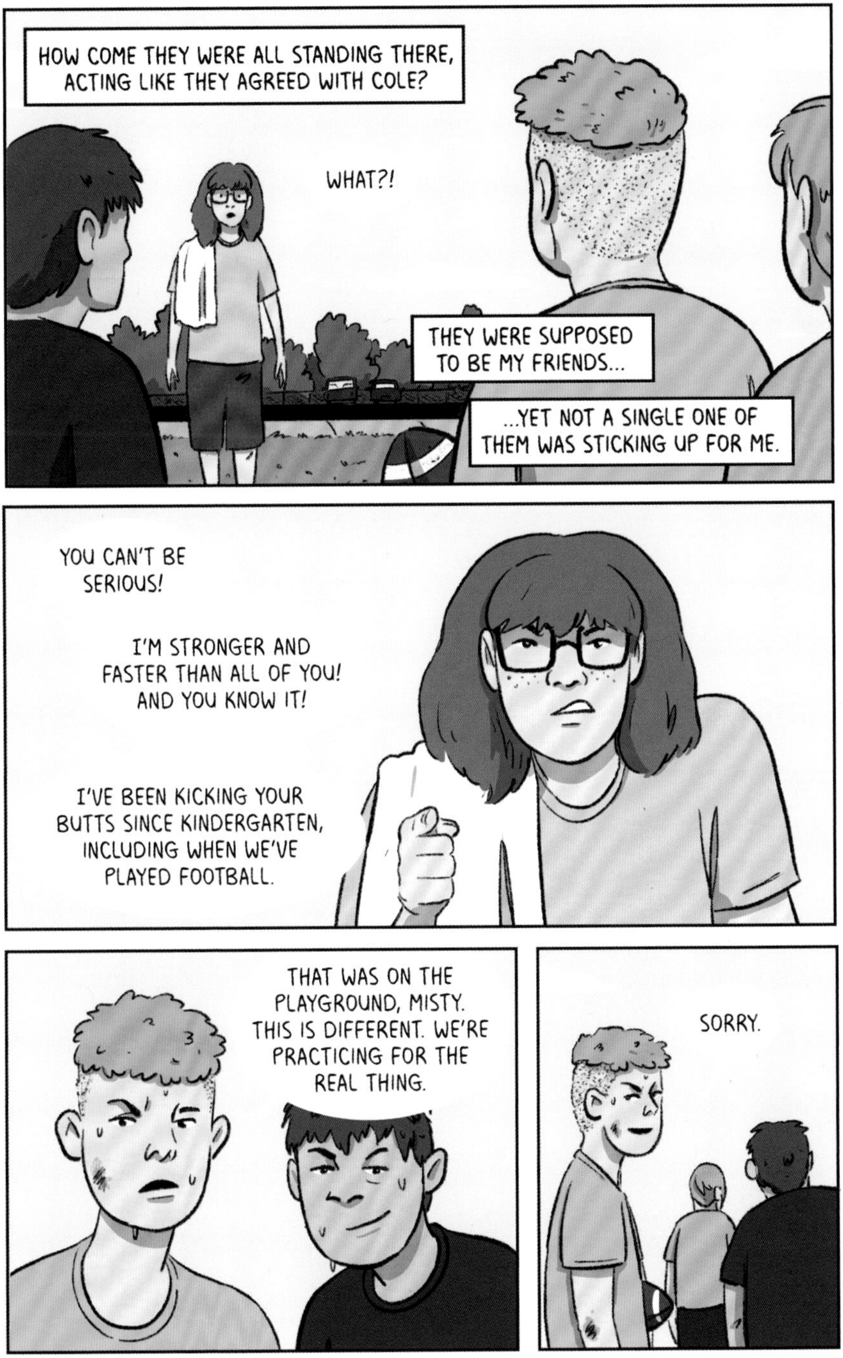
HOW COME THEY WERE ALL STANDING THERE, ACTING LIKE THEY AGREED WITH COLE?
WHAT?!
THEY WERE SUPPOSED TO BE MY FRIENDS...
...YET NOT A SINGLE ONE OF THEM WAS STICKING UP FOR ME.
YOU CAN'T BE SERIOUS!
I'M STRONGER AND FASTER THAN ALL OF YOU! AND YOU KNOW IT!
I'VE BEEN KICKING YOUR BUTTS SINCE KINDERGARTEN, INCLUDING WHEN WE'VE PLAYED FOOTBALL.
THAT WAS ON THE PLAYGROUND, MISTY. THIS IS DIFFERENT. WE'RE PRACTICING FOR THE REAL THING.
SORRY.

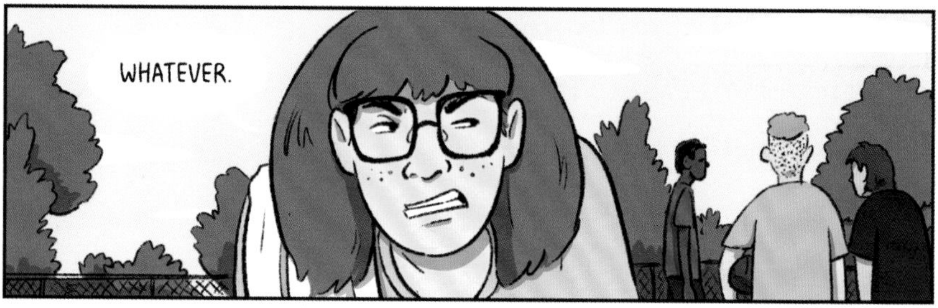
WHATEVER.

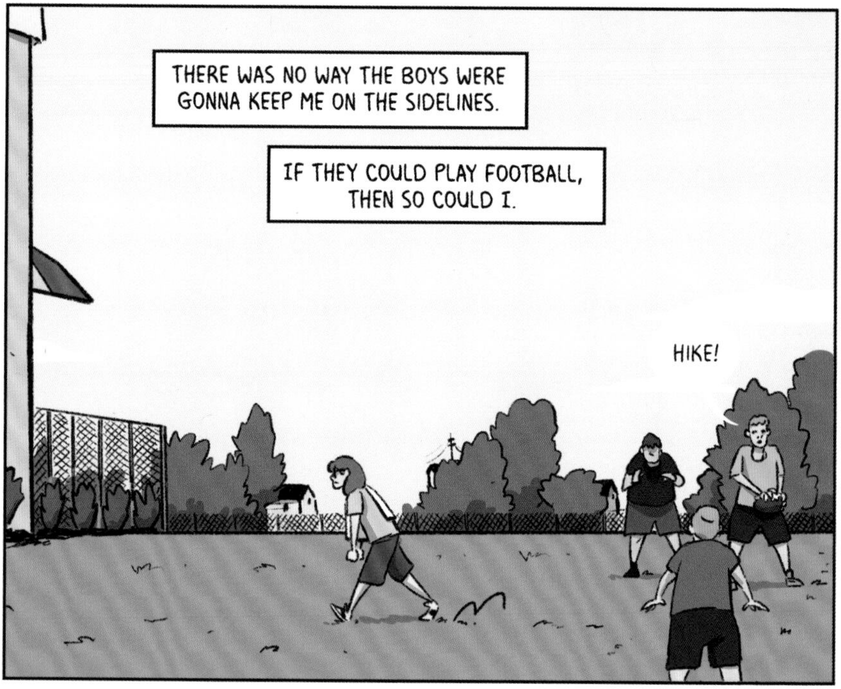
THERE WAS NO WAY THE BOYS WERE GONNA KEEP ME ON THE SIDELINES.
IF THEY COULD PLAY FOOTBALL, THEN SO COULD I.
HIKE!

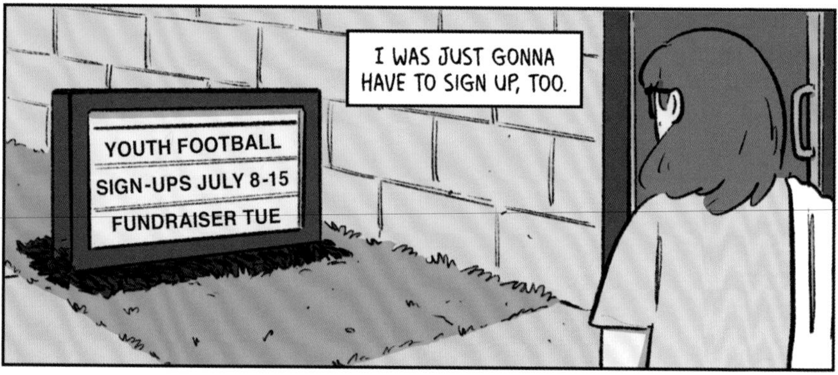
YOUTH FOOTBALL
SIGN-UPS JULY 8-15
FUNDRAISER TUE
I WAS JUST GONNA HAVE TO SIGN UP, TOO.

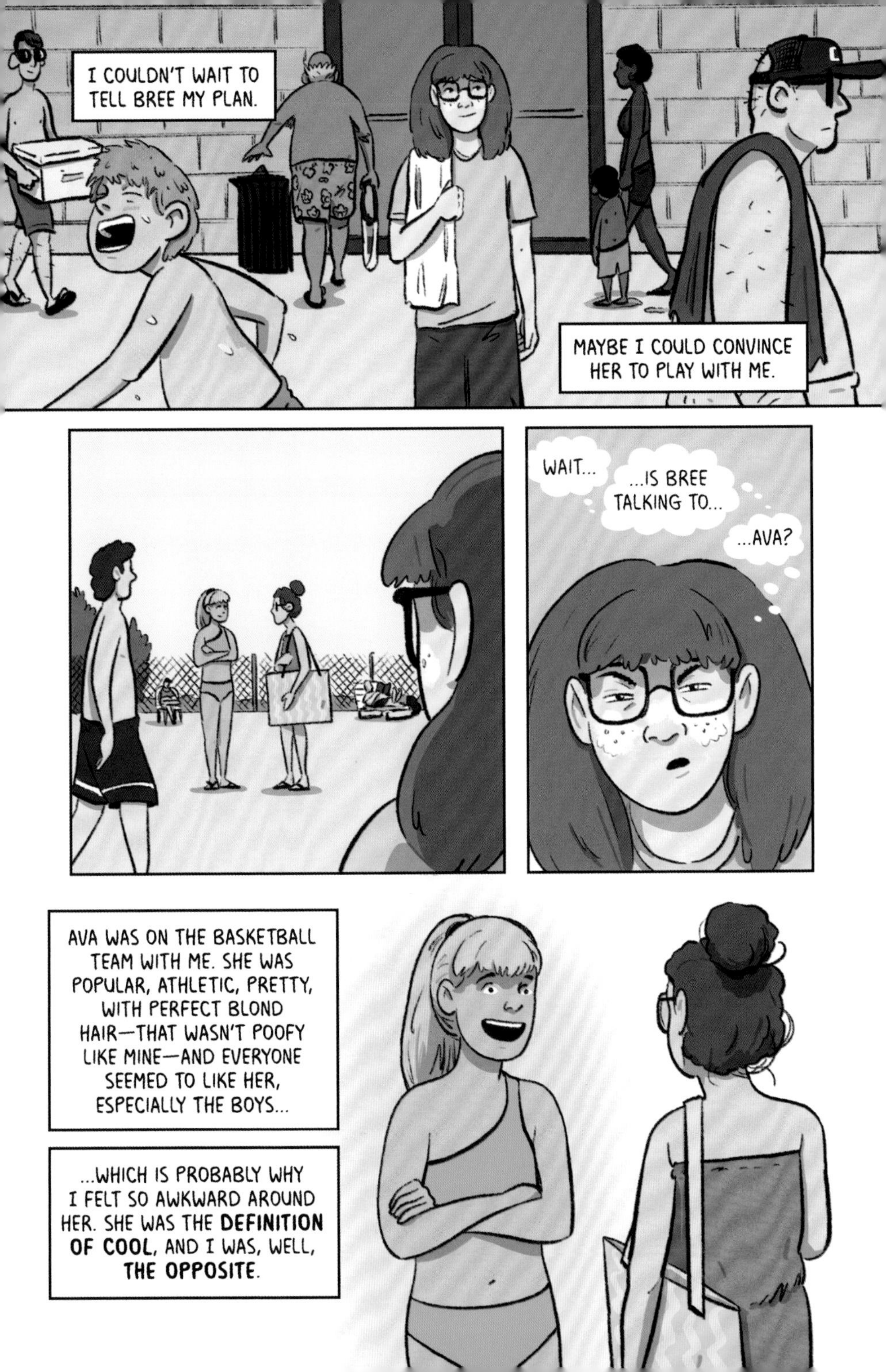
I COULDN'T WAIT TO TELL BREE MY PLAN.
MAYBE I COULD CONVINCE HER TO PLAY WITH ME.
WAIT...
...IS BREE TALKING TO...
...AVA?
AVA WAS ON THE BASKETBALL TEAM WITH ME. SHE WAS POPULAR, ATHLETIC, PRETTY, WITH PERFECT BLOND HAIR—THAT WASN'T POOFY LIKE MINE—AND EVERYONE SEEMED TO LIKE HER, ESPECIALLY THE BOYS...
...WHICH IS PROBABLY WHY I FELT SO AWKWARD AROUND HER. SHE WAS THE **DEFINITION OF COOL**, AND I WAS, WELL, **THE OPPOSITE**.

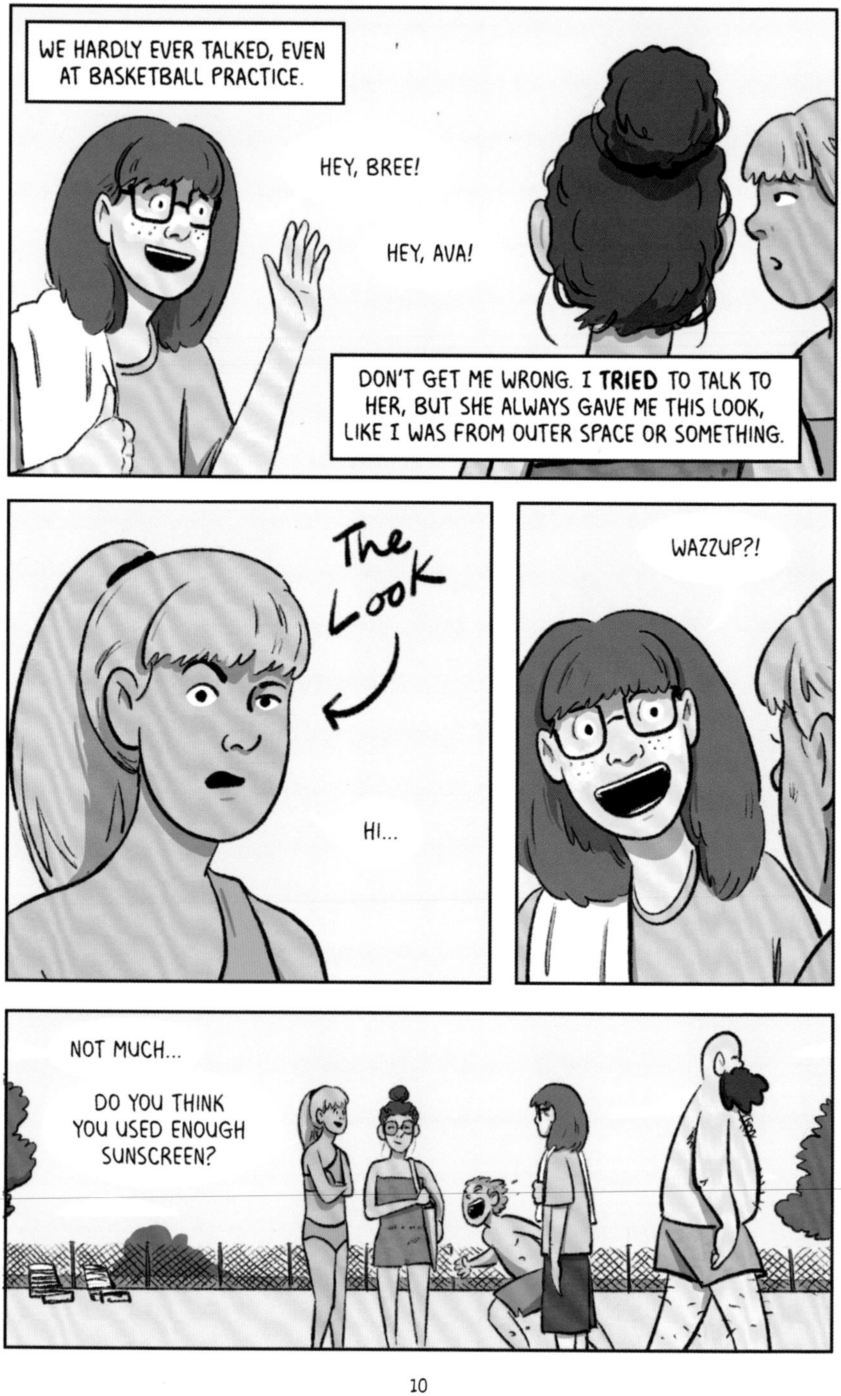
WE HARDLY EVER TALKED, EVEN AT BASKETBALL PRACTICE.
HEY, BREE!
HEY, AVA!
DON'T GET ME WRONG. I **TRIED** TO TALK TO HER, BUT SHE ALWAYS GAVE ME THIS LOOK, LIKE I WAS FROM OUTER SPACE OR SOMETHING.
The Look
HI...
WAZZUP?!
NOT MUCH...
DO YOU THINK YOU USED ENOUGH SUNSCREEN?

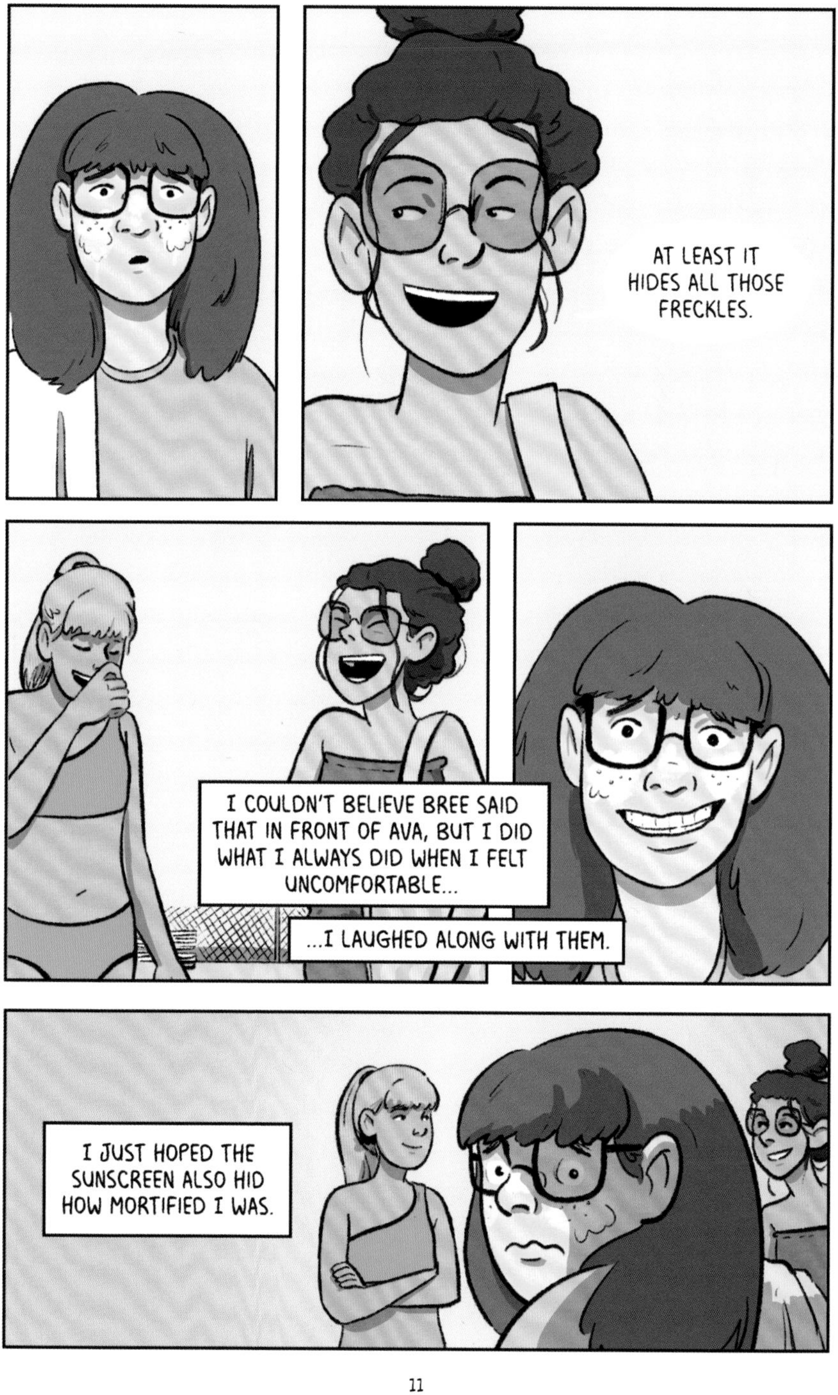
AT LEAST IT HIDES ALL THOSE FRECKLES.
I COULDN'T BELIEVE BREE SAID THAT IN FRONT OF AVA, BUT I DID WHAT I ALWAYS DID WHEN I FELT UNCOMFORTABLE...
...I LAUGHED ALONG WITH THEM.
I JUST HOPED THE SUNSCREEN ALSO HID HOW MORTIFIED I WAS.

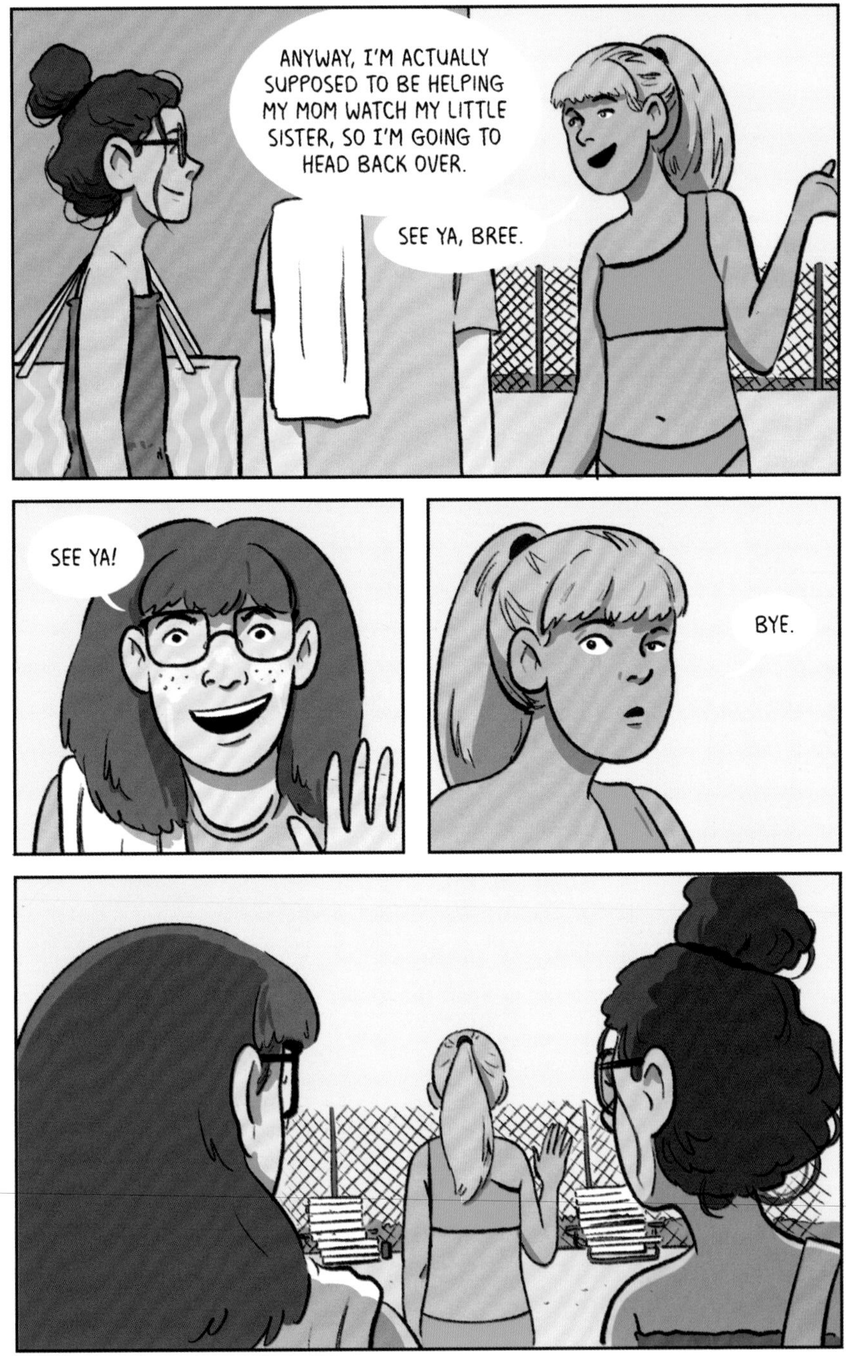
ANYWAY, I'M ACTUALLY SUPPOSED TO BE HELPING MY MOM WATCH MY LITTLE SISTER, SO I'M GOING TO HEAD BACK OVER.
SEE YA, BREE.
SEE YA!
BYE.

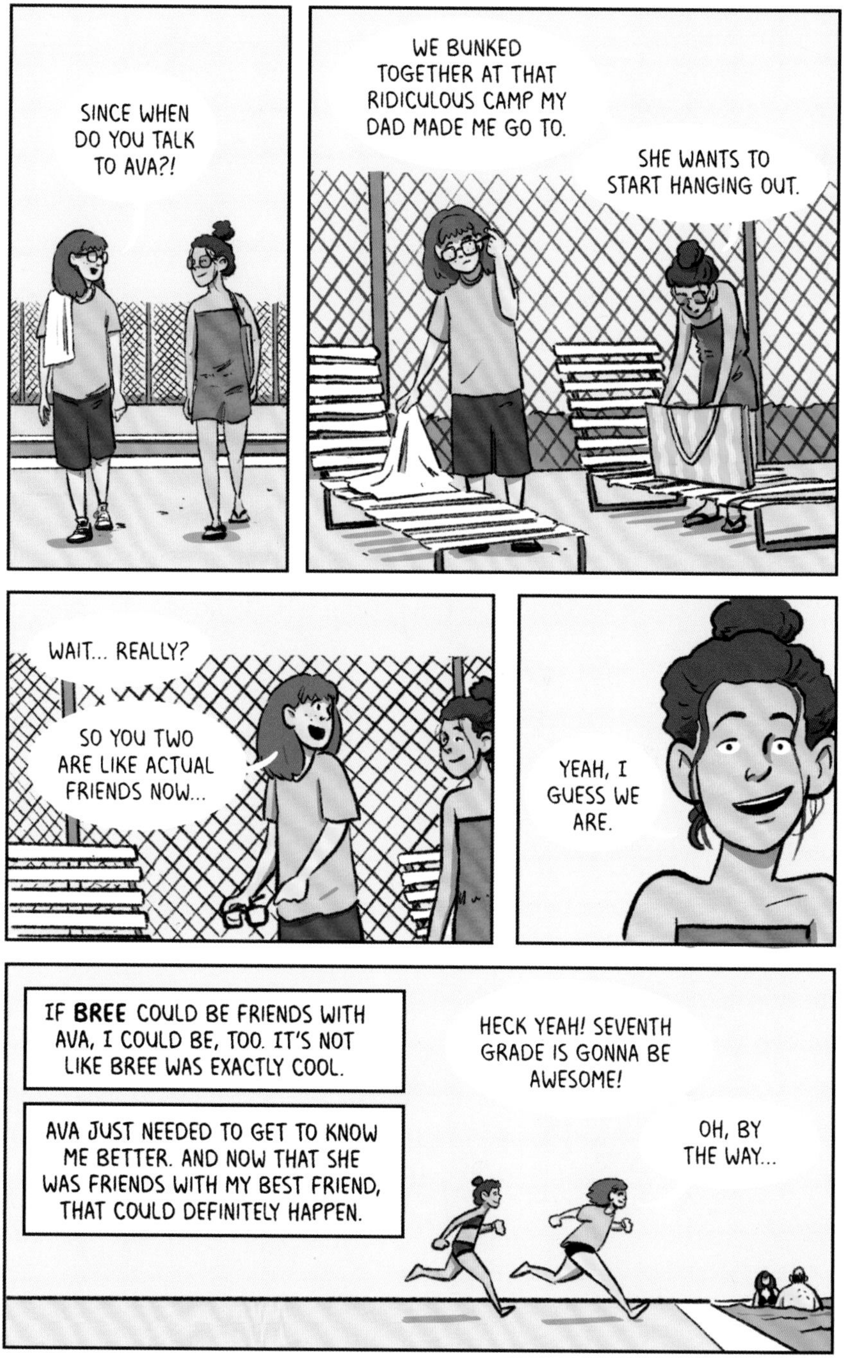
SINCE WHEN DO YOU TALK TO AVA?!
WE BUNKED TOGETHER AT THAT RIDICULOUS CAMP MY DAD MADE ME GO TO.
SHE WANTS TO START HANGING OUT.
WAIT... REALLY?
SO YOU TWO ARE LIKE ACTUAL FRIENDS NOW...
YEAH, I GUESS WE ARE.
IF **BREE** COULD BE FRIENDS WITH AVA, I COULD BE, TOO. IT'S NOT LIKE BREE WAS EXACTLY COOL.
AVA JUST NEEDED TO GET TO KNOW ME BETTER. AND NOW THAT SHE WAS FRIENDS WITH MY BEST FRIEND, THAT COULD DEFINITELY HAPPEN.
HECK YEAH! SEVENTH GRADE IS GONNA BE AWESOME!
OH, BY THE WAY...

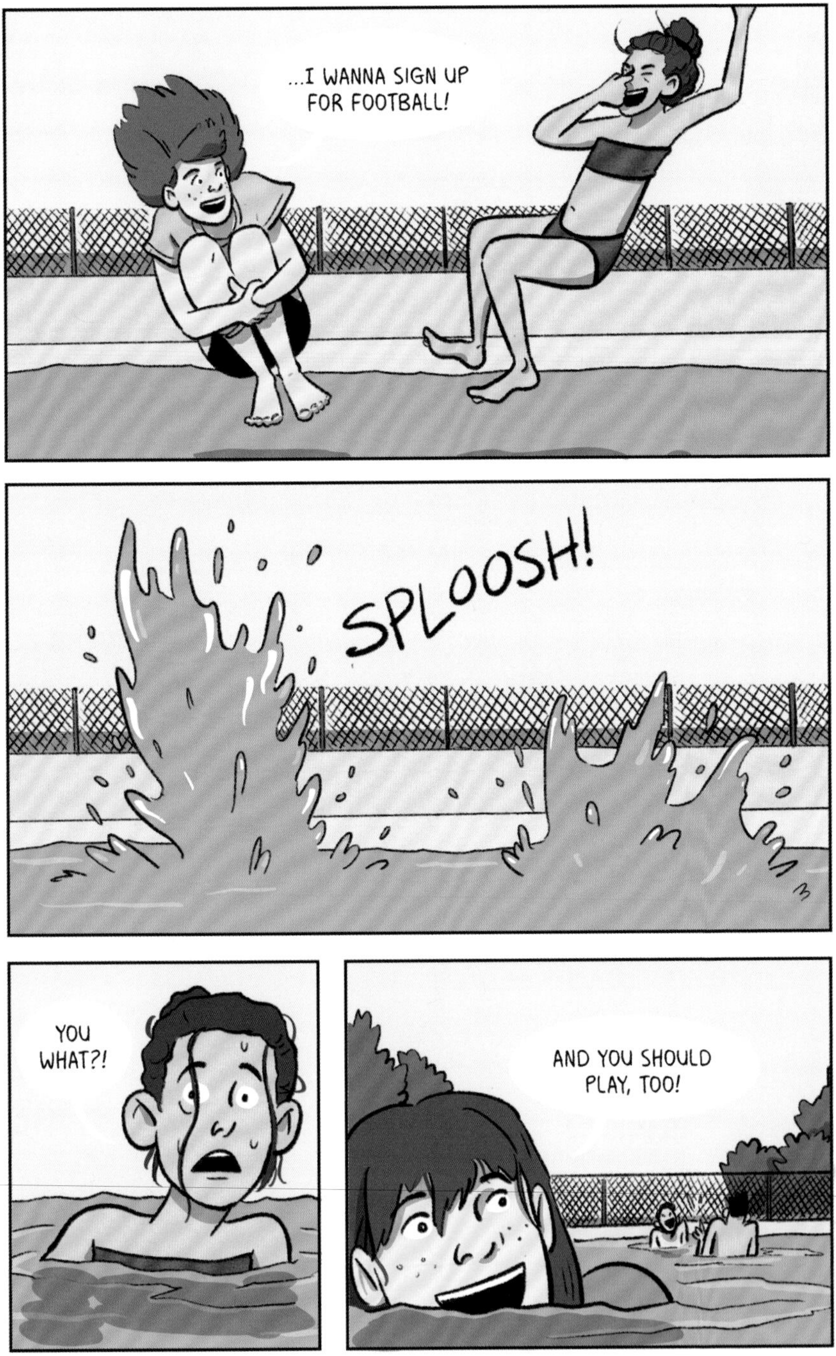
...I WANNA SIGN UP FOR FOOTBALL!
SPLOOSH!
YOU WHAT?!
AND YOU SHOULD PLAY, TOO!

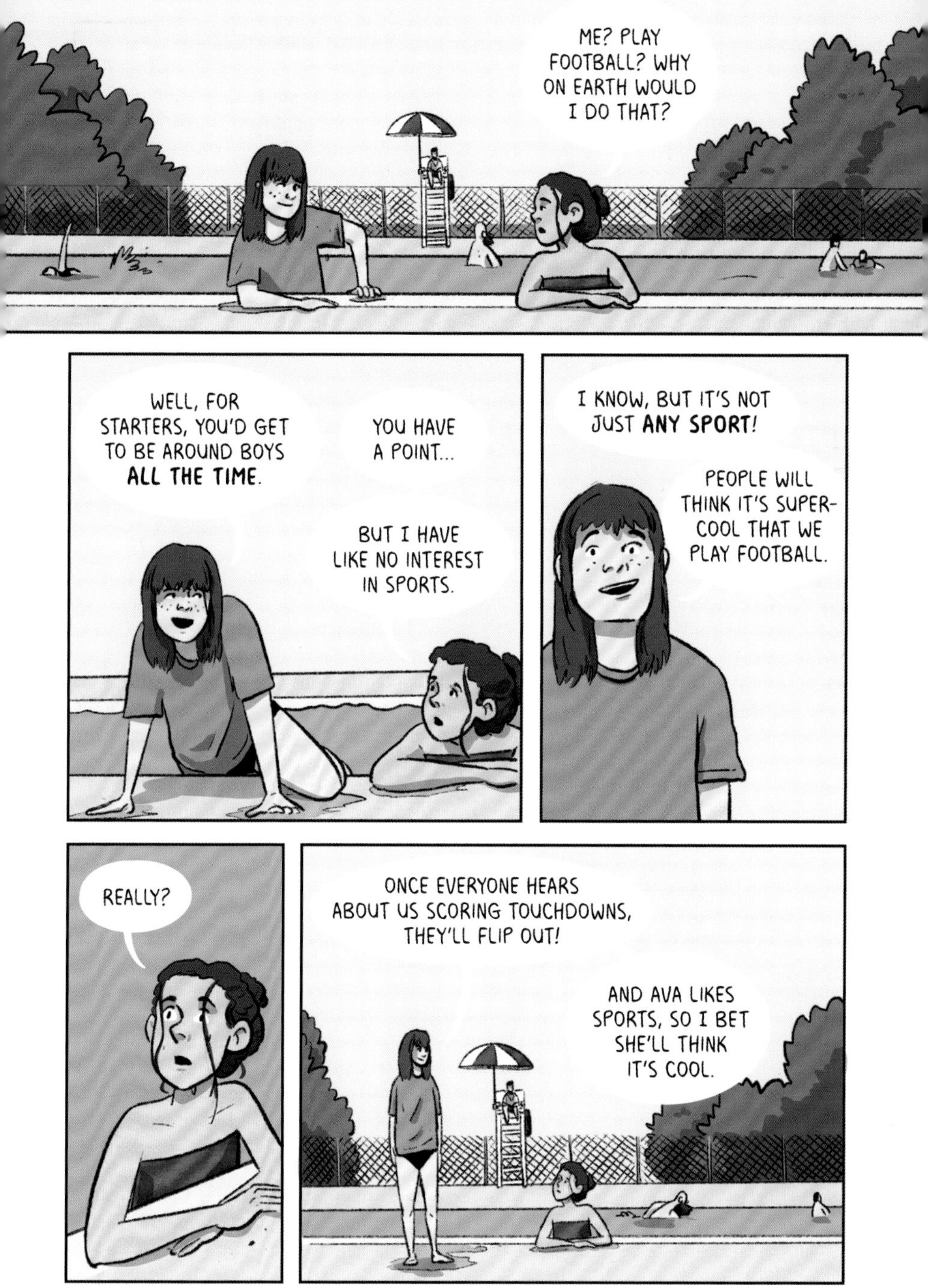
ME? PLAY FOOTBALL? WHY ON EARTH WOULD I DO THAT?
WELL, FOR STARTERS, YOU'D GET TO BE AROUND BOYS **ALL THE TIME**.
YOU HAVE A POINT...
BUT I HAVE LIKE NO INTEREST IN SPORTS.
I KNOW, BUT IT'S NOT JUST **ANY SPORT**!
PEOPLE WILL THINK IT'S SUPER-COOL THAT WE PLAY FOOTBALL.
REALLY?
ONCE EVERYONE HEARS ABOUT US SCORING TOUCHDOWNS, THEY'LL FLIP OUT!
AND AVA LIKES SPORTS, SO I BET SHE'LL THINK IT'S COOL.

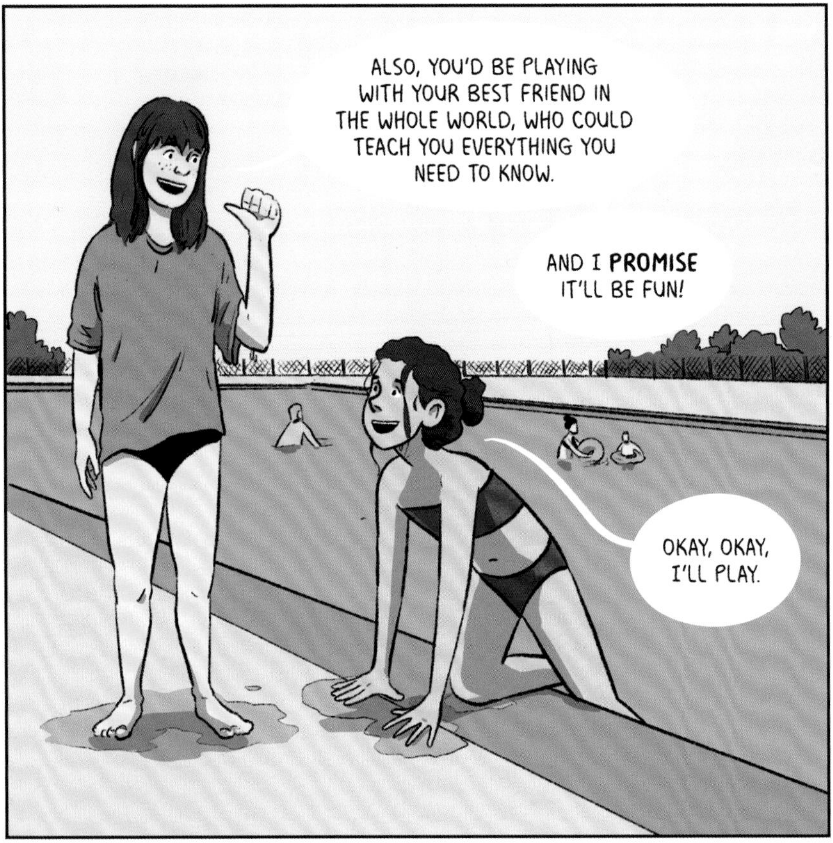
ALSO, YOU'D BE PLAYING WITH YOUR BEST FRIEND IN THE WHOLE WORLD, WHO COULD TEACH YOU EVERYTHING YOU NEED TO KNOW.
AND I **PROMISE** IT'LL BE FUN!
OKAY, OKAY, I'LL PLAY.

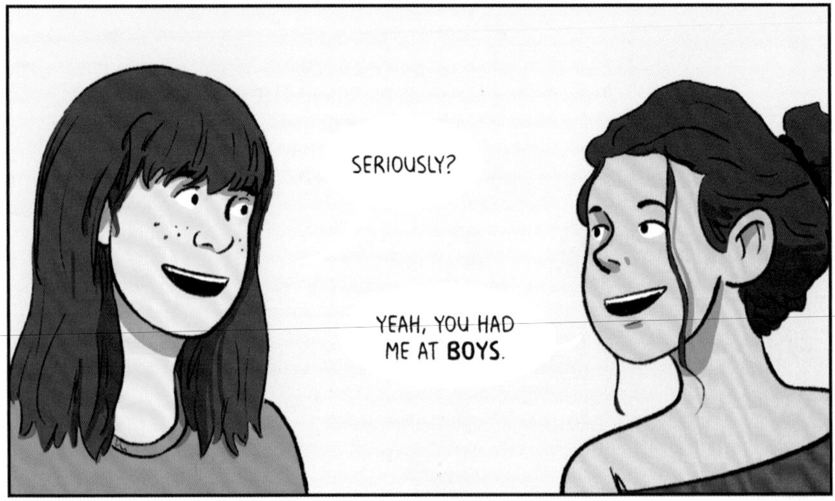
SERIOUSLY?
YEAH, YOU HAD ME AT **BOYS**.

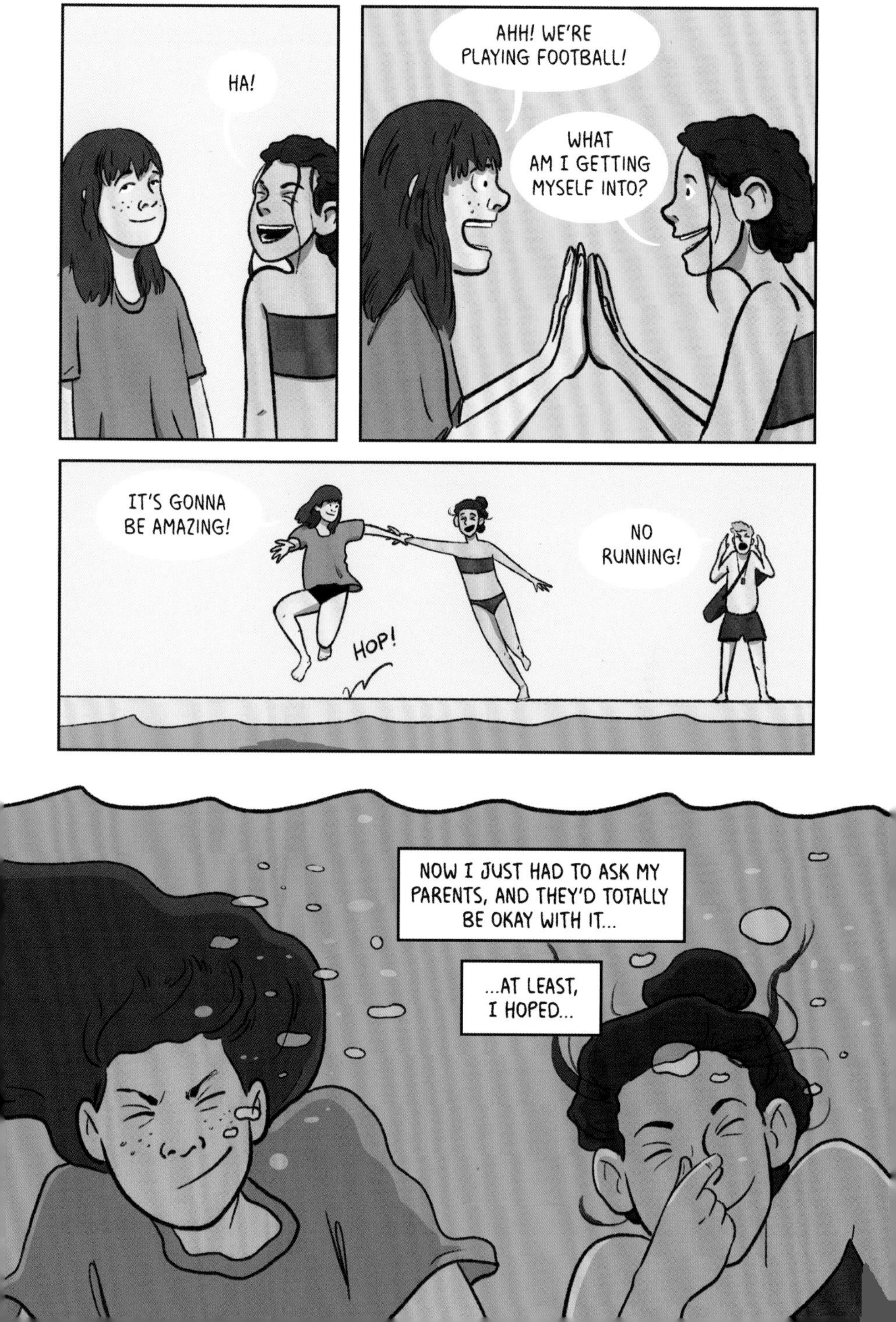
HA!
AHH! WE'RE PLAYING FOOTBALL!
WHAT AM I GETTING MYSELF INTO?
IT'S GONNA BE AMAZING!
HOP!
NO RUNNING!
NOW I JUST HAD TO ASK MY PARENTS, AND THEY'D TOTALLY BE OKAY WITH IT...
...AT LEAST, I HOPED...

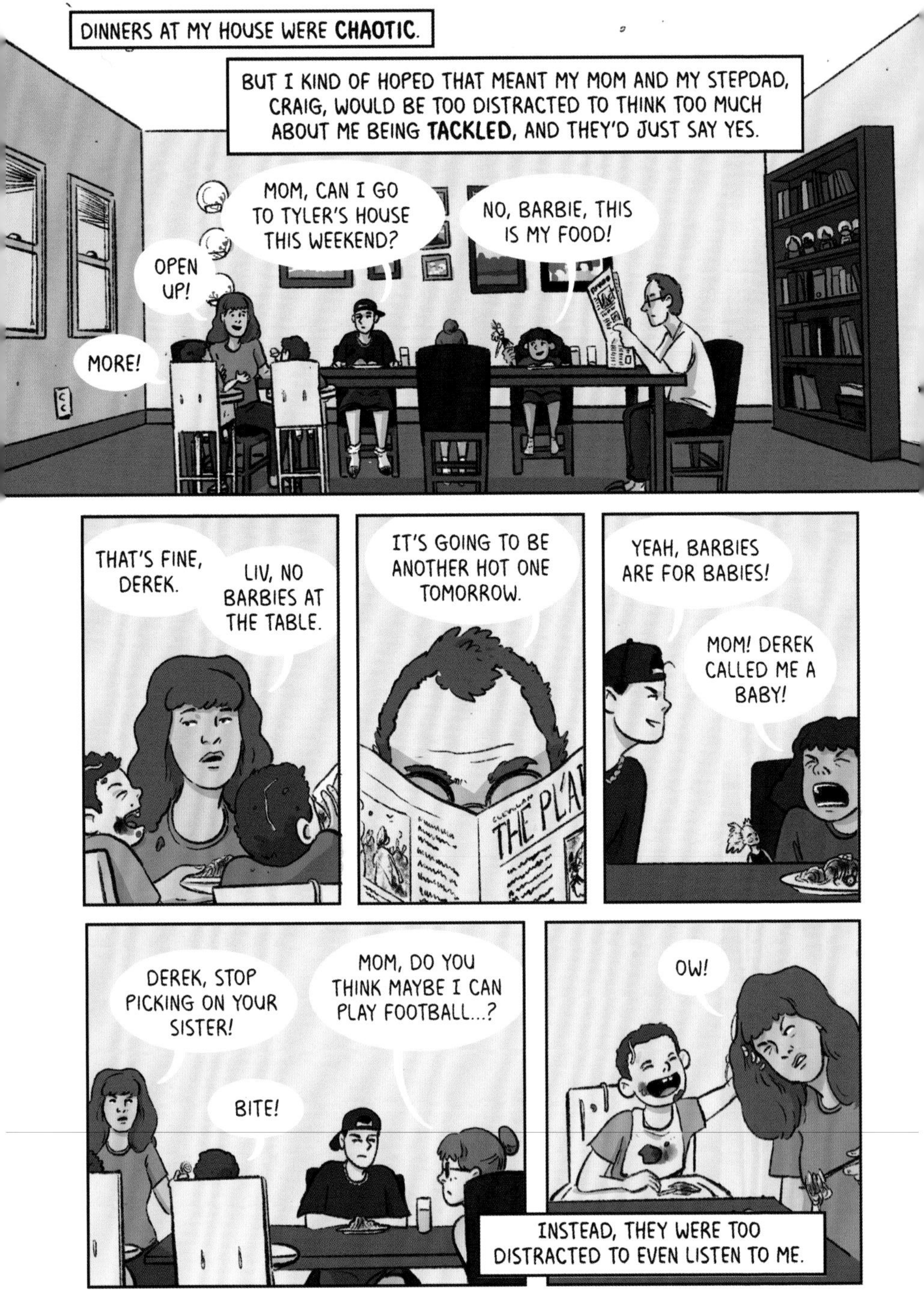
DINNERS AT MY HOUSE WERE **CHAOTIC**.
BUT I KIND OF HOPED THAT MEANT MY MOM AND MY STEPDAD, CRAIG, WOULD BE TOO DISTRACTED TO THINK TOO MUCH ABOUT ME BEING **TACKLED**, AND THEY'D JUST SAY YES.
OPEN UP!
MORE!
MOM, CAN I GO TO TYLER'S HOUSE THIS WEEKEND?
NO, BARBIE, THIS IS MY FOOD!
THAT'S FINE, DEREK.
LIV, NO BARBIES AT THE TABLE.
IT'S GOING TO BE ANOTHER HOT ONE TOMORROW.
THE PLA
YEAH, BARBIES ARE FOR BABIES!
MOM! DEREK CALLED ME A BABY!
DEREK, STOP PICKING ON YOUR SISTER!
MOM, DO YOU THINK MAYBE I CAN PLAY FOOTBALL...?
BITE!
OW!
INSTEAD, THEY WERE TOO DISTRACTED TO EVEN LISTEN TO ME.

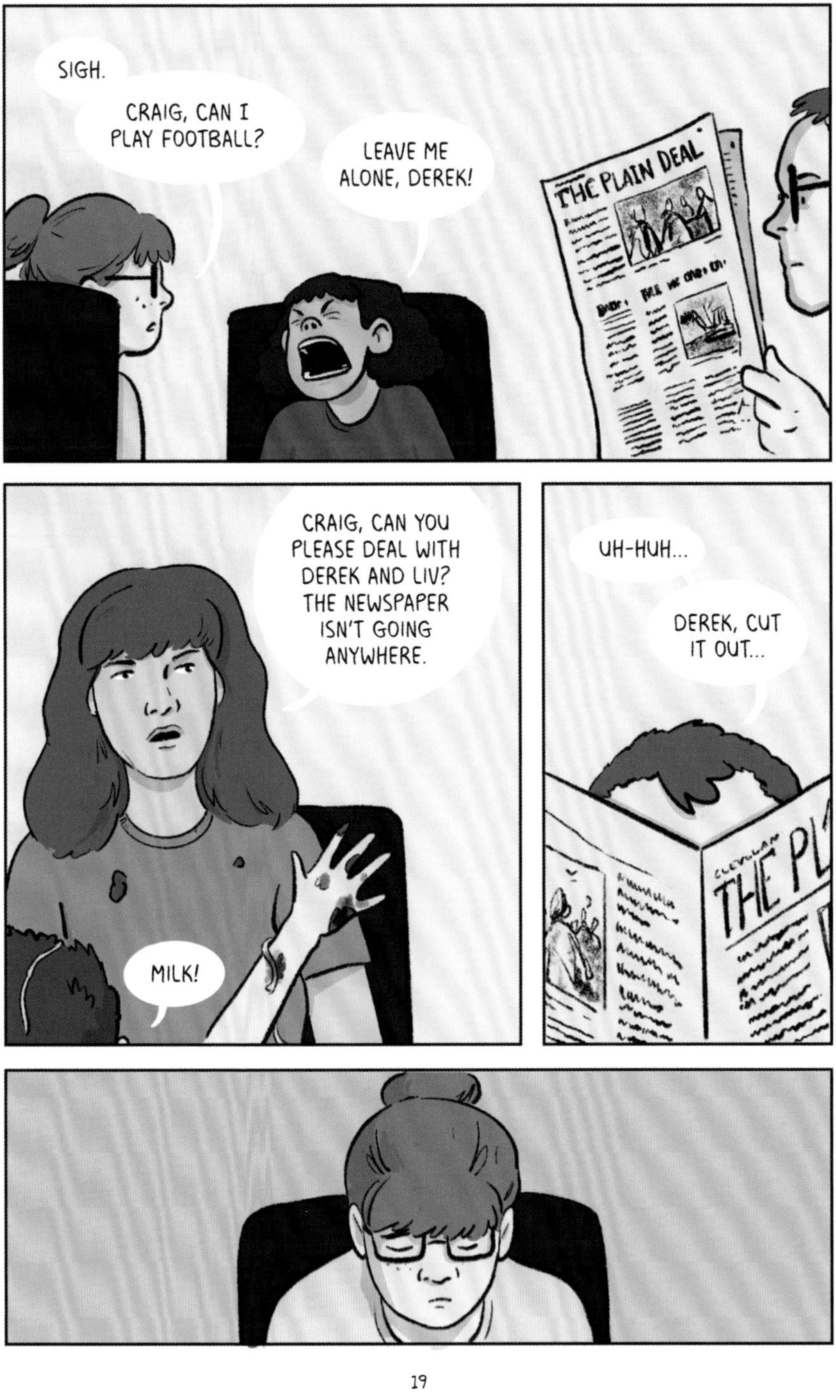
SIGH.
CRAIG, CAN I PLAY FOOTBALL?
LEAVE ME ALONE, DEREK!
THE PLAIN DEAL
CRAIG, CAN YOU PLEASE DEAL WITH DEREK AND LIV? THE NEWSPAPER ISN'T GOING ANYWHERE.
MILK!
UH-HUH...
DEREK, CUT IT OUT...
THE PL

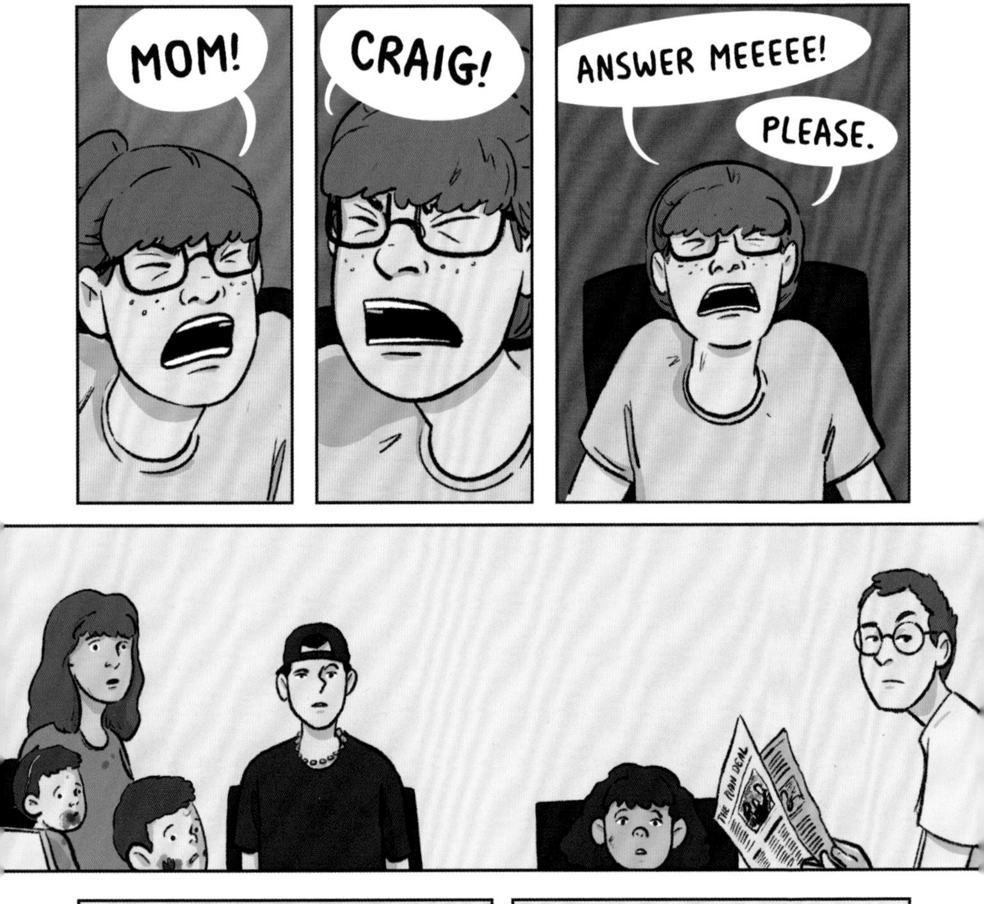
MOM!
CRAIG!
ANSWER MEEEEE!
PLEASE.
WHAT?
I WANT TO PLAY FOOTBALL!

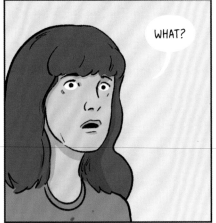

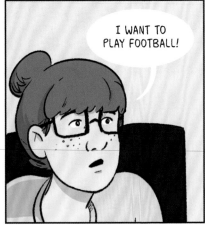

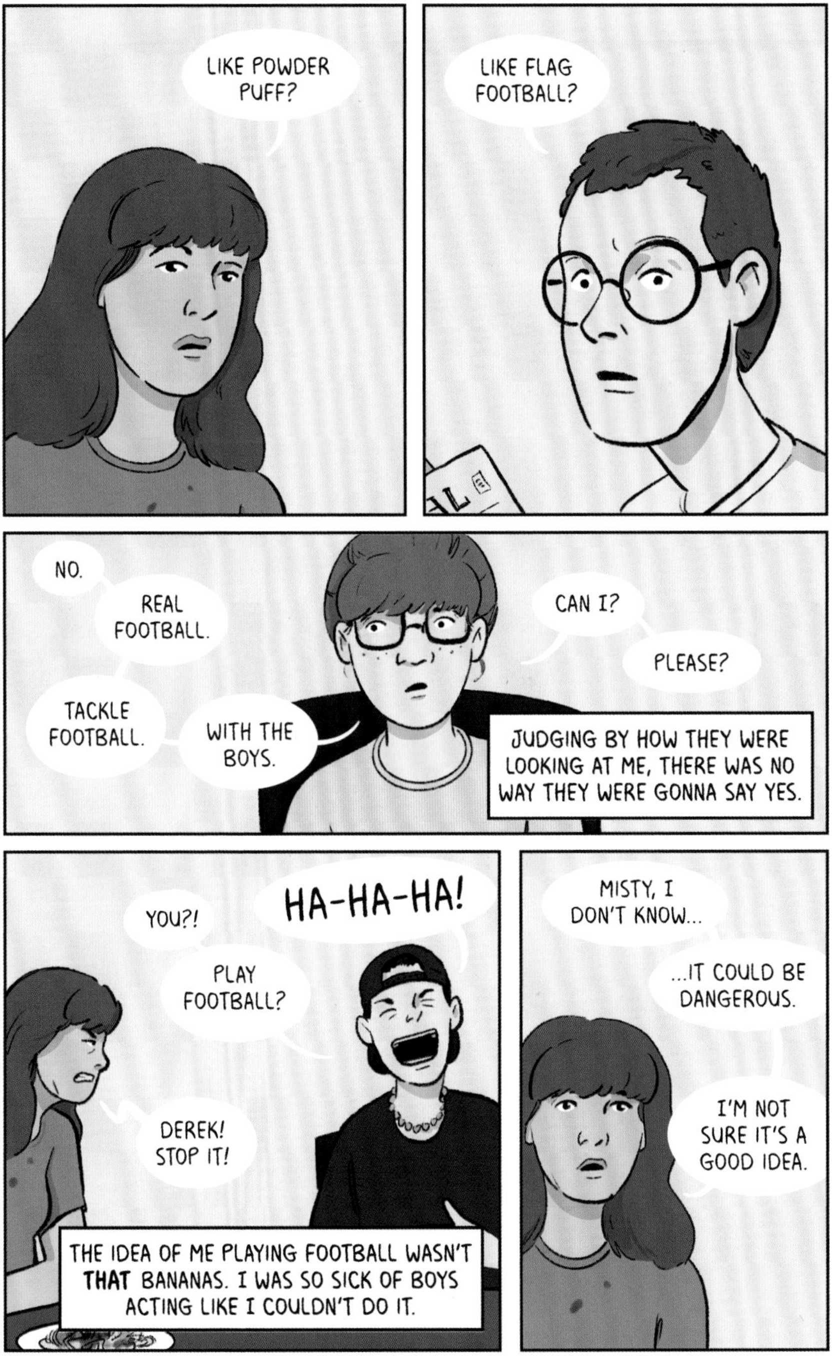
LIKE POWDER PUFF?
LIKE FLAG FOOTBALL?
NO.
REAL FOOTBALL.
TACKLE FOOTBALL.
WITH THE BOYS.
CAN I?
PLEASE?
JUDGING BY HOW THEY WERE LOOKING AT ME, THERE WAS NO WAY THEY WERE GONNA SAY YES.
YOU?!
HA-HA-HA!
PLAY FOOTBALL?
DEREK! STOP IT!
THE IDEA OF ME PLAYING FOOTBALL WASN'T **THAT** BANANAS. I WAS SO SICK OF BOYS ACTING LIKE I COULDN'T DO IT.
MISTY, I DON'T KNOW...
...IT COULD BE DANGEROUS.
I'M NOT SURE IT'S A GOOD IDEA.

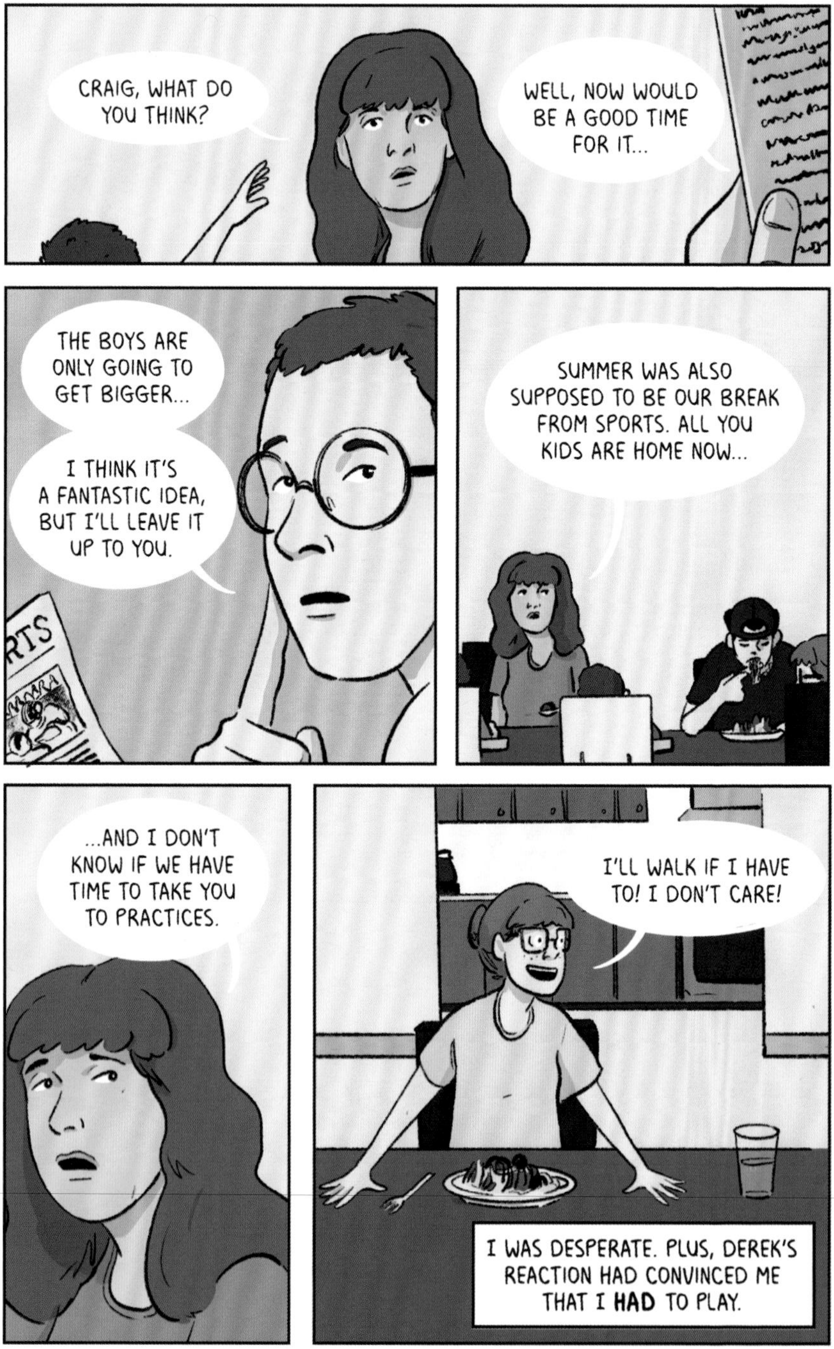
CRAIG, WHAT DO YOU THINK?
WELL, NOW WOULD BE A GOOD TIME FOR IT...
THE BOYS ARE ONLY GOING TO GET BIGGER...
I THINK IT'S A FANTASTIC IDEA, BUT I'LL LEAVE IT UP TO YOU.
RTS
SUMMER WAS ALSO SUPPOSED TO BE OUR BREAK FROM SPORTS. ALL YOU KIDS ARE HOME NOW...
...AND I DON'T KNOW IF WE HAVE TIME TO TAKE YOU TO PRACTICES.
I'LL WALK IF I HAVE TO! I DON'T CARE!
I WAS DESPERATE. PLUS, DEREK'S REACTION HAD CONVINCED ME THAT I **HAD** TO PLAY.

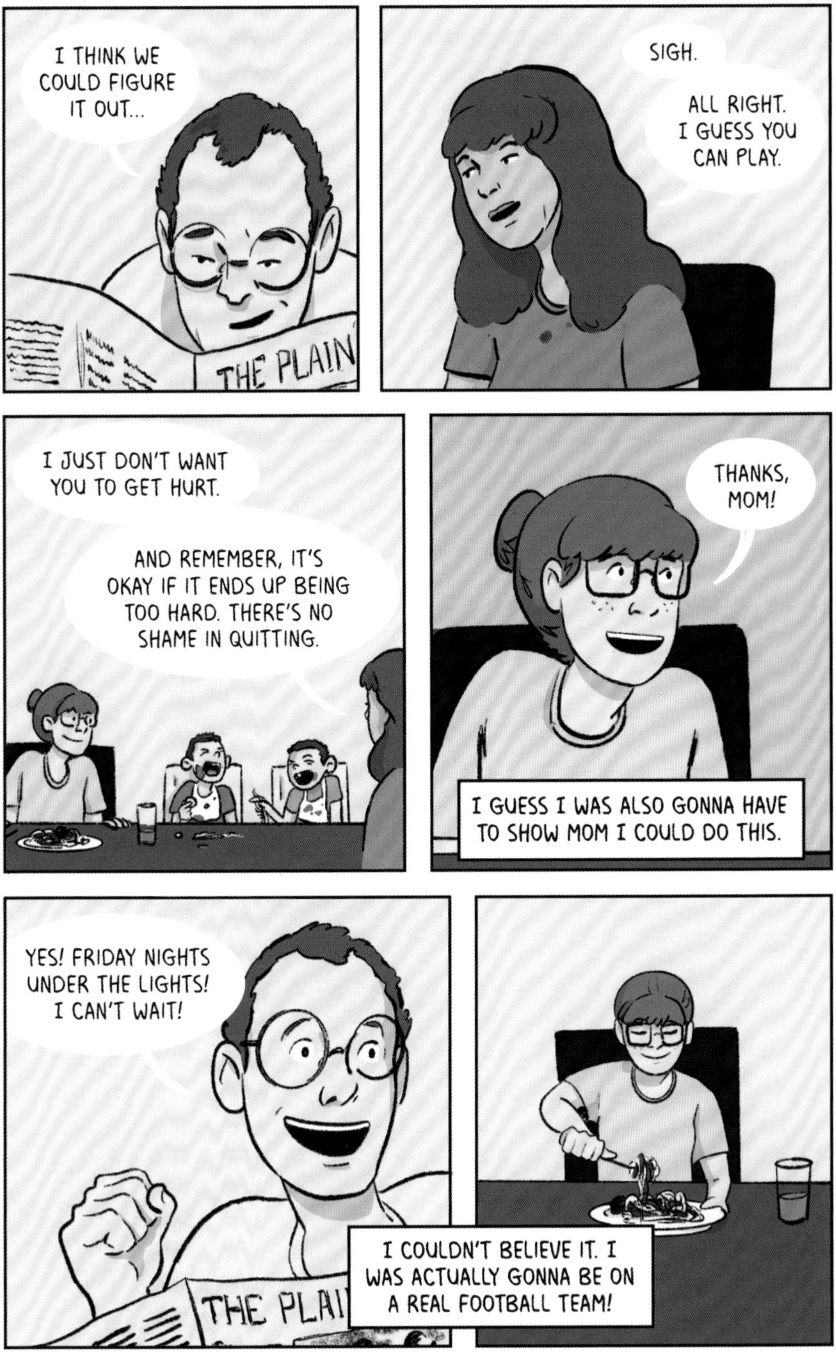
I THINK WE COULD FIGURE IT OUT...
THE PLAIN
SIGH.
ALL RIGHT. I GUESS YOU CAN PLAY.
I JUST DON'T WANT YOU TO GET HURT.
AND REMEMBER, IT'S OKAY IF IT ENDS UP BEING TOO HARD. THERE'S NO SHAME IN QUITTING.
THANKS, MOM!
I GUESS I WAS ALSO GONNA HAVE TO SHOW MOM I COULD DO THIS.
YES! FRIDAY NIGHTS UNDER THE LIGHTS! I CAN'T WAIT!
THE PLAI
I COULDN'T BELIEVE IT. I WAS ACTUALLY GONNA BE ON A REAL FOOTBALL TEAM!

CHAPTER 2

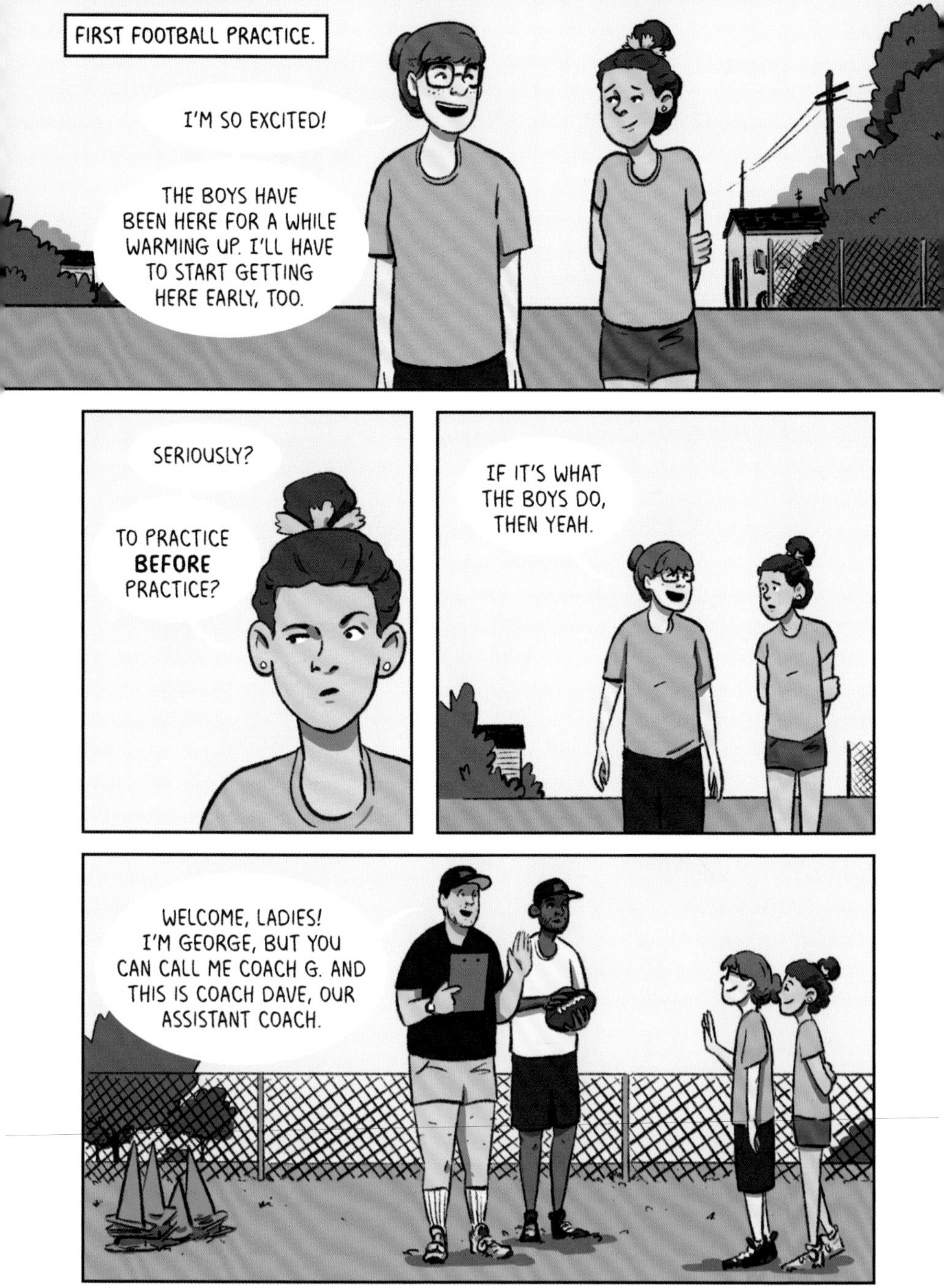
FIRST FOOTBALL PRACTICE.
I'M SO EXCITED!
THE BOYS HAVE BEEN HERE FOR A WHILE WARMING UP. I'LL HAVE TO START GETTING HERE EARLY, TOO.
SERIOUSLY?
TO PRACTICE **BEFORE** PRACTICE?
IF IT'S WHAT THE BOYS DO, THEN YEAH.
WELCOME, LADIES! I'M GEORGE, BUT YOU CAN CALL ME COACH G. AND THIS IS COACH DAVE, OUR ASSISTANT COACH.

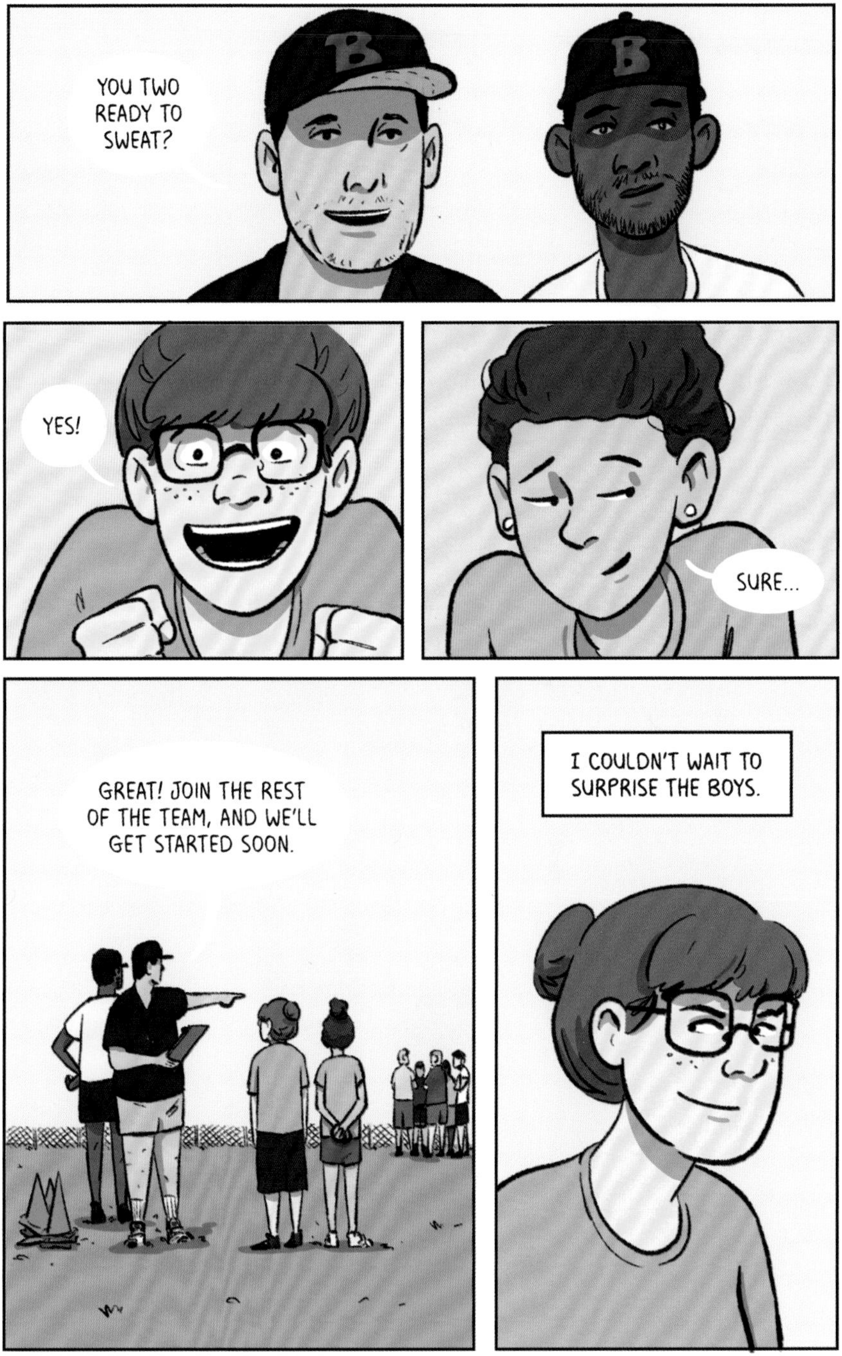
YOU TWO READY TO SWEAT?
YES!
SURE...
GREAT! JOIN THE REST OF THE TEAM, AND WE'LL GET STARTED SOON.
I COULDN'T WAIT TO SURPRISE THE BOYS.

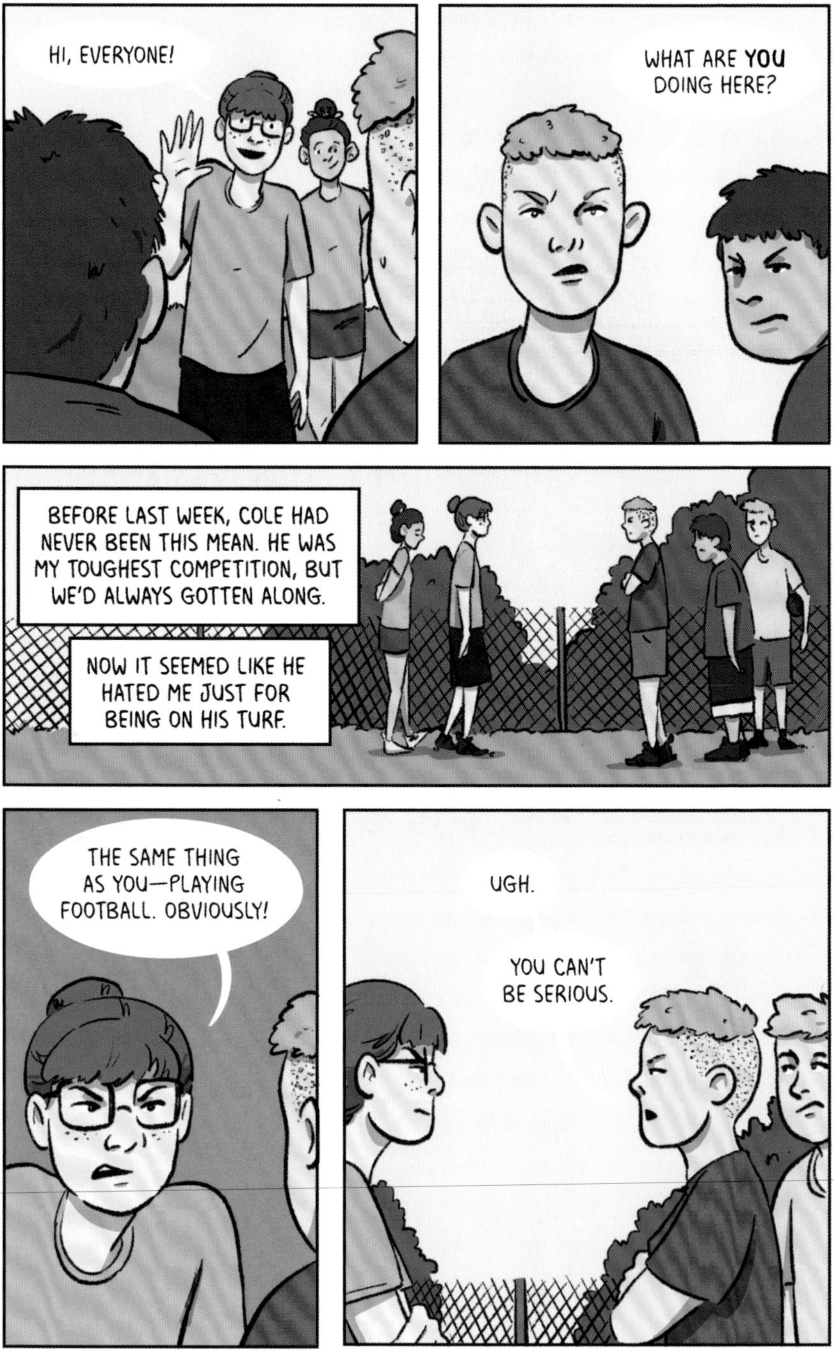
HI, EVERYONE!
WHAT ARE **YOU** DOING HERE?
BEFORE LAST WEEK, COLE HAD NEVER BEEN THIS MEAN. HE WAS MY TOUGHEST COMPETITION, BUT WE'D ALWAYS GOTTEN ALONG.
NOW IT SEEMED LIKE HE HATED ME JUST FOR BEING ON HIS TURF.
THE SAME THING AS YOU—PLAYING FOOTBALL. OBVIOUSLY!
UGH.
YOU CAN'T BE SERIOUS.

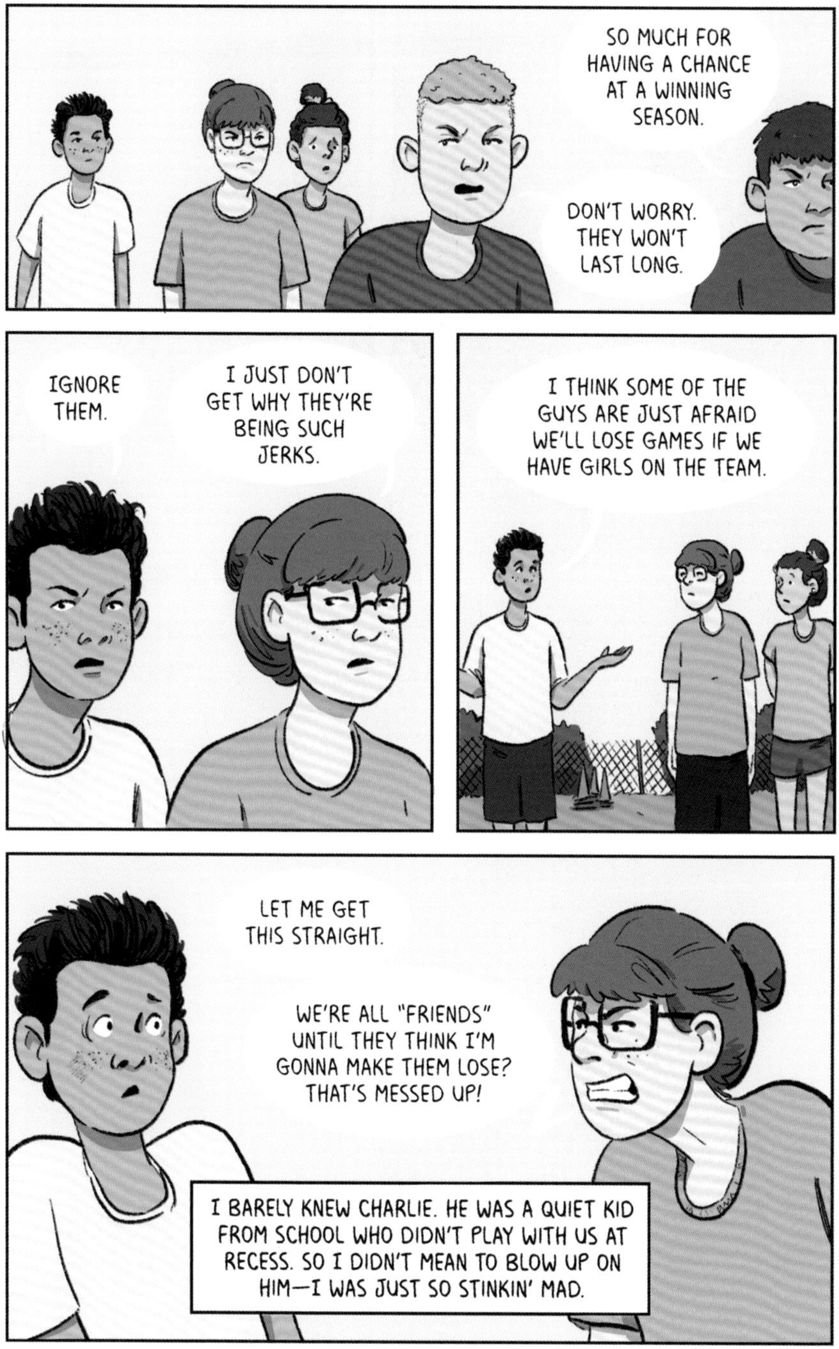
SO MUCH FOR HAVING A CHANCE AT A WINNING SEASON.
DON'T WORRY. THEY WON'T LAST LONG.
IGNORE THEM.
I JUST DON'T GET WHY THEY'RE BEING SUCH JERKS.
I THINK SOME OF THE GUYS ARE JUST AFRAID WE'LL LOSE GAMES IF WE HAVE GIRLS ON THE TEAM.
LET ME GET THIS STRAIGHT.
WE'RE ALL "FRIENDS" UNTIL THEY THINK I'M GONNA MAKE THEM LOSE? THAT'S MESSED UP!
I BARELY KNEW CHARLIE. HE WAS A QUIET KID FROM SCHOOL WHO DIDN'T PLAY WITH US AT RECESS. SO I DIDN'T MEAN TO BLOW UP ON HIM—I WAS JUST SO STINKIN' MAD.

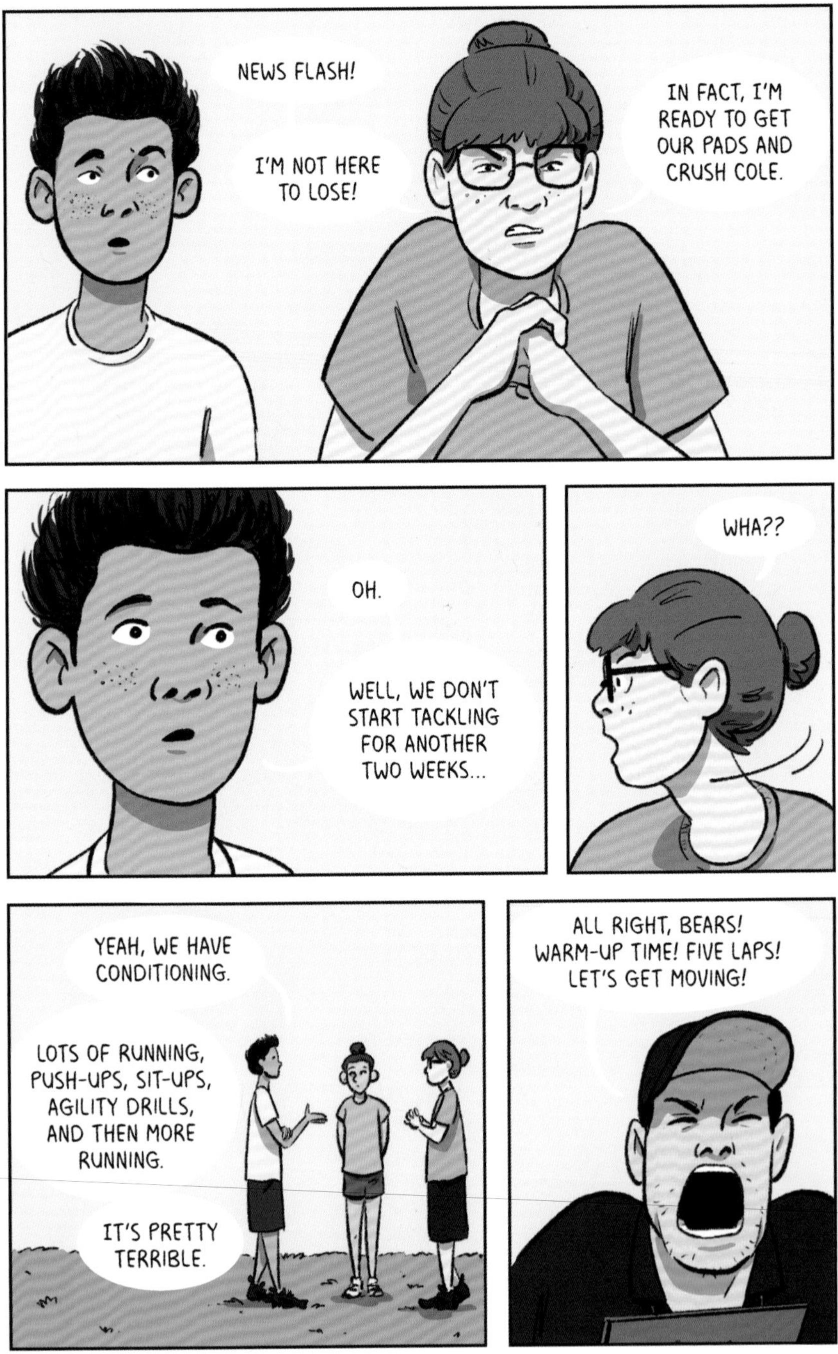
NEWS FLASH!
I'M NOT HERE TO LOSE!
IN FACT, I'M READY TO GET OUR PADS AND CRUSH COLE.
OH.
WELL, WE DON'T START TACKLING FOR ANOTHER TWO WEEKS...
WHA??
YEAH, WE HAVE CONDITIONING.
LOTS OF RUNNING, PUSH-UPS, SIT-UPS, AGILITY DRILLS, AND THEN MORE RUNNING.
IT'S PRETTY TERRIBLE.
ALL RIGHT, BEARS! WARM-UP TIME! FIVE LAPS! LET'S GET MOVING!

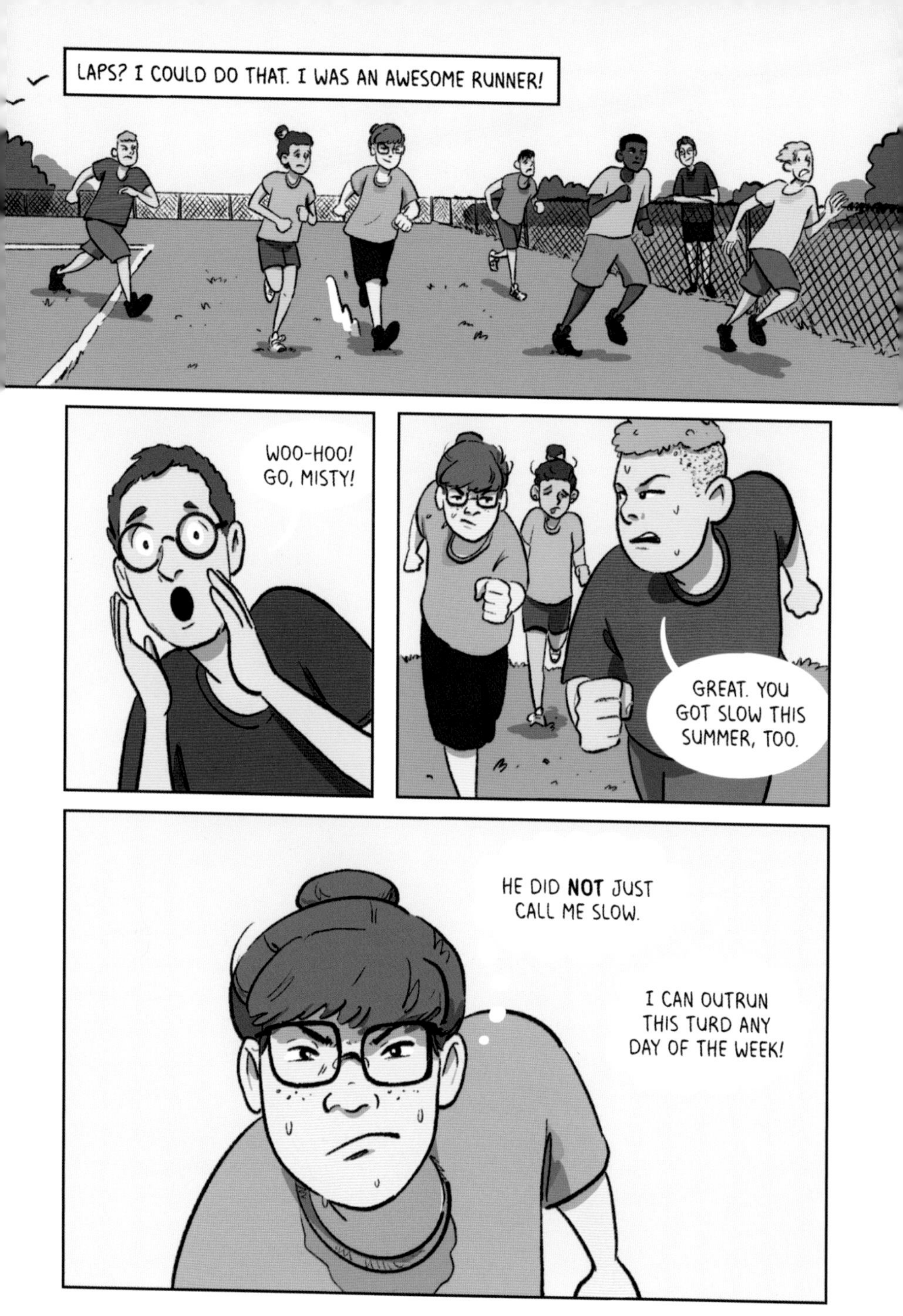
LAPS? I COULD DO THAT. I WAS AN AWESOME RUNNER!
WOO-HOO! GO, MISTY!
GREAT. YOU GOT SLOW THIS SUMMER, TOO.
HE DID **NOT** JUST CALL ME SLOW.
I CAN OUTRUN THIS TURD ANY DAY OF THE WEEK!

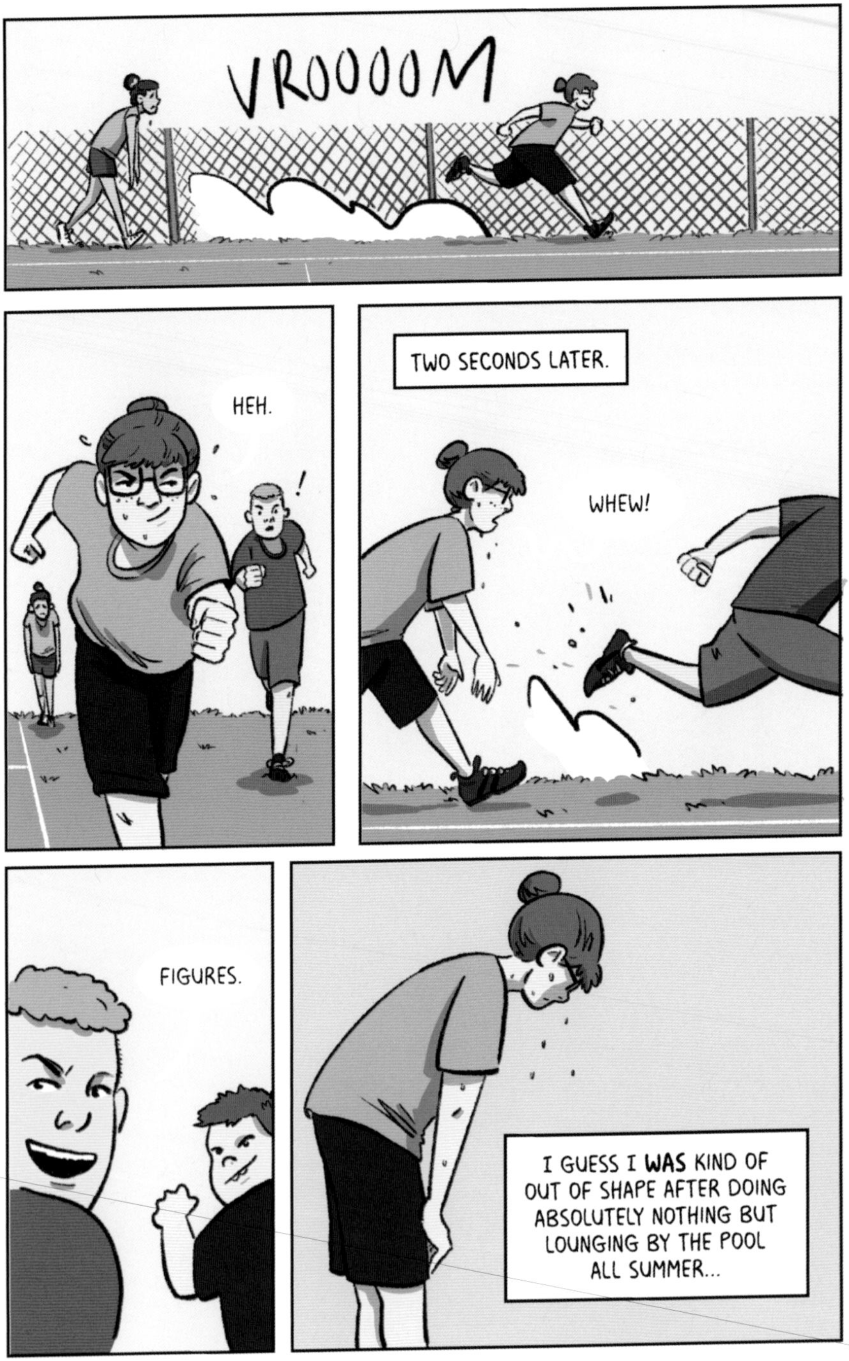
VROOOOM
HEH.
!
TWO SECONDS LATER.
WHEW!
FIGURES.
I GUESS I **WAS** KIND OF OUT OF SHAPE AFTER DOING ABSOLUTELY NOTHING BUT LOUNGING BY THE POOL ALL SUMMER...

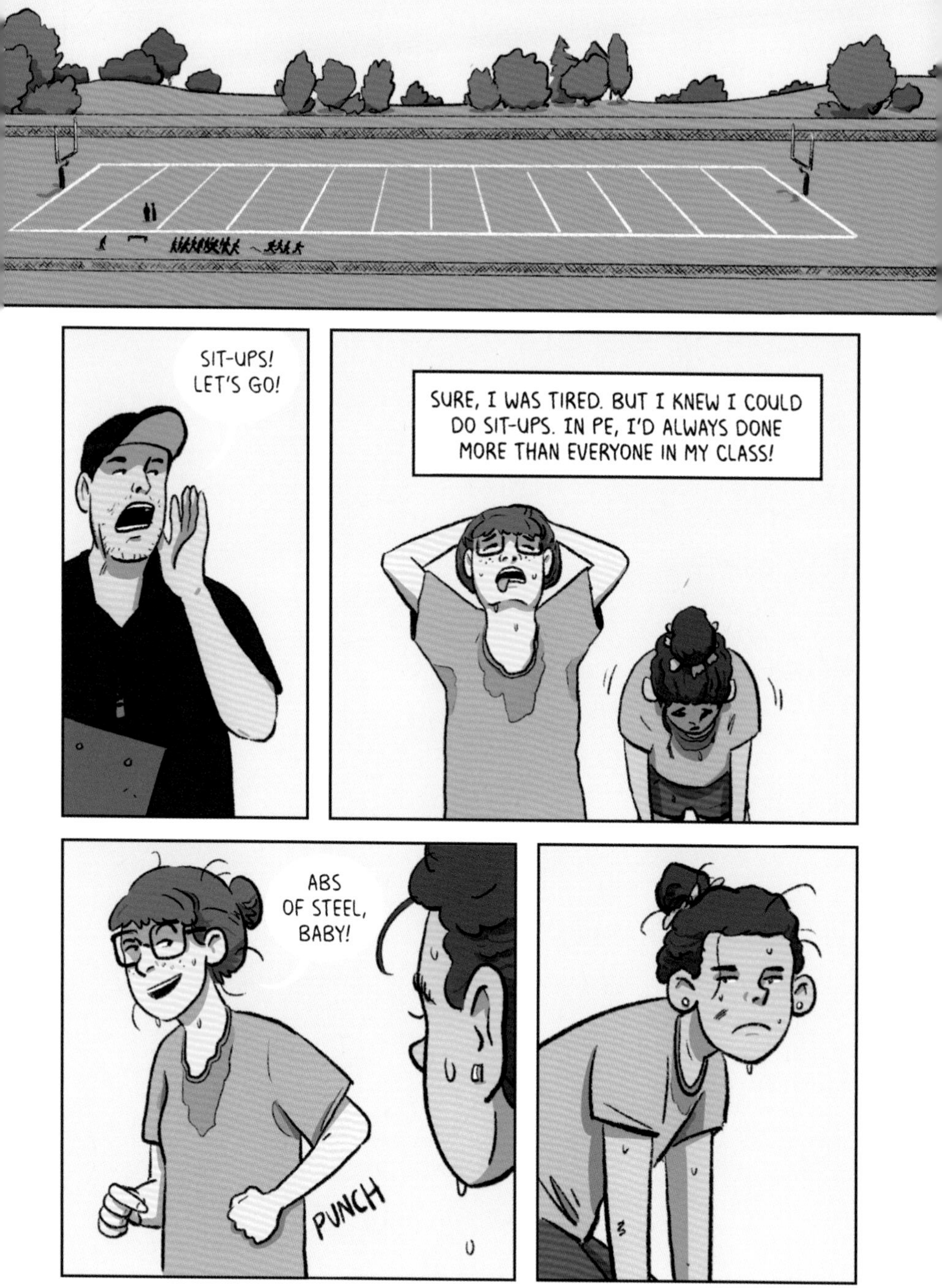
SIT-UPS! LET'S GO!
SURE, I WAS TIRED. BUT I KNEW I COULD DO SIT-UPS. IN PE, I'D ALWAYS DONE MORE THAN EVERYONE IN MY CLASS!
ABS OF STEEL, BABY!
PUNCH

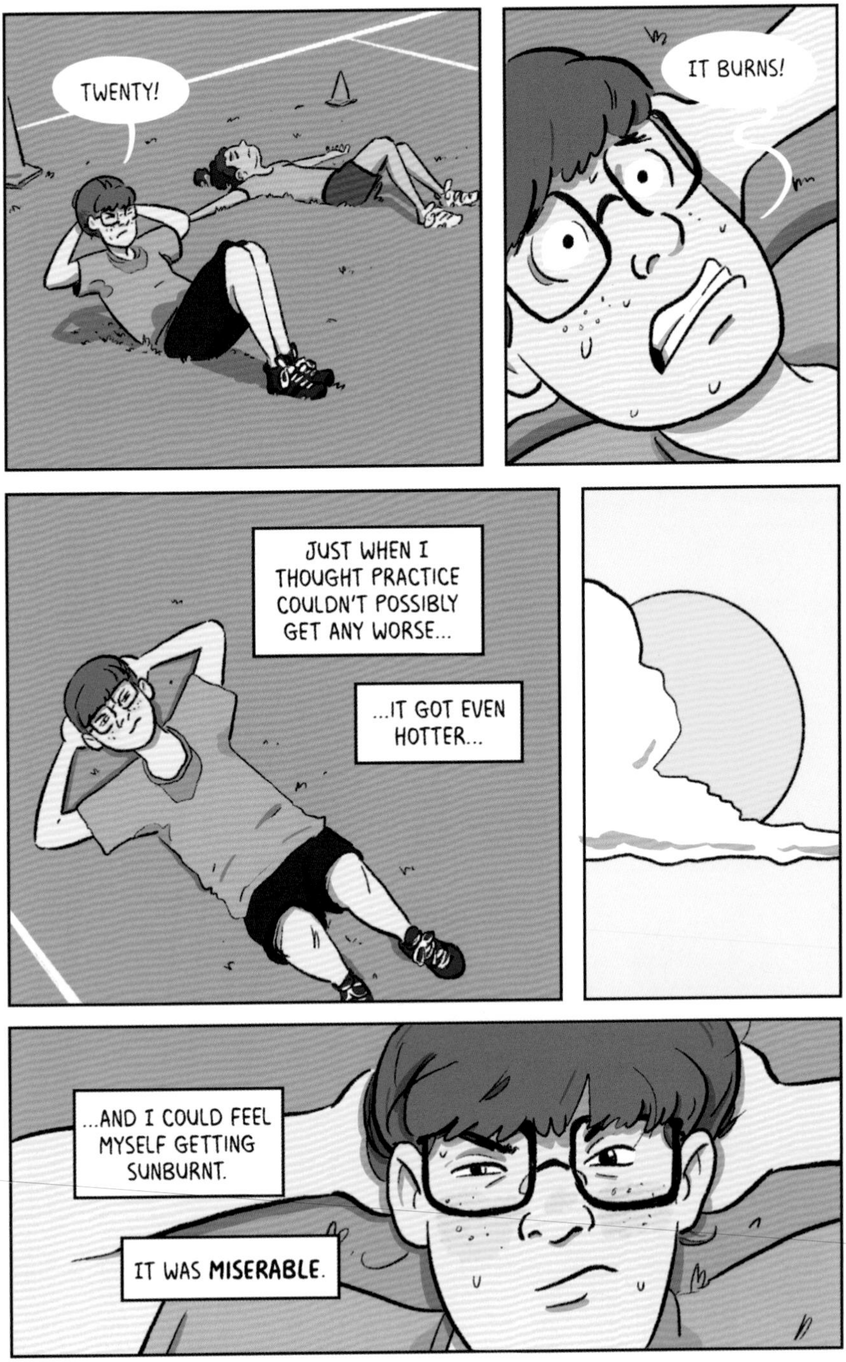
TWENTY!
IT BURNS!
JUST WHEN I THOUGHT PRACTICE COULDN'T POSSIBLY GET ANY WORSE...
...IT GOT EVEN HOTTER...
...AND I COULD FEEL MYSELF GETTING SUNBURNT.
IT WAS **MISERABLE**.

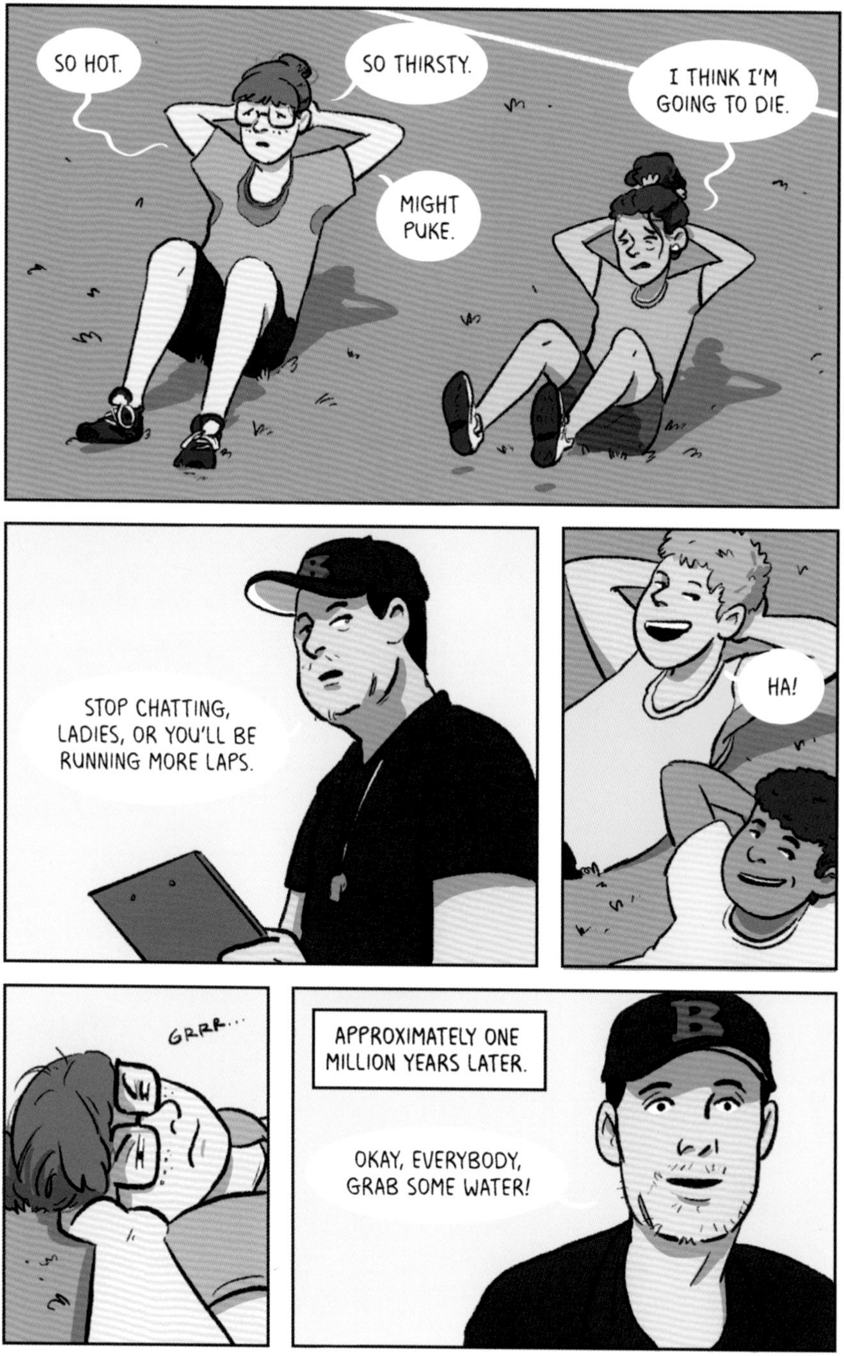
SO HOT.
SO THIRSTY.
I THINK I'M GOING TO DIE.
MIGHT PUKE.
STOP CHATTING, LADIES, OR YOU'LL BE RUNNING MORE LAPS.
HA!
GRRR...
APPROXIMATELY ONE MILLION YEARS LATER.
OKAY, EVERYBODY, GRAB SOME WATER!

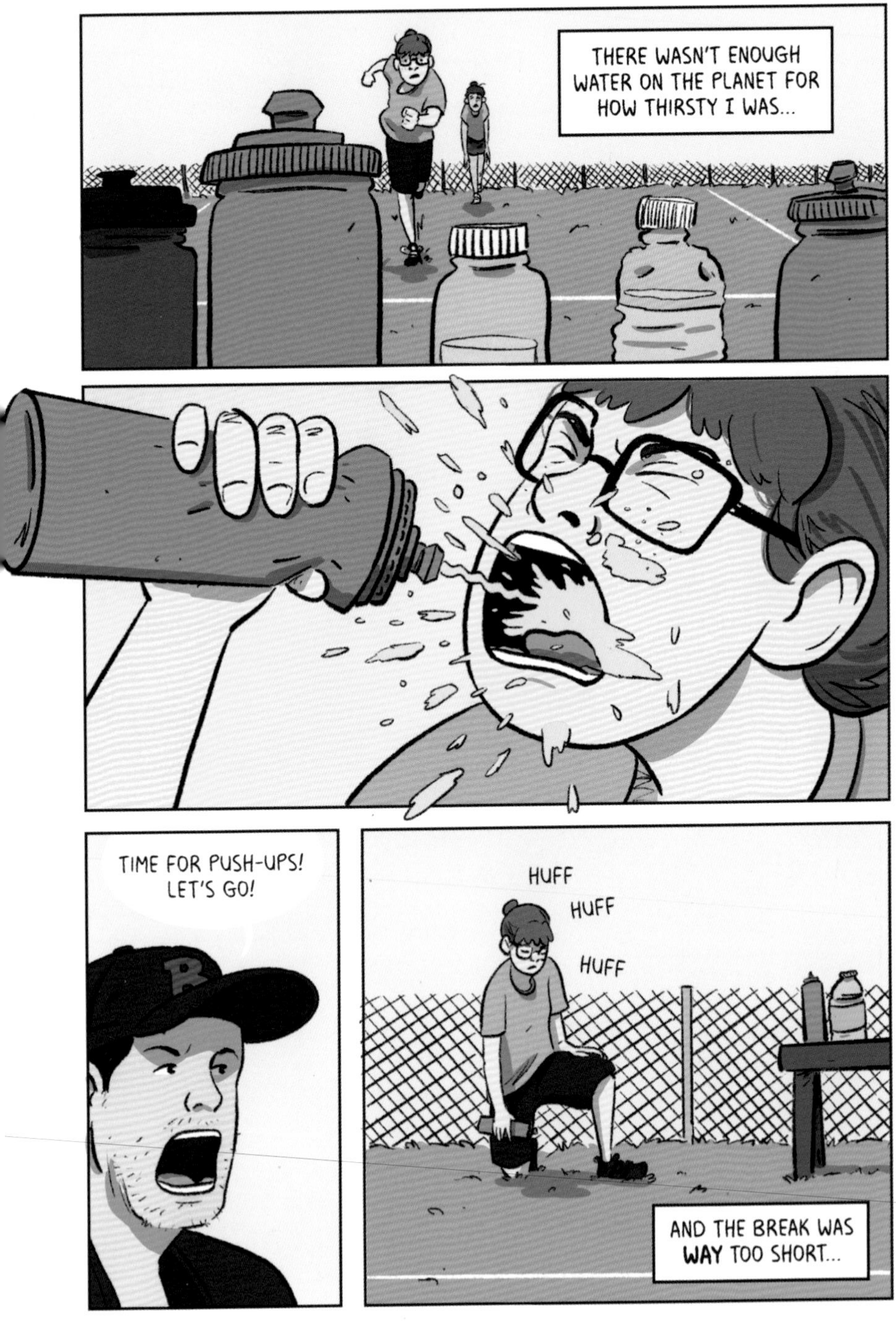
THERE WASN'T ENOUGH WATER ON THE PLANET FOR HOW THIRSTY I WAS...
TIME FOR PUSH-UPS! LET'S GO!
HUFF
HUFF
HUFF
AND THE BREAK WAS **WAY** TOO SHORT...

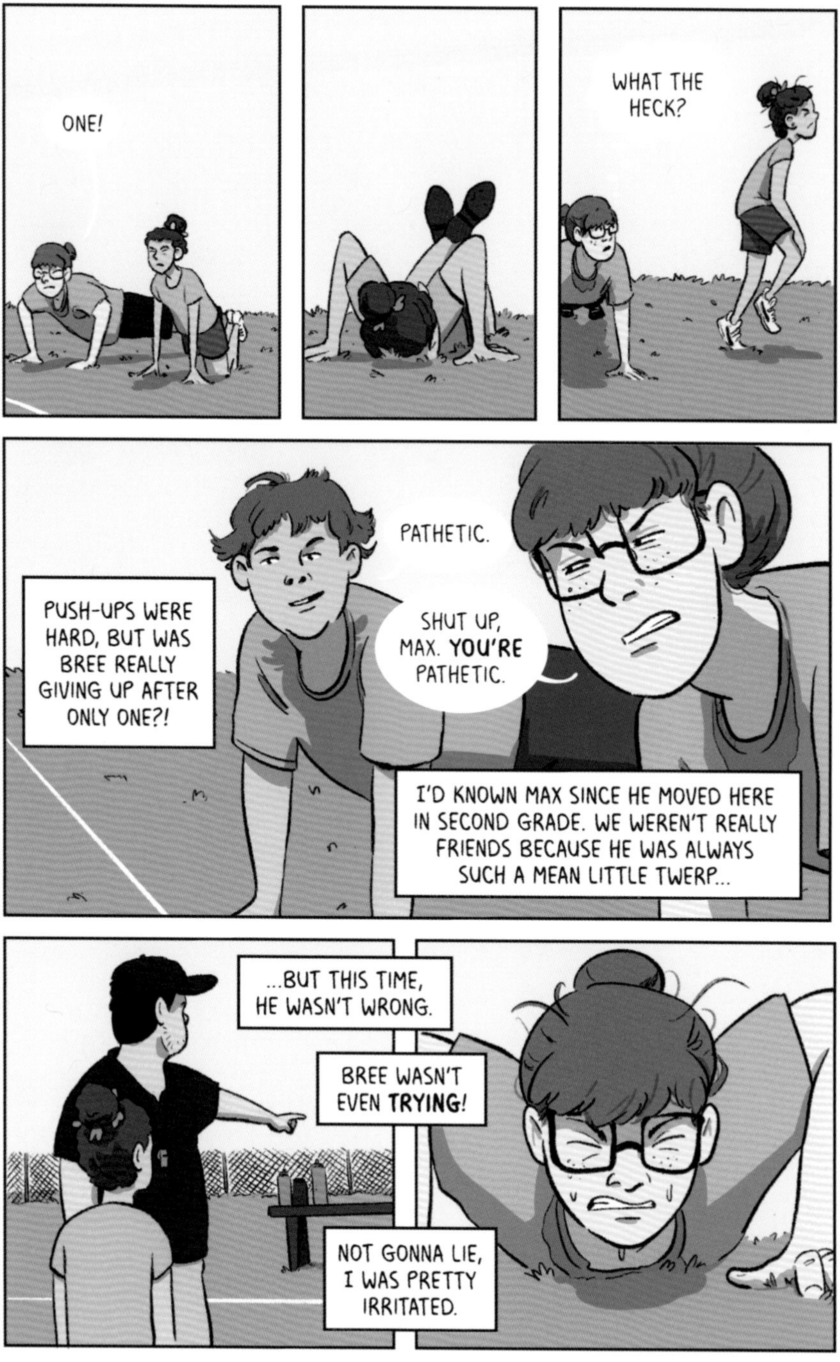

ONE!
WHAT THE HECK?
PATHETIC.
PUSH-UPS WERE HARD, BUT WAS BREE REALLY GIVING UP AFTER ONLY ONE?!
SHUT UP, MAX. **YOU'RE** PATHETIC.
I'D KNOWN MAX SINCE HE MOVED HERE IN SECOND GRADE. WE WEREN'T REALLY FRIENDS BECAUSE HE WAS ALWAYS SUCH A MEAN LITTLE TWERP...
...BUT THIS TIME, HE WASN'T WRONG.
BREE WASN'T EVEN **TRYING**!
NOT GONNA LIE, I WAS PRETTY IRRITATED.

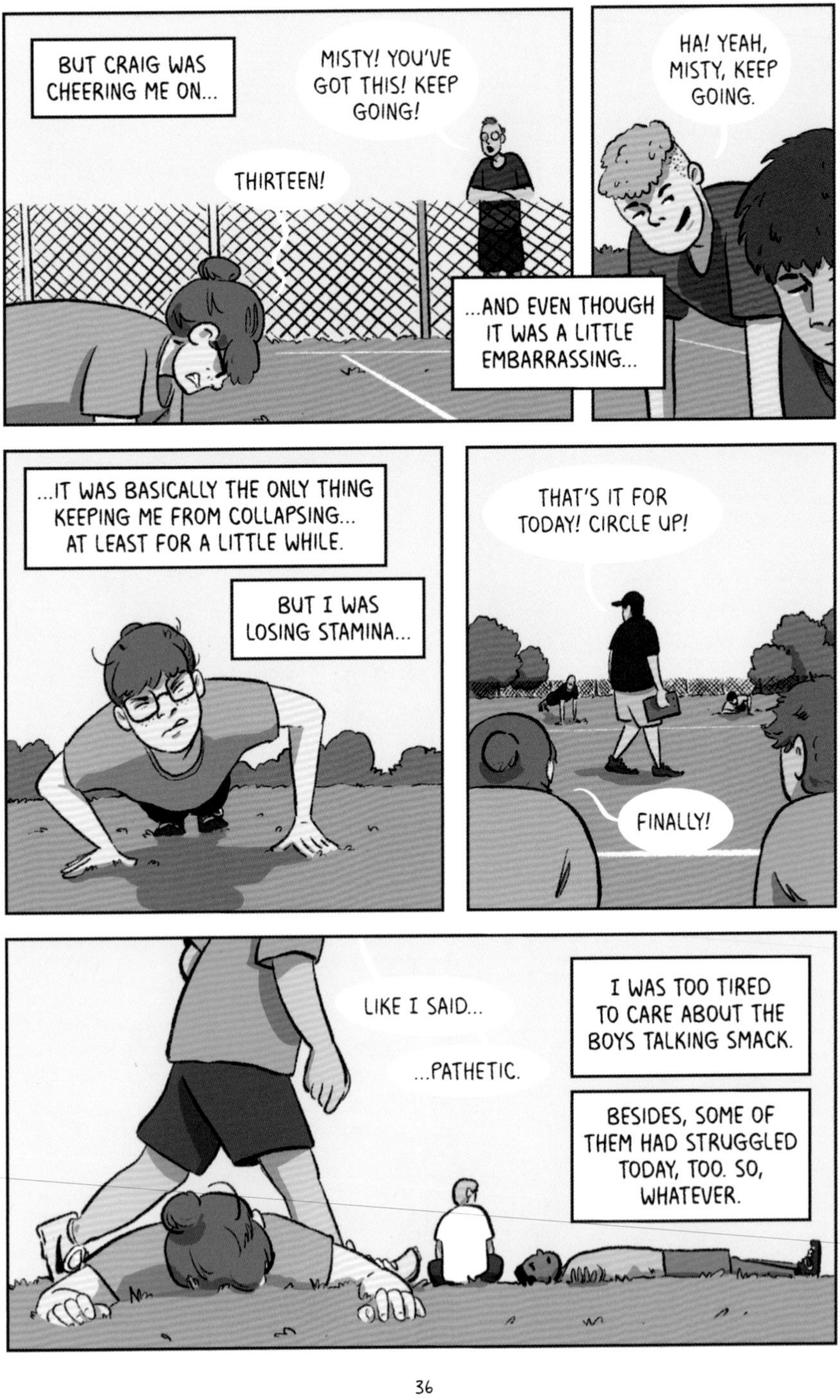
BUT CRAIG WAS CHEERING ME ON...
MISTY! YOU'VE GOT THIS! KEEP GOING!
THIRTEEN!
HA! YEAH, MISTY, KEEP GOING.
...AND EVEN THOUGH IT WAS A LITTLE EMBARRASSING...
...IT WAS BASICALLY THE ONLY THING KEEPING ME FROM COLLAPSING... AT LEAST FOR A LITTLE WHILE.
BUT I WAS LOSING STAMINA...
THAT'S IT FOR TODAY! CIRCLE UP!
FINALLY!
LIKE I SAID...
...PATHETIC.
I WAS TOO TIRED TO CARE ABOUT THE BOYS TALKING SMACK.
BESIDES, SOME OF THEM HAD STRUGGLED TODAY, TOO. SO, WHATEVER.

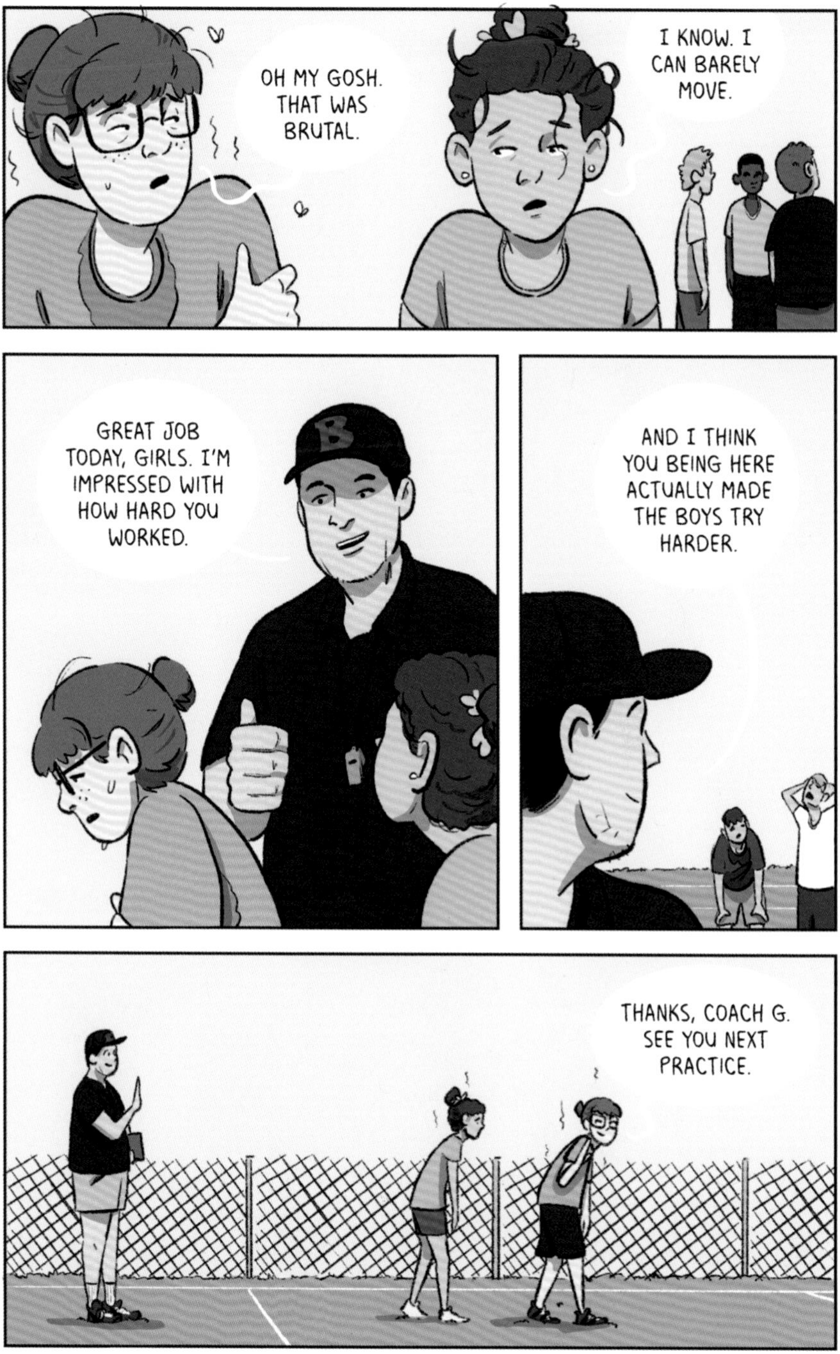
OH MY GOSH. THAT WAS BRUTAL.
I KNOW. I CAN BARELY MOVE.
GREAT JOB TODAY, GIRLS. I'M IMPRESSED WITH HOW HARD YOU WORKED.
AND I THINK YOU BEING HERE ACTUALLY MADE THE BOYS TRY HARDER.
THANKS, COACH G. SEE YOU NEXT PRACTICE.

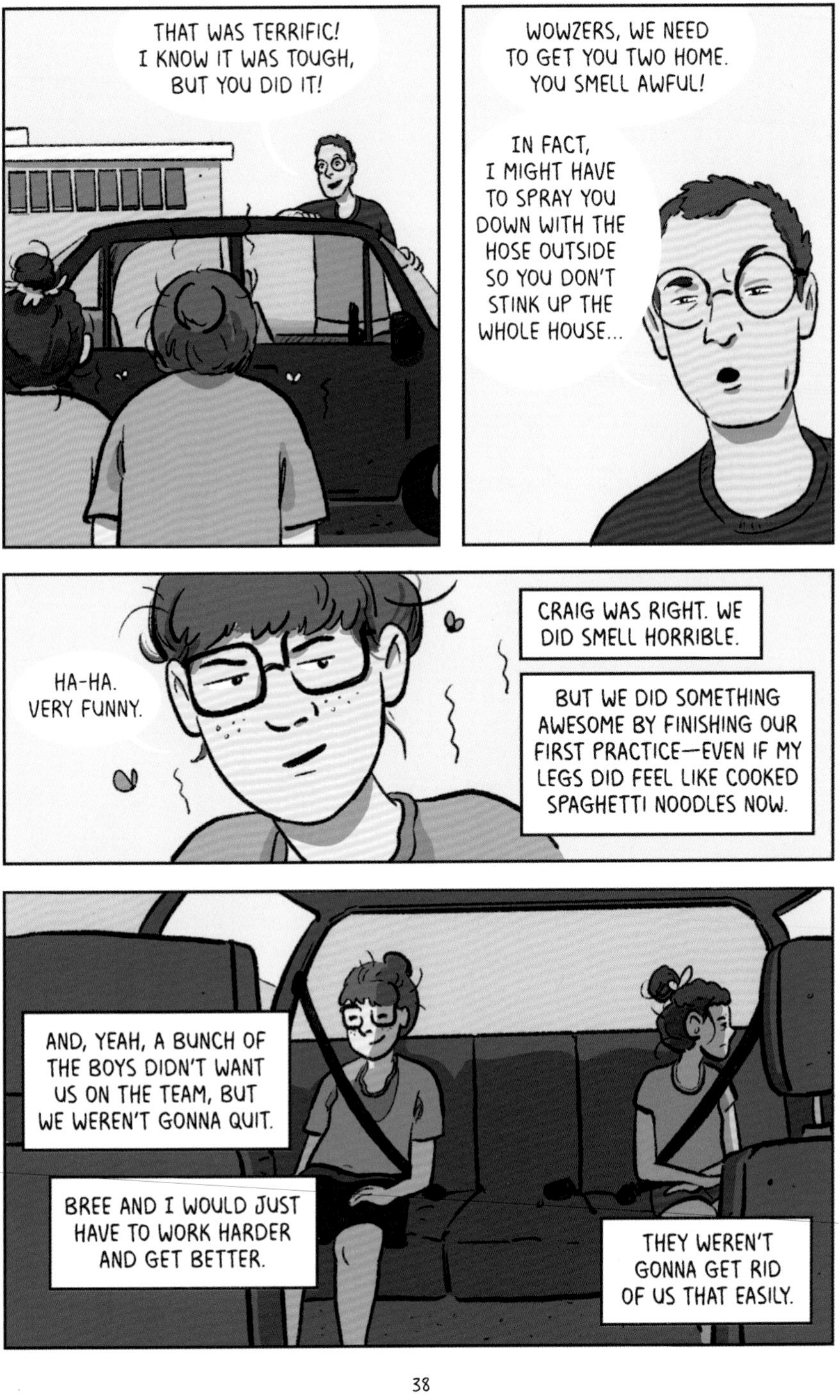
THAT WAS TERRIFIC! I KNOW IT WAS TOUGH, BUT YOU DID IT!
WOWZERS, WE NEED TO GET YOU TWO HOME. YOU SMELL AWFUL!
IN FACT, I MIGHT HAVE TO SPRAY YOU DOWN WITH THE HOSE OUTSIDE SO YOU DON'T STINK UP THE WHOLE HOUSE...
HA-HA. VERY FUNNY.
CRAIG WAS RIGHT. WE DID SMELL HORRIBLE.
BUT WE DID SOMETHING AWESOME BY FINISHING OUR FIRST PRACTICE—EVEN IF MY LEGS DID FEEL LIKE COOKED SPAGHETTI NOODLES NOW.
AND, YEAH, A BUNCH OF THE BOYS DIDN'T WANT US ON THE TEAM, BUT WE WEREN'T GONNA QUIT.
BREE AND I WOULD JUST HAVE TO WORK HARDER AND GET BETTER.
THEY WEREN'T GONNA GET RID OF US THAT EASILY.

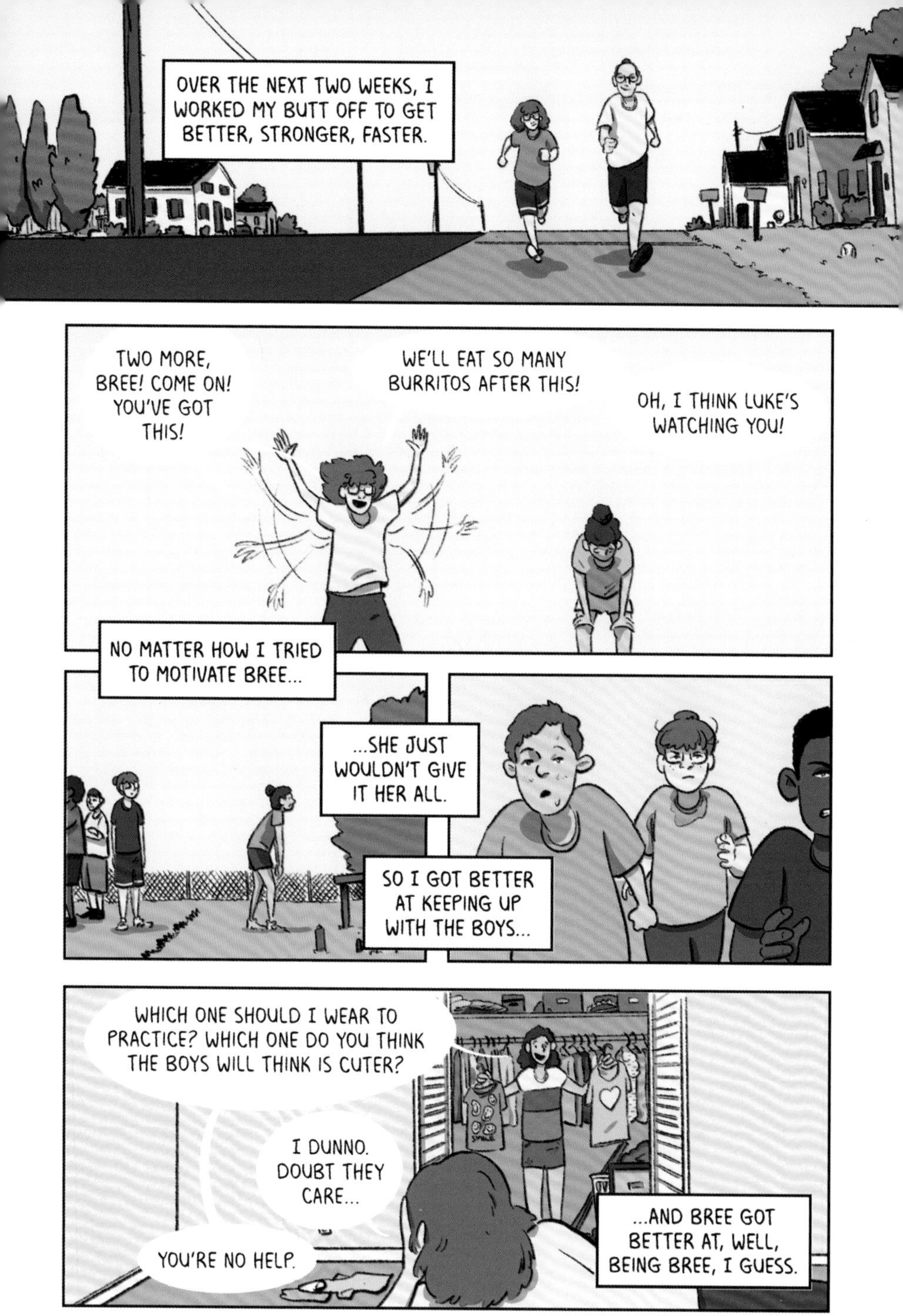
OVER THE NEXT TWO WEEKS, I WORKED MY BUTT OFF TO GET BETTER, STRONGER, FASTER.
TWO MORE, BREE! COME ON! YOU'VE GOT THIS!
WE'LL EAT SO MANY BURRITOS AFTER THIS!
OH, I THINK LUKE'S WATCHING YOU!
NO MATTER HOW I TRIED TO MOTIVATE BREE...
...SHE JUST WOULDN'T GIVE IT HER ALL.
SO I GOT BETTER AT KEEPING UP WITH THE BOYS...
WHICH ONE SHOULD I WEAR TO PRACTICE? WHICH ONE DO YOU THINK THE BOYS WILL THINK IS CUTER?
I DUNNO. DOUBT THEY CARE...
YOU'RE NO HELP.
...AND BREE GOT BETTER AT, WELL, BEING BREE, I GUESS.

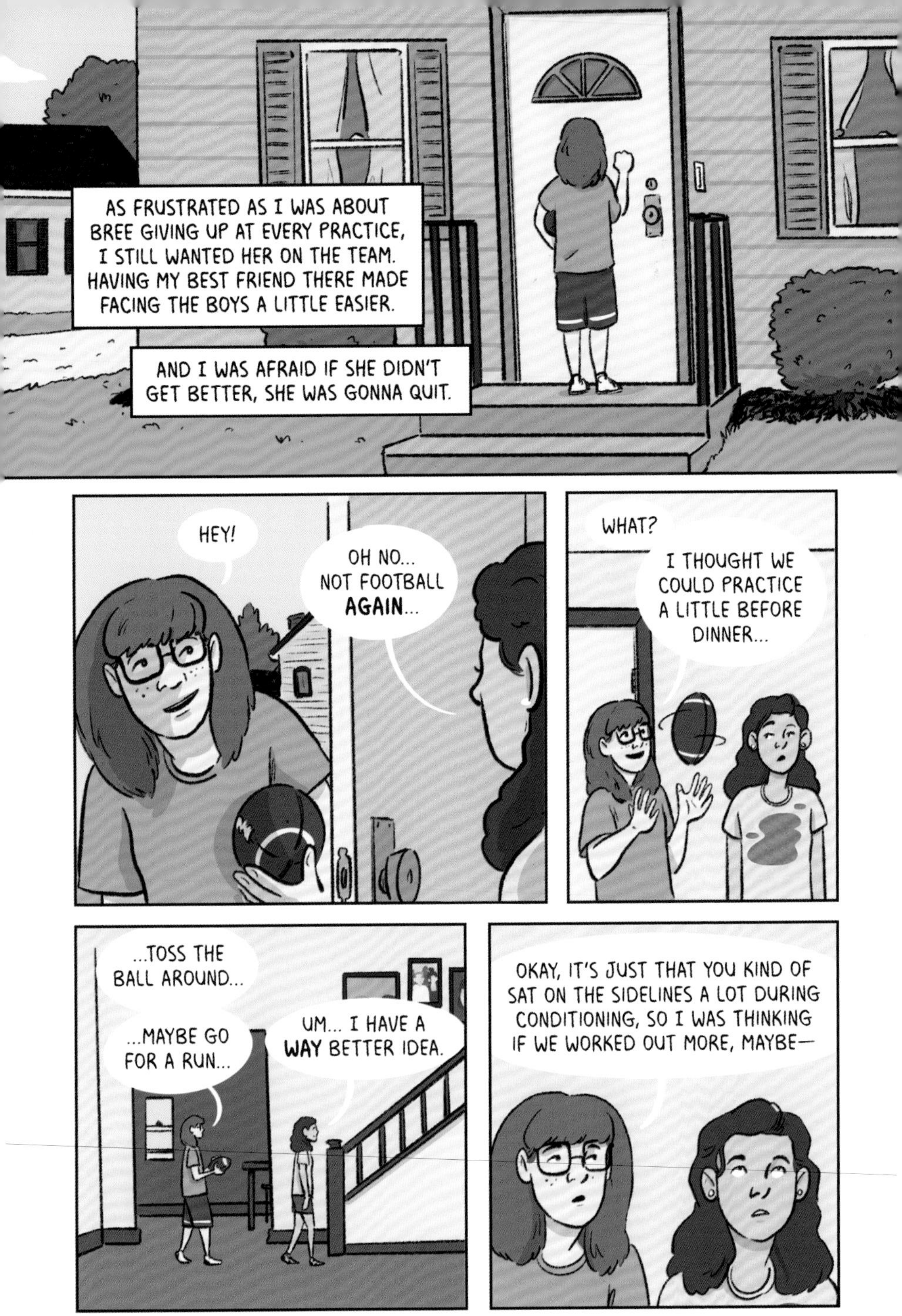
AS FRUSTRATED AS I WAS ABOUT BREE GIVING UP AT EVERY PRACTICE, I STILL WANTED HER ON THE TEAM. HAVING MY BEST FRIEND THERE MADE FACING THE BOYS A LITTLE EASIER.
AND I WAS AFRAID IF SHE DIDN'T GET BETTER, SHE WAS GONNA QUIT.
HEY!
OH NO... NOT FOOTBALL **AGAIN**...
WHAT?
I THOUGHT WE COULD PRACTICE A LITTLE BEFORE DINNER...
...TOSS THE BALL AROUND...
...MAYBE GO FOR A RUN...
UM... I HAVE A **WAY** BETTER IDEA.
OKAY, IT'S JUST THAT YOU KIND OF SAT ON THE SIDELINES A LOT DURING CONDITIONING, SO I WAS THINKING IF WE WORKED OUT MORE, MAYBE—

41

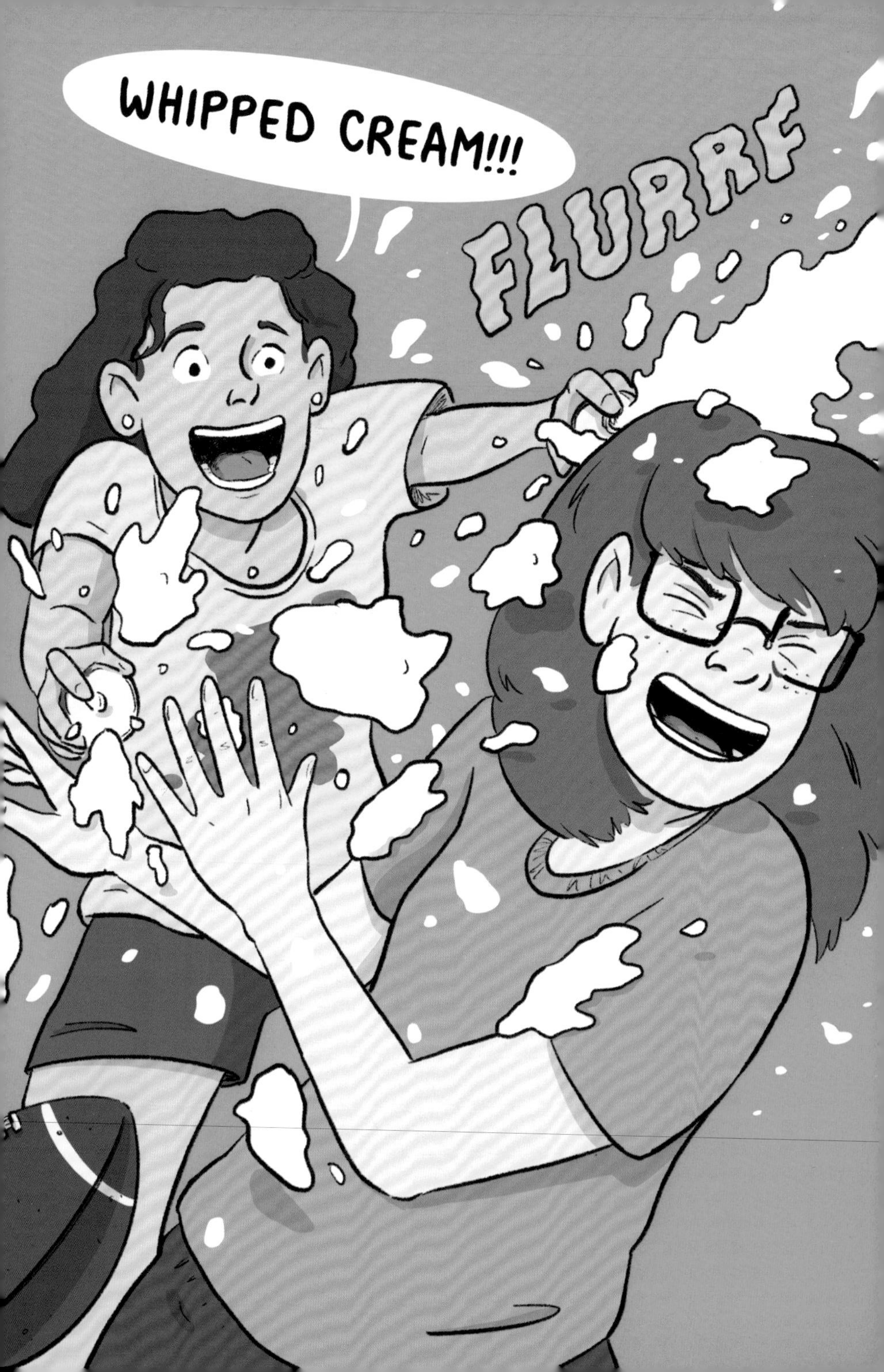
WHIPPED CREAM!!!
FLURRF

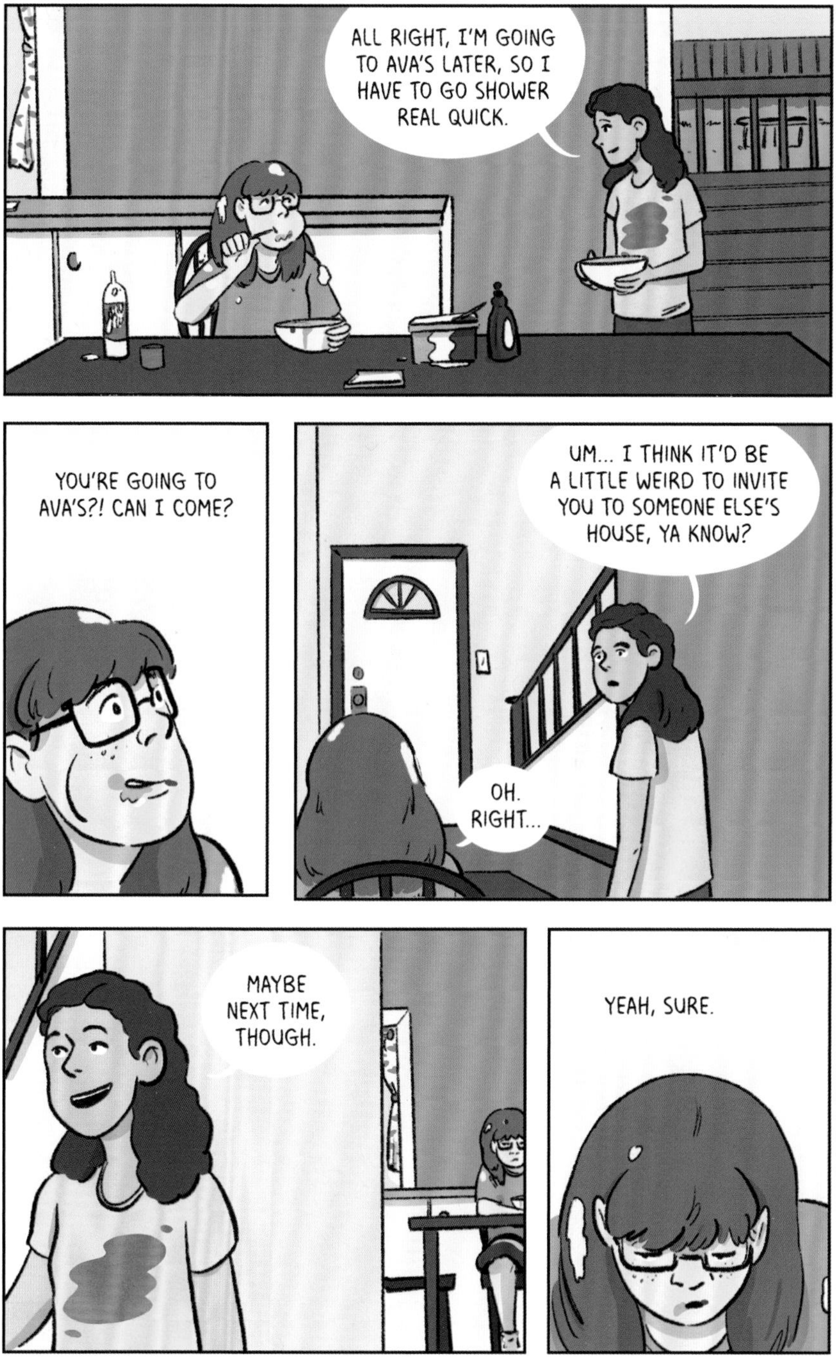
ALL RIGHT, I'M GOING TO AVA'S LATER, SO I HAVE TO GO SHOWER REAL QUICK.
YOU'RE GOING TO AVA'S?! CAN I COME?
UM... I THINK IT'D BE A LITTLE WEIRD TO INVITE YOU TO SOMEONE ELSE'S HOUSE, YA KNOW?
OH. RIGHT...
MAYBE NEXT TIME, THOUGH.
YEAH, SURE.

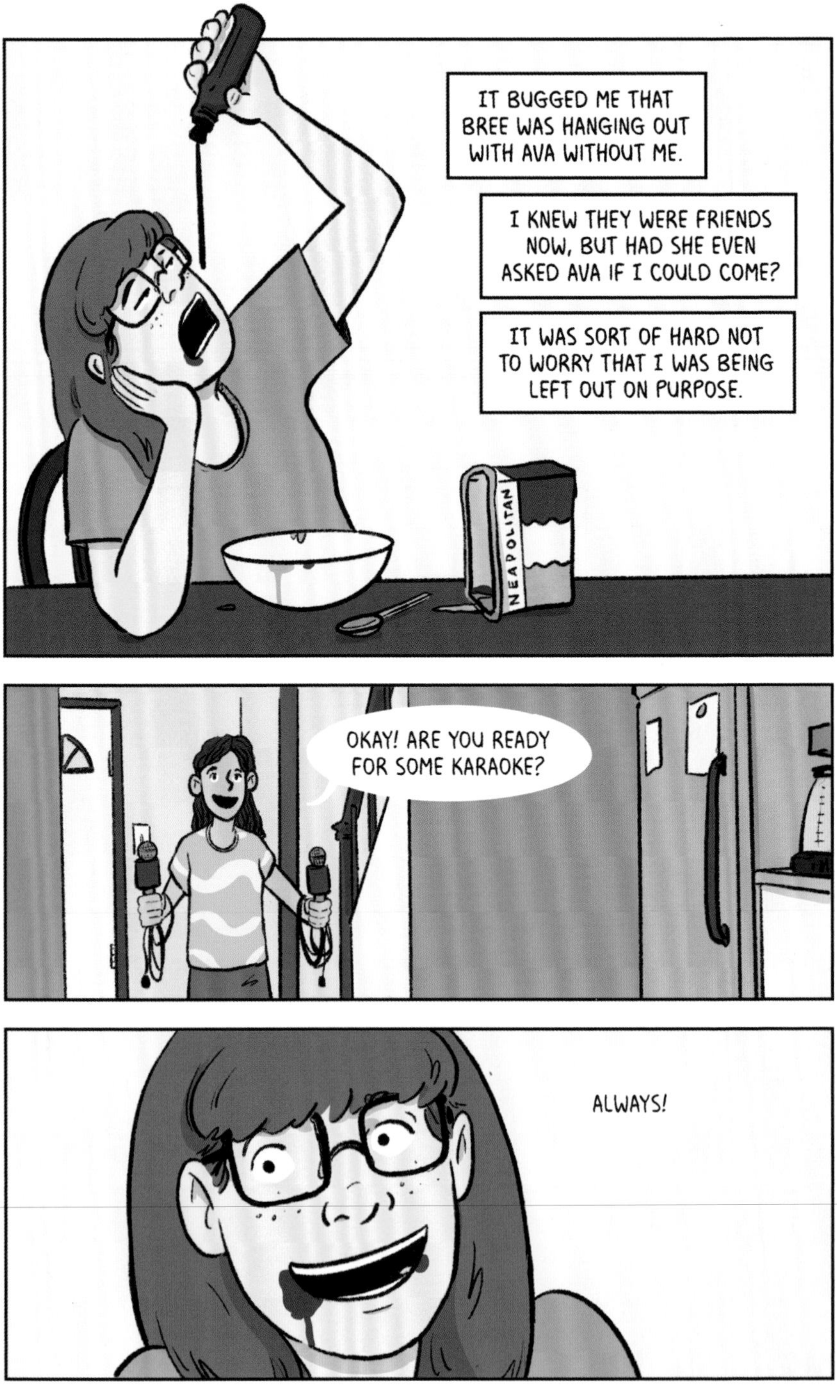
IT BUGGED ME THAT BREE WAS HANGING OUT WITH AVA WITHOUT ME.
I KNEW THEY WERE FRIENDS NOW, BUT HAD SHE EVEN ASKED AVA IF I COULD COME?
IT WAS SORT OF HARD NOT TO WORRY THAT I WAS BEING LEFT OUT ON PURPOSE.
NEAPOLITAN
OKAY! ARE YOU READY FOR SOME KARAOKE?
ALWAYS!

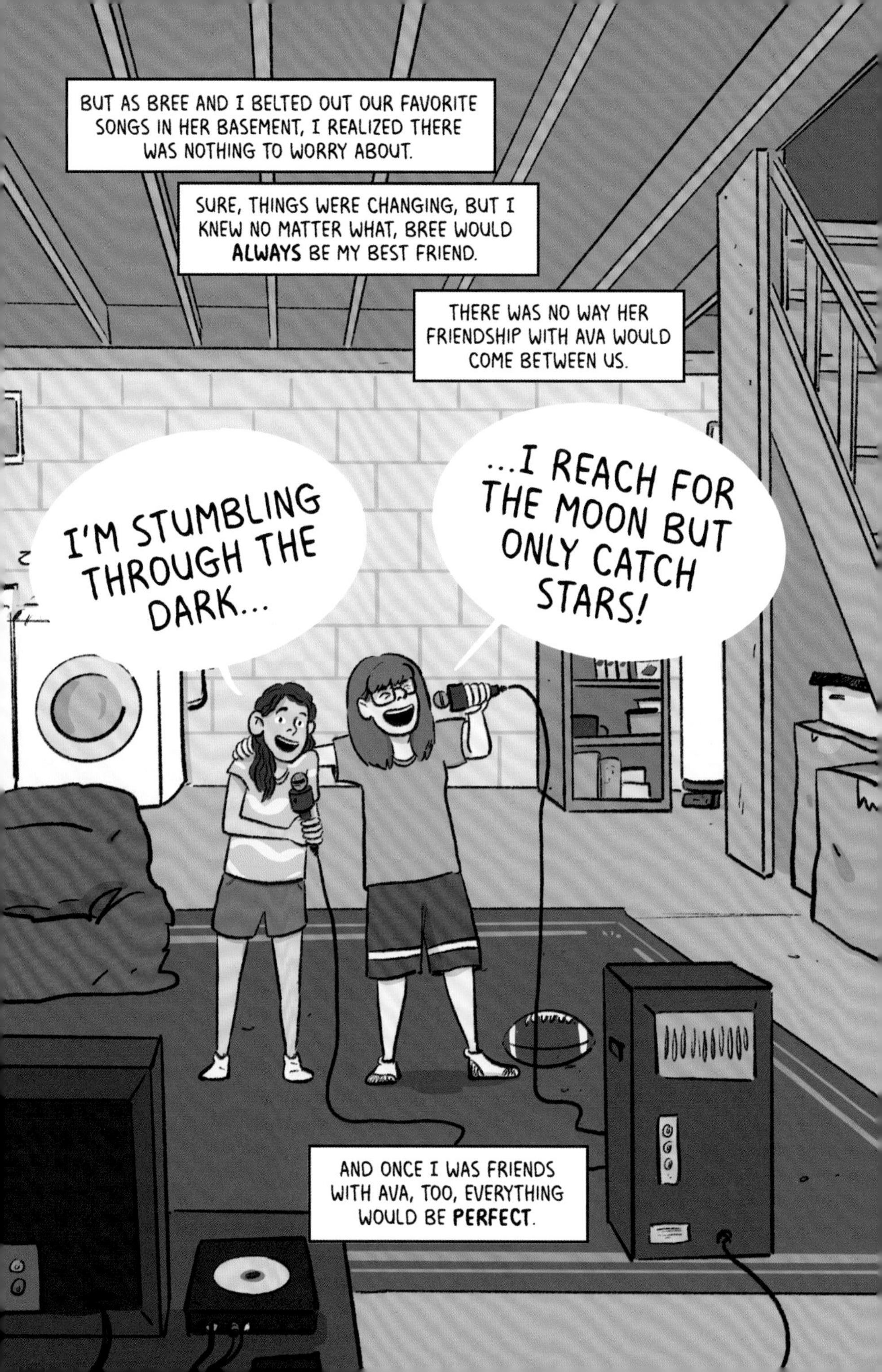
BUT AS BREE AND I BELTED OUT OUR FAVORITE SONGS IN HER BASEMENT, I REALIZED THERE WAS NOTHING TO WORRY ABOUT.
SURE, THINGS WERE CHANGING, BUT I KNEW NO MATTER WHAT, BREE WOULD **ALWAYS** BE MY BEST FRIEND.
THERE WAS NO WAY HER FRIENDSHIP WITH AVA WOULD COME BETWEEN US.
I'M STUMBLING THROUGH THE DARK...
...I REACH FOR THE MOON BUT ONLY CATCH STARS!
AND ONCE I WAS FRIENDS WITH AVA, TOO, EVERYTHING WOULD BE **PERFECT**.

CHAPTER 3

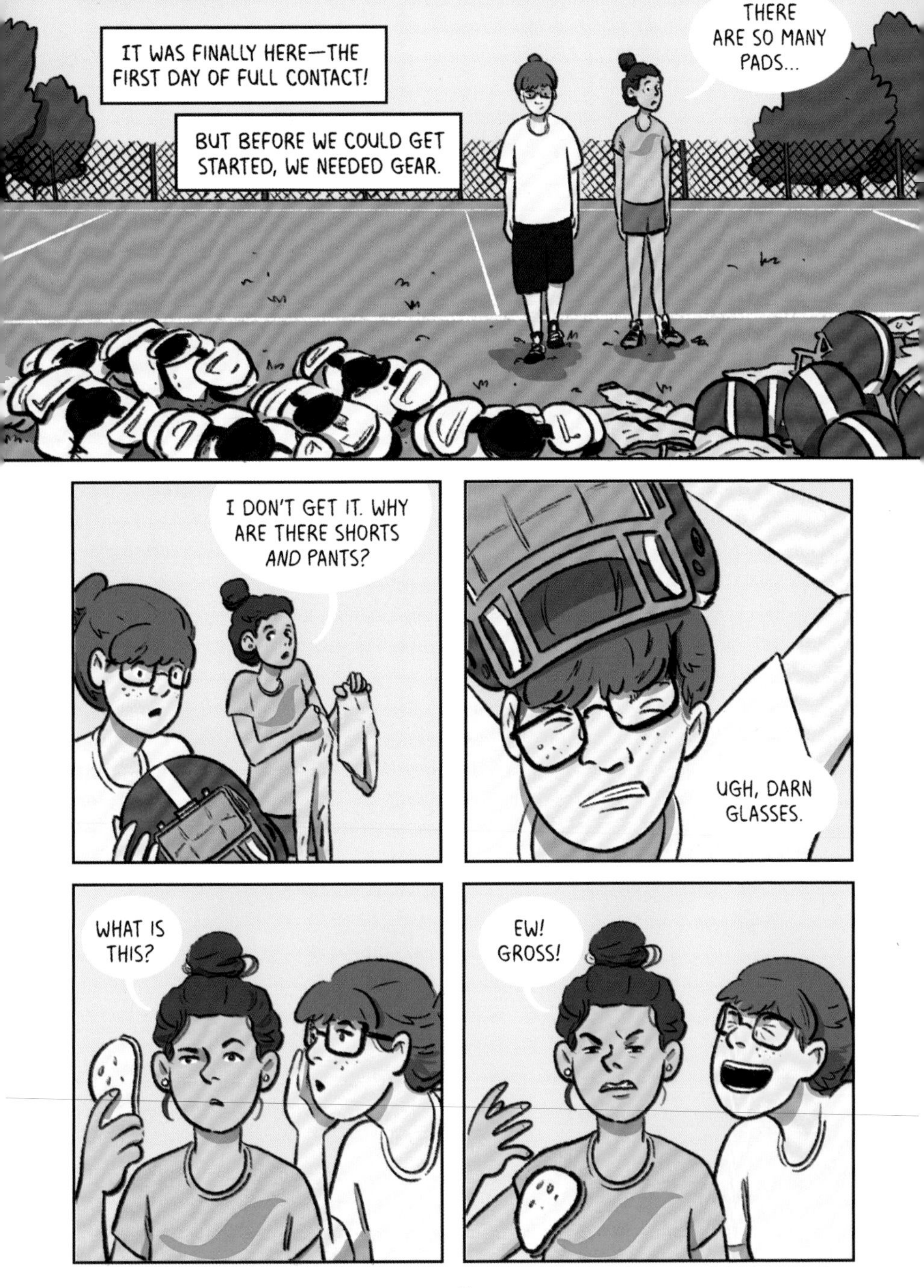
IT WAS FINALLY HERE—THE FIRST DAY OF FULL CONTACT!
BUT BEFORE WE COULD GET STARTED, WE NEEDED GEAR.
THERE ARE SO MANY PADS...
I DON'T GET IT. WHY ARE THERE SHORTS *AND* PANTS?
UGH, DARN GLASSES.
WHAT IS THIS?
EW! GROSS!

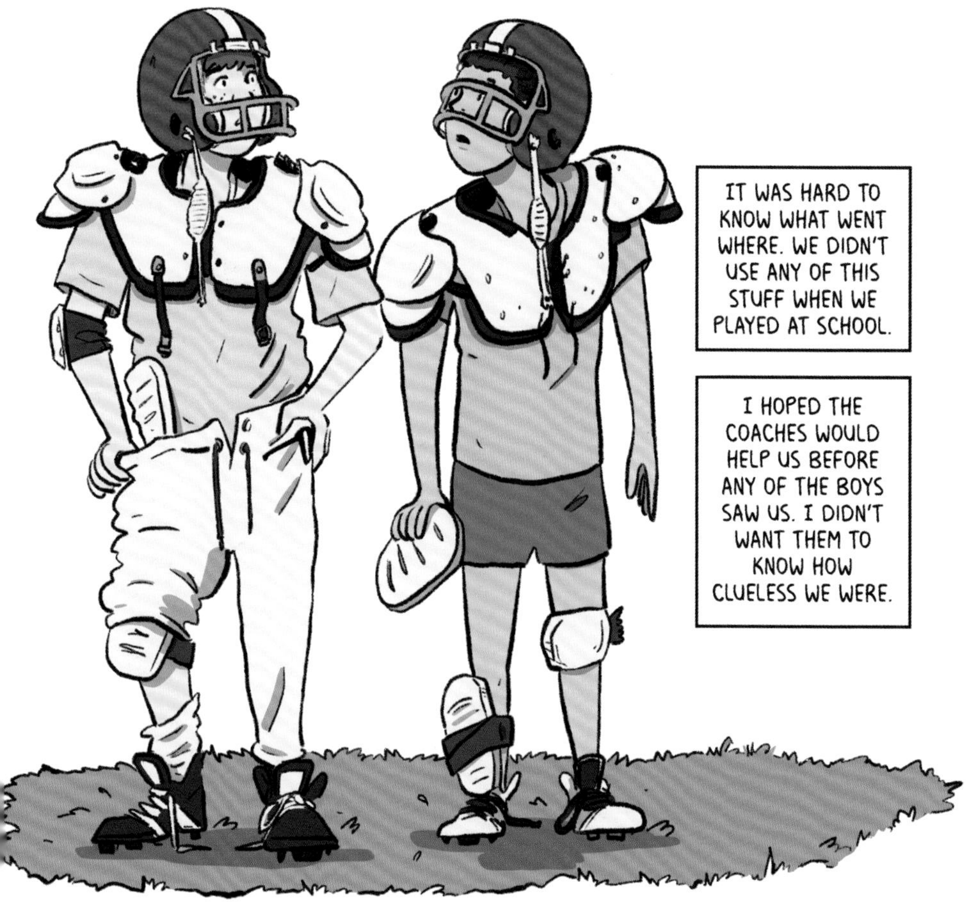
IT WAS HARD TO KNOW WHAT WENT WHERE. WE DIDN'T USE ANY OF THIS STUFF WHEN WE PLAYED AT SCHOOL.
I HOPED THE COACHES WOULD HELP US BEFORE ANY OF THE BOYS SAW US. I DIDN'T WANT THEM TO KNOW HOW CLUELESS WE WERE.

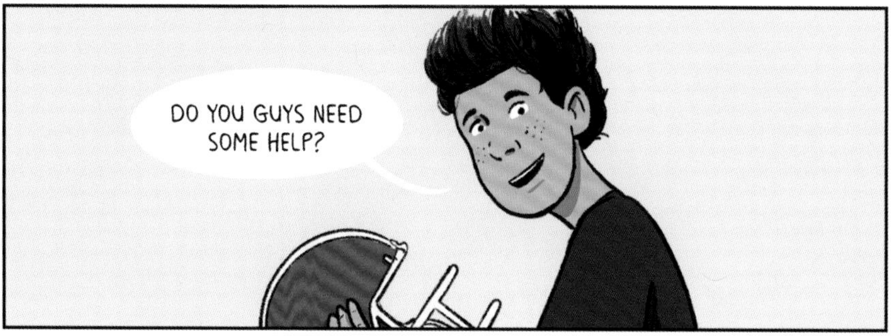
DO YOU GUYS NEED SOME HELP?

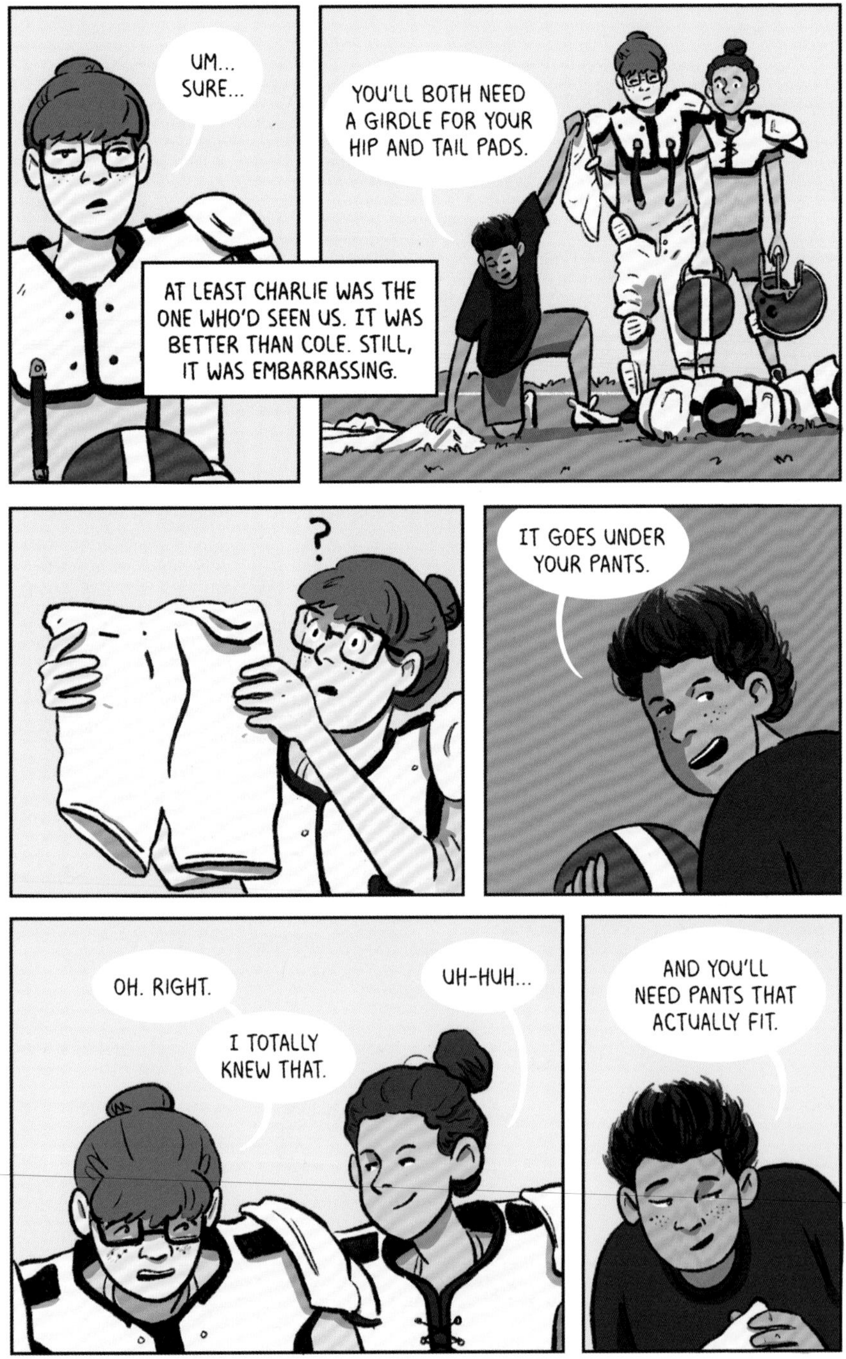
UM... SURE...
YOU'LL BOTH NEED A GIRDLE FOR YOUR HIP AND TAIL PADS.
AT LEAST CHARLIE WAS THE ONE WHO'D SEEN US. IT WAS BETTER THAN COLE. STILL, IT WAS EMBARRASSING.
?
IT GOES UNDER YOUR PANTS.
OH. RIGHT.
I TOTALLY KNEW THAT.
UH-HUH...
AND YOU'LL NEED PANTS THAT ACTUALLY FIT.

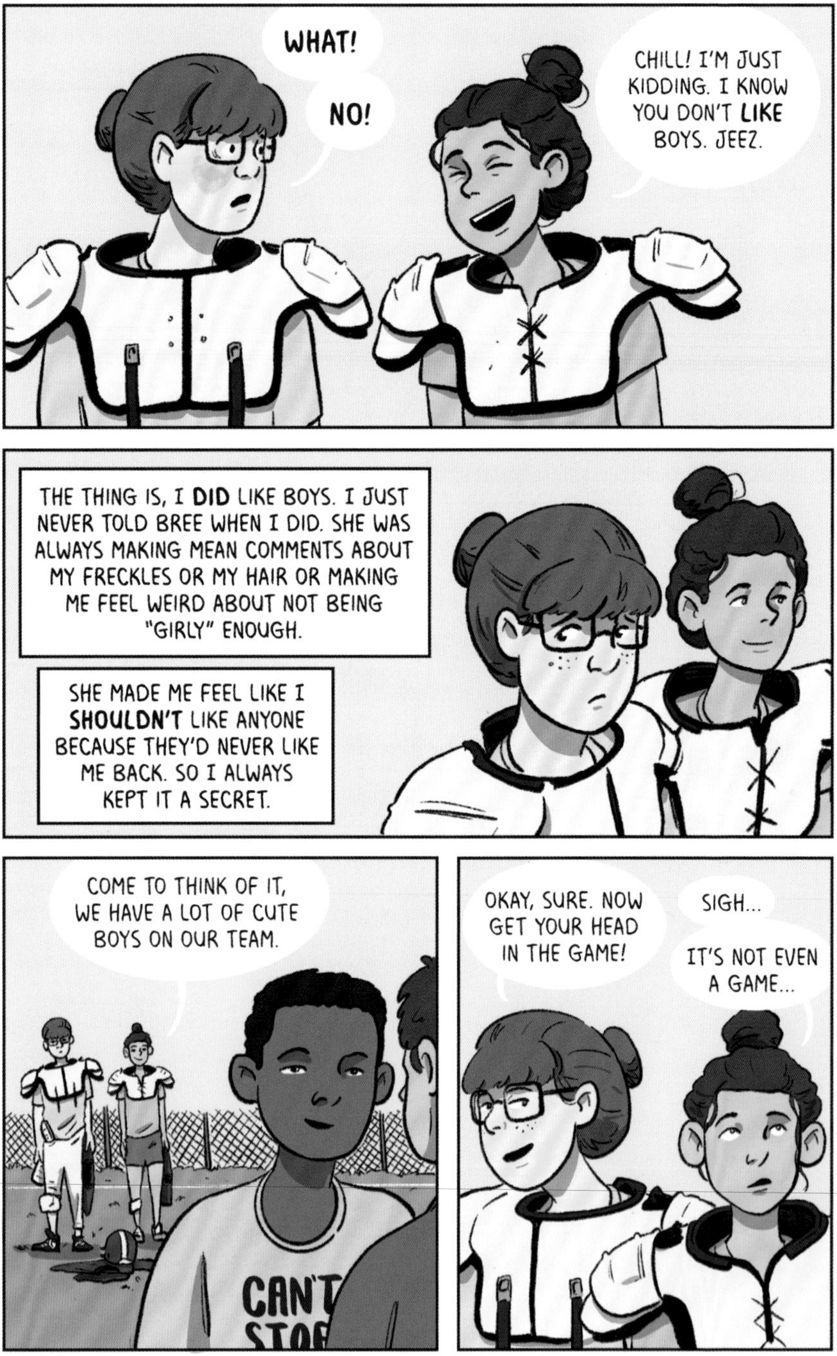
WHAT!
NO!
CHILL! I'M JUST KIDDING. I KNOW YOU DON'T **LIKE** BOYS. JEEZ.
THE THING IS, I **DID** LIKE BOYS. I JUST NEVER TOLD BREE WHEN I DID. SHE WAS ALWAYS MAKING MEAN COMMENTS ABOUT MY FRECKLES OR MY HAIR OR MAKING ME FEEL WEIRD ABOUT NOT BEING "GIRLY" ENOUGH.
SHE MADE ME FEEL LIKE I **SHOULDN'T** LIKE ANYONE BECAUSE THEY'D NEVER LIKE ME BACK. SO I ALWAYS KEPT IT A SECRET.
COME TO THINK OF IT, WE HAVE A LOT OF CUTE BOYS ON OUR TEAM.
CAN'T
STOP
OKAY, SURE. NOW GET YOUR HEAD IN THE GAME!
SIGH...
IT'S NOT EVEN A GAME...

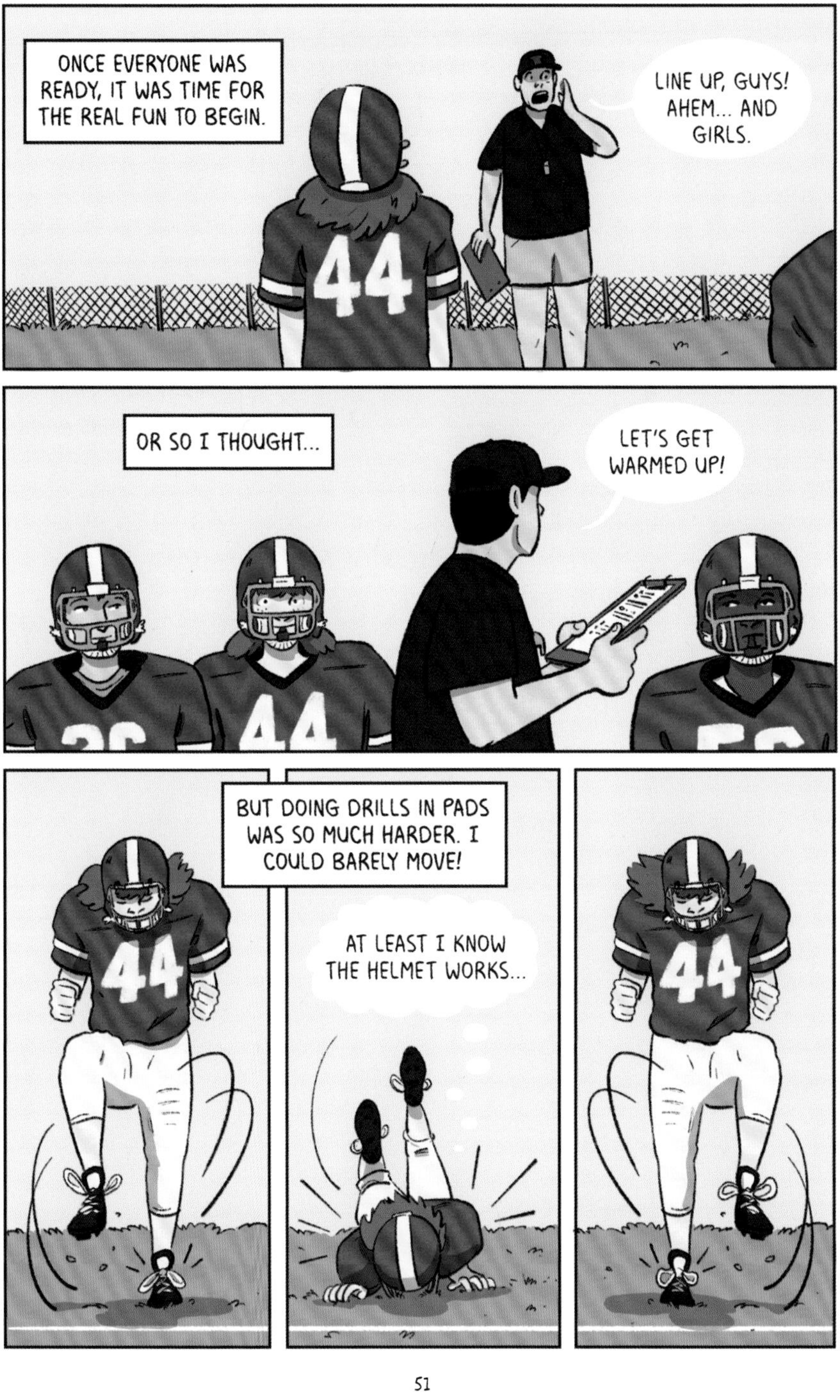
ONCE EVERYONE WAS READY, IT WAS TIME FOR THE REAL FUN TO BEGIN.
LINE UP, GUYS! AHEM... AND GIRLS.
OR SO I THOUGHT...
LET'S GET WARMED UP!
BUT DOING DRILLS IN PADS WAS SO MUCH HARDER. I COULD BARELY MOVE!
AT LEAST I KNOW THE HELMET WORKS...

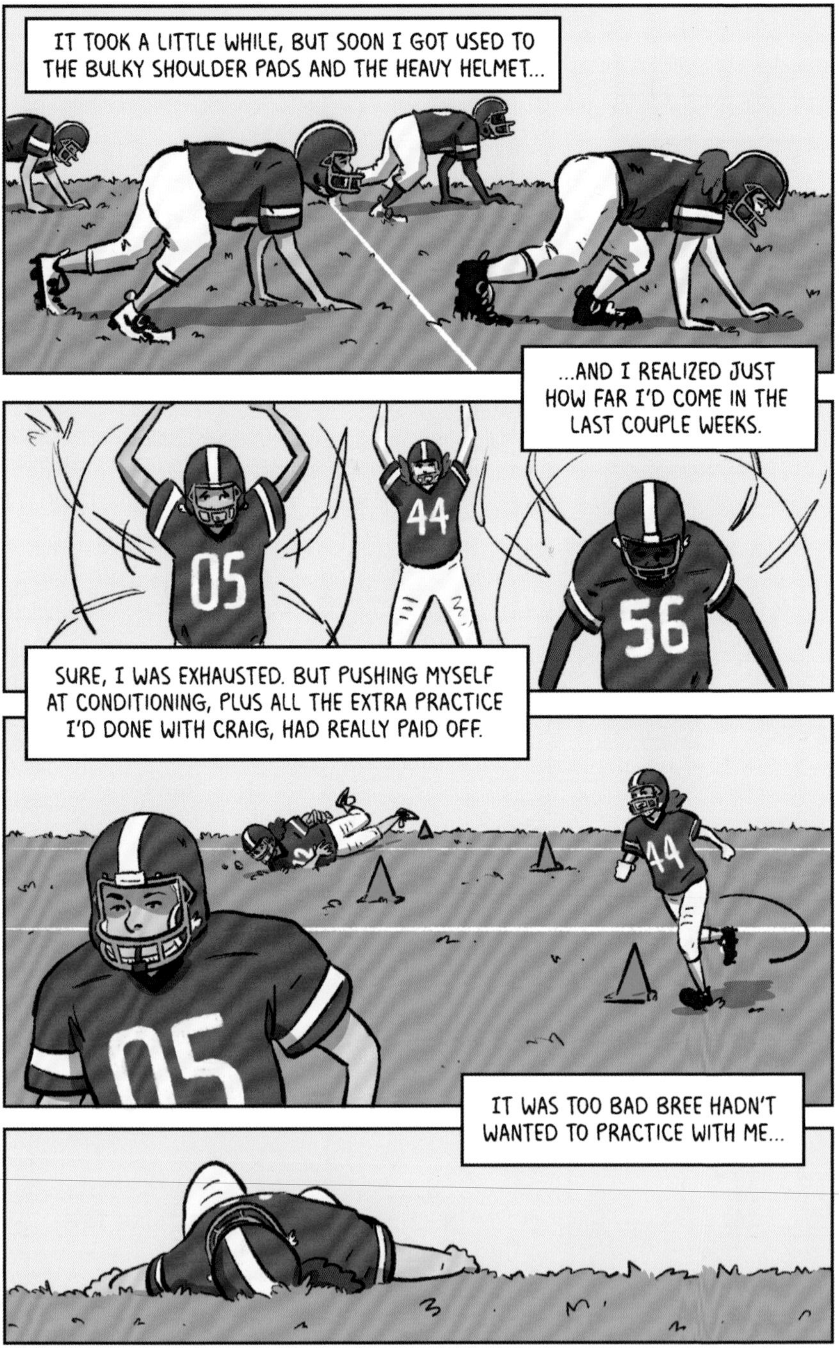
IT TOOK A LITTLE WHILE, BUT SOON I GOT USED TO THE BULKY SHOULDER PADS AND THE HEAVY HELMET...
...AND I REALIZED JUST HOW FAR I'D COME IN THE LAST COUPLE WEEKS.
05
44
56
SURE, I WAS EXHAUSTED. BUT PUSHING MYSELF AT CONDITIONING, PLUS ALL THE EXTRA PRACTICE I'D DONE WITH CRAIG, HAD REALLY PAID OFF.
44
05
IT WAS TOO BAD BREE HADN'T WANTED TO PRACTICE WITH ME...

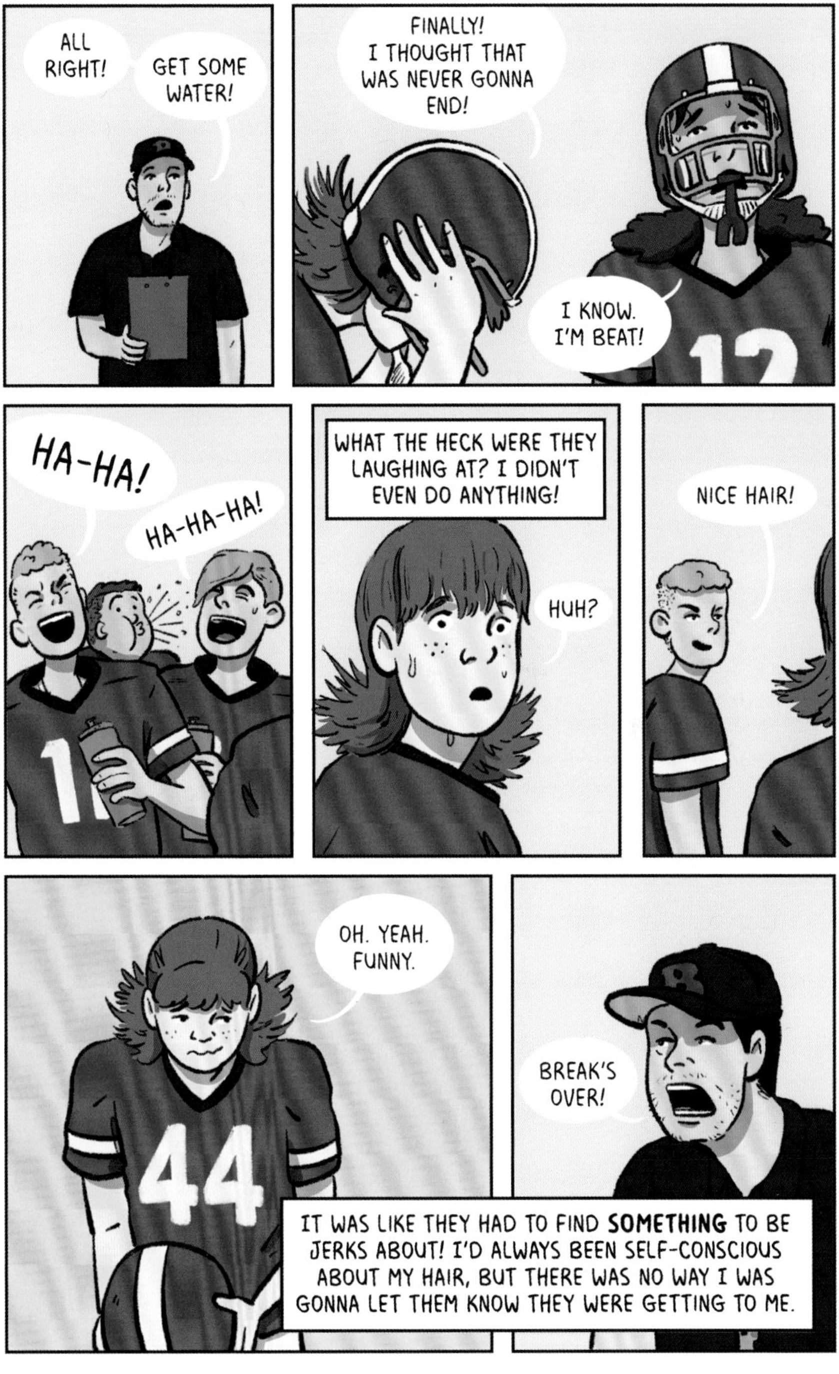
ALL RIGHT!
GET SOME WATER!
FINALLY! I THOUGHT THAT WAS NEVER GONNA END!
I KNOW. I'M BEAT!
HA-HA!
HA-HA-HA!
WHAT THE HECK WERE THEY LAUGHING AT? I DIDN'T EVEN DO ANYTHING!
HUH?
NICE HAIR!
OH. YEAH. FUNNY.
BREAK'S OVER!
IT WAS LIKE THEY HAD TO FIND **SOMETHING** TO BE JERKS ABOUT! I'D ALWAYS BEEN SELF-CONSCIOUS ABOUT MY HAIR, BUT THERE WAS NO WAY I WAS GONNA LET THEM KNOW THEY WERE GETTING TO ME.

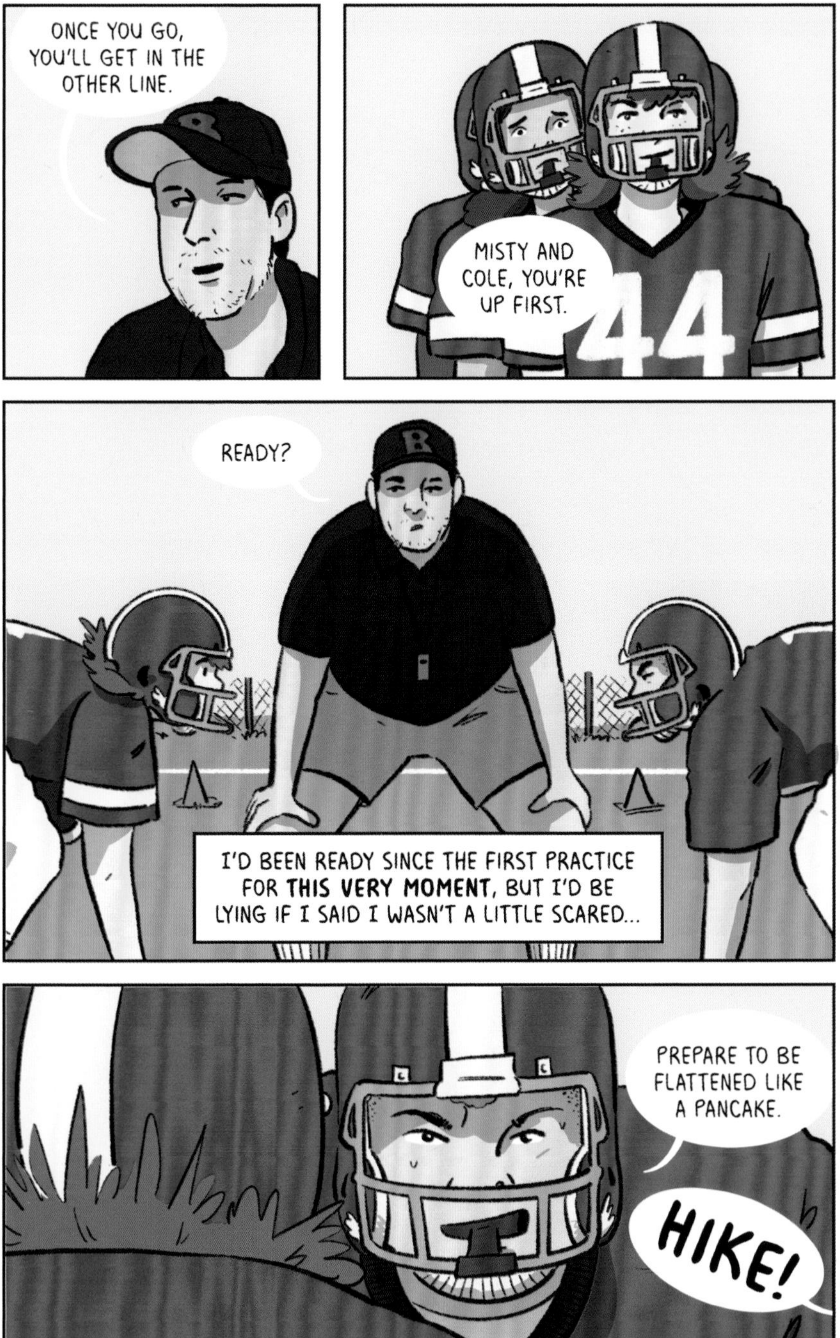
ONCE YOU GO, YOU'LL GET IN THE OTHER LINE.
MISTY AND COLE, YOU'RE UP FIRST.
READY?
I'D BEEN READY SINCE THE FIRST PRACTICE FOR **THIS VERY MOMENT**, BUT I'D BE LYING IF I SAID I WASN'T A LITTLE SCARED...
PREPARE TO BE FLATTENED LIKE A PANCAKE.
HIKE!

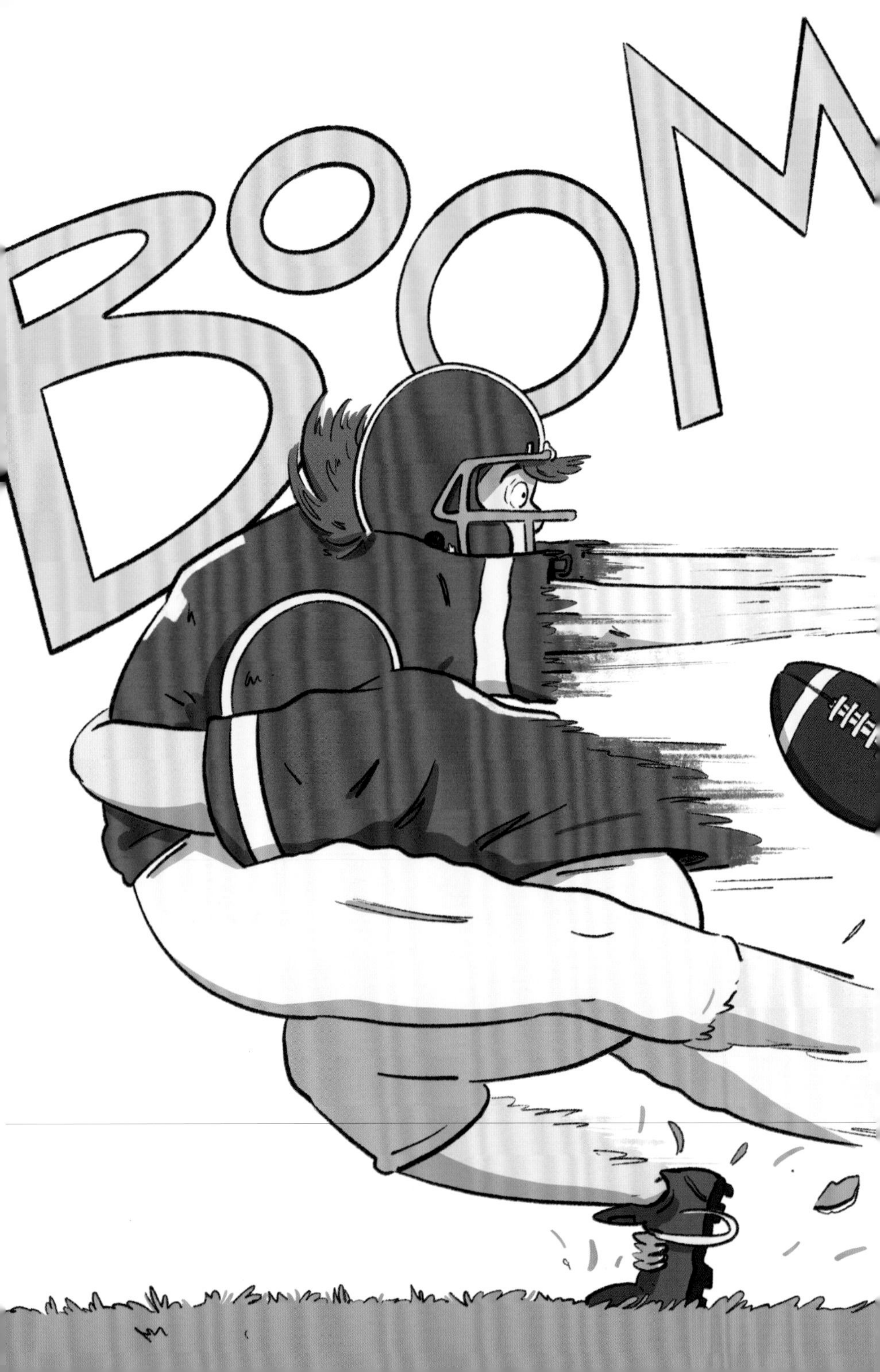
BOOM

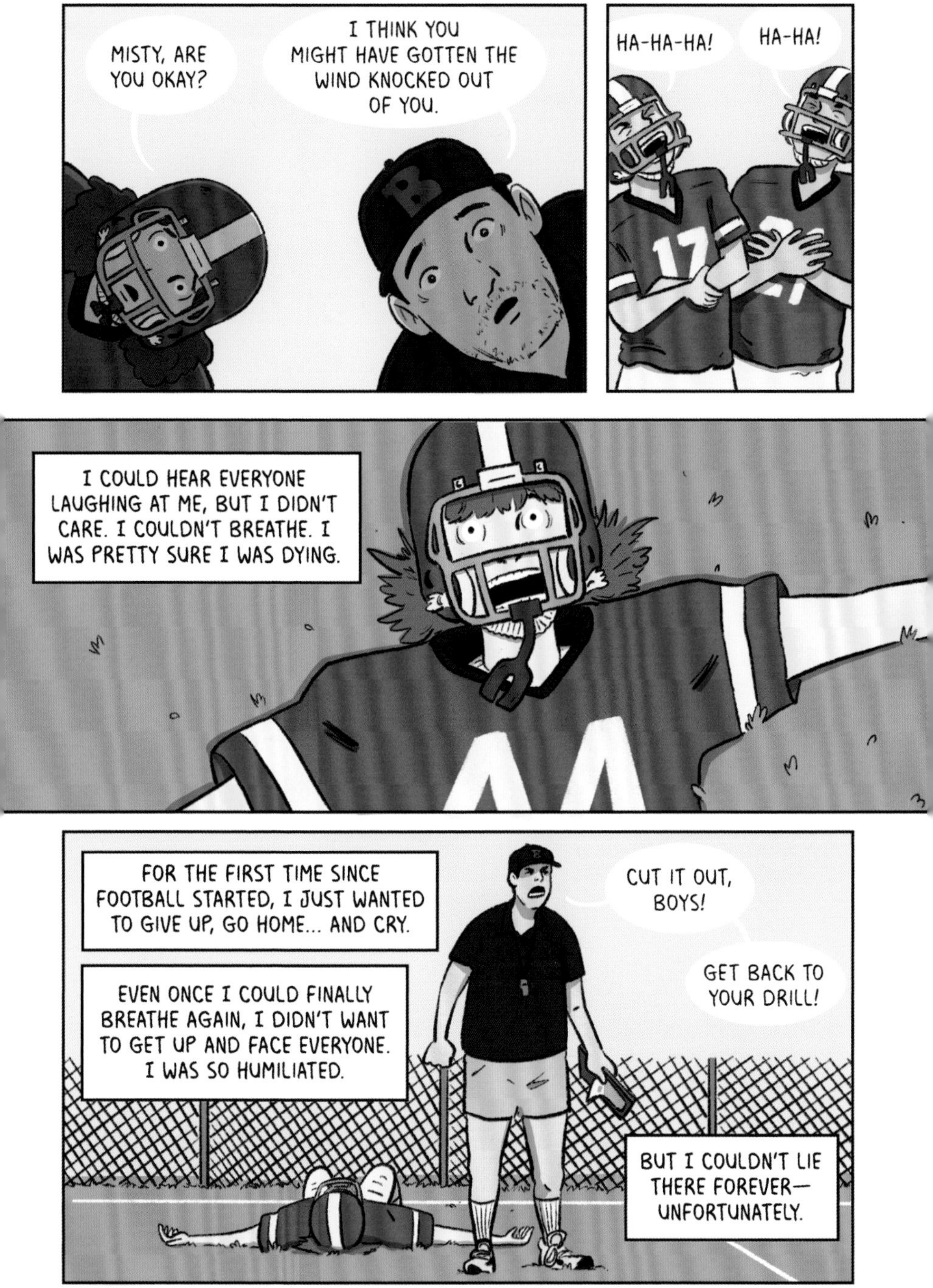
MISTY, ARE YOU OKAY?
I THINK YOU MIGHT HAVE GOTTEN THE WIND KNOCKED OUT OF YOU.
HA-HA-HA!
HA-HA!
I COULD HEAR EVERYONE LAUGHING AT ME, BUT I DIDN'T CARE. I COULDN'T BREATHE. I WAS PRETTY SURE I WAS DYING.
FOR THE FIRST TIME SINCE FOOTBALL STARTED, I JUST WANTED TO GIVE UP, GO HOME... AND CRY.
EVEN ONCE I COULD FINALLY BREATHE AGAIN, I DIDN'T WANT TO GET UP AND FACE EVERYONE. I WAS SO HUMILIATED.
CUT IT OUT, BOYS!
GET BACK TO YOUR DRILL!
BUT I COULDN'T LIE THERE FOREVER—UNFORTUNATELY.

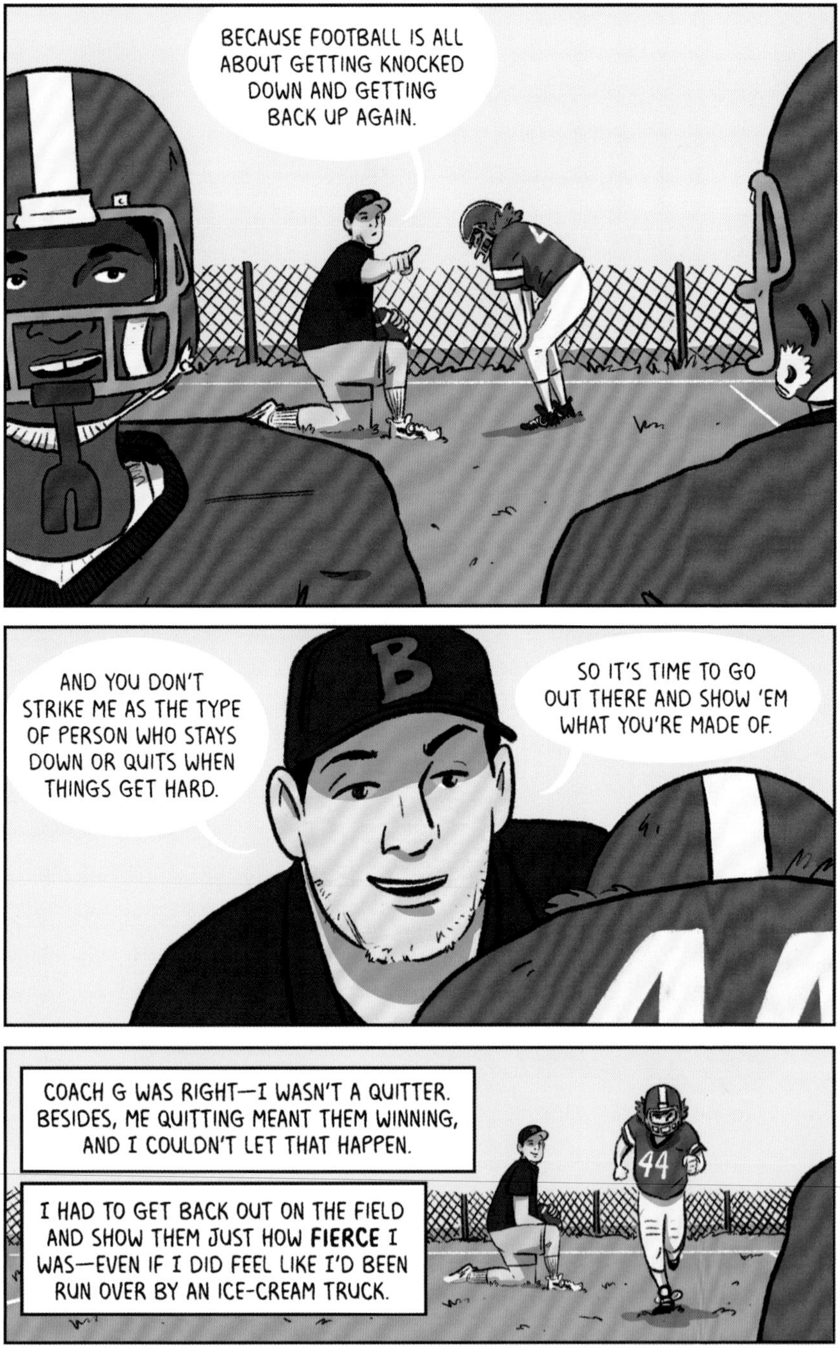
BECAUSE FOOTBALL IS ALL ABOUT GETTING KNOCKED DOWN AND GETTING BACK UP AGAIN.
AND YOU DON'T STRIKE ME AS THE TYPE OF PERSON WHO STAYS DOWN OR QUITS WHEN THINGS GET HARD.
SO IT'S TIME TO GO OUT THERE AND SHOW 'EM WHAT YOU'RE MADE OF.
COACH G WAS RIGHT—I WASN'T A QUITTER. BESIDES, ME QUITTING MEANT THEM WINNING, AND I COULDN'T LET THAT HAPPEN.
I HAD TO GET BACK OUT ON THE FIELD AND SHOW THEM JUST HOW **FIERCE** I WAS—EVEN IF I DID FEEL LIKE I'D BEEN RUN OVER BY AN ICE-CREAM TRUCK.
44

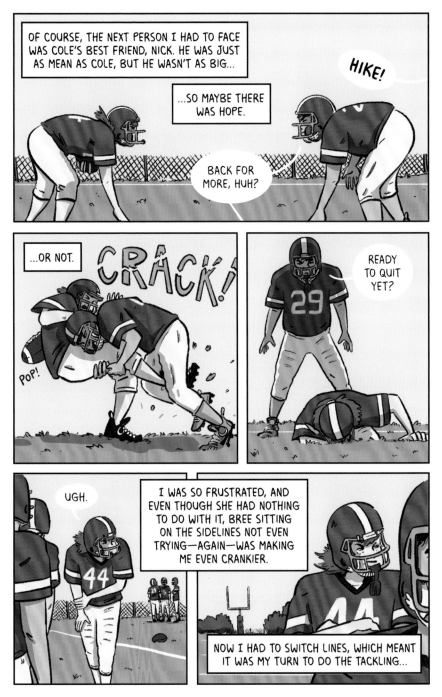

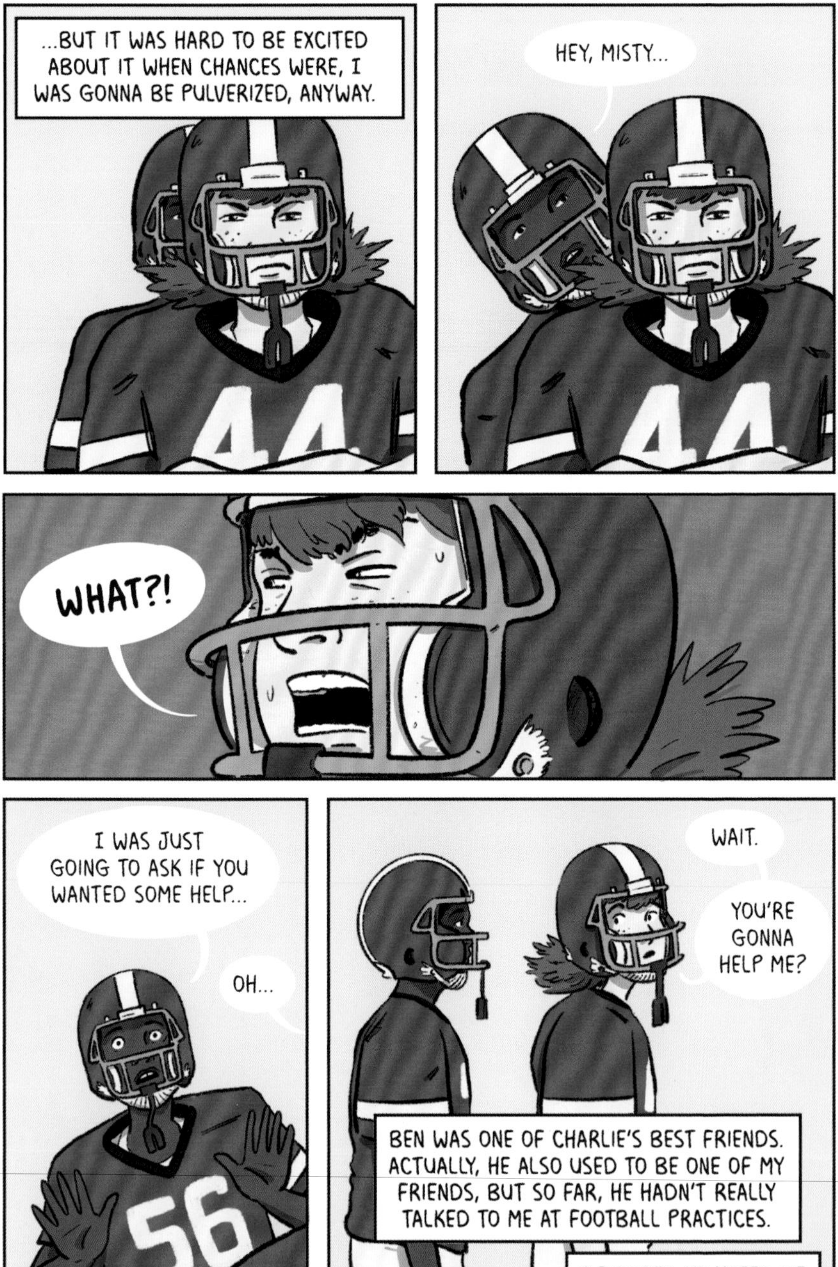

...BUT IT WAS HARD TO BE EXCITED ABOUT IT WHEN CHANCES WERE, I WAS GONNA BE PULVERIZED, ANYWAY.
HEY, MISTY...
WHAT?!
I WAS JUST GOING TO ASK IF YOU WANTED SOME HELP...
OH...
WAIT.
YOU'RE GONNA HELP ME?
BEN WAS ONE OF CHARLIE'S BEST FRIENDS. ACTUALLY, HE ALSO USED TO BE ONE OF MY FRIENDS, BUT SO FAR, HE HADN'T REALLY TALKED TO ME AT FOOTBALL PRACTICES.
I FIGURED HE HATED ME FOR BEING HERE, TOO.

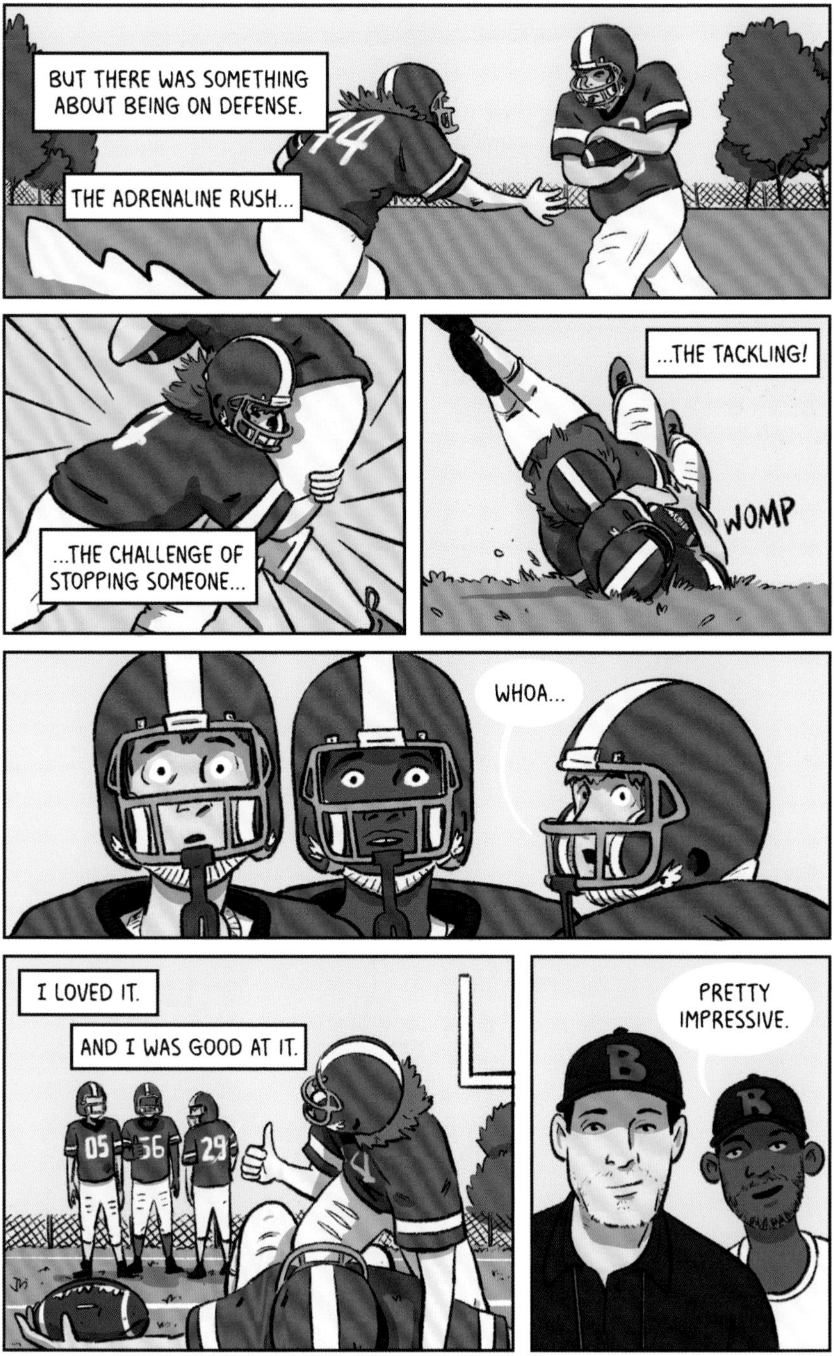
BUT THERE WAS SOMETHING ABOUT BEING ON DEFENSE.
THE ADRENALINE RUSH...
...THE CHALLENGE OF STOPPING SOMEONE...
...THE TACKLING!
WOMP
WHOA...
I LOVED IT.
AND I WAS GOOD AT IT.
05
56
29
PRETTY IMPRESSIVE.

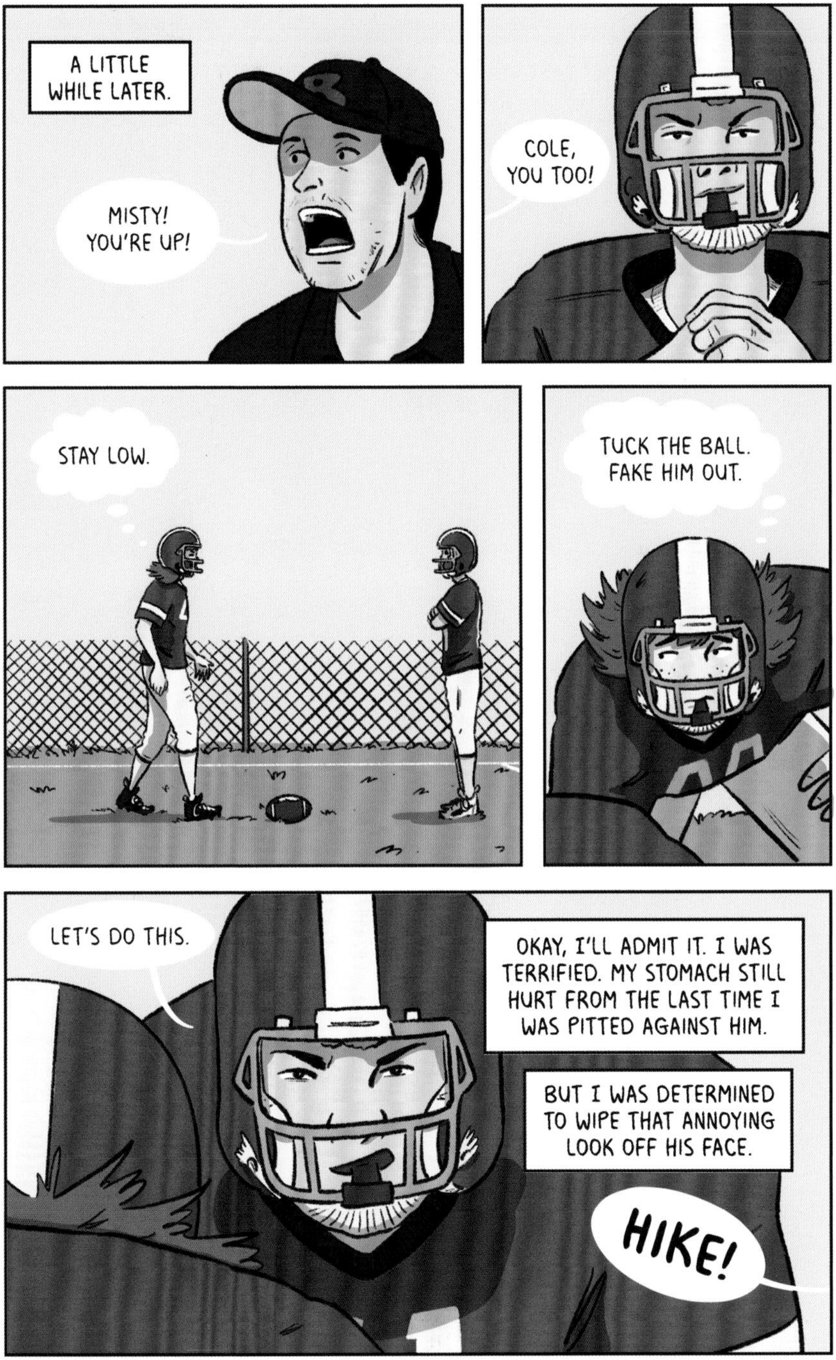
A LITTLE WHILE LATER.
MISTY! YOU'RE UP!
COLE, YOU TOO!
STAY LOW.
TUCK THE BALL. FAKE HIM OUT.
LET'S DO THIS.
OKAY, I'LL ADMIT IT. I WAS TERRIFIED. MY STOMACH STILL HURT FROM THE LAST TIME I WAS PITTED AGAINST HIM.
BUT I WAS DETERMINED TO WIPE THAT ANNOYING LOOK OFF HIS FACE.
HIKE!

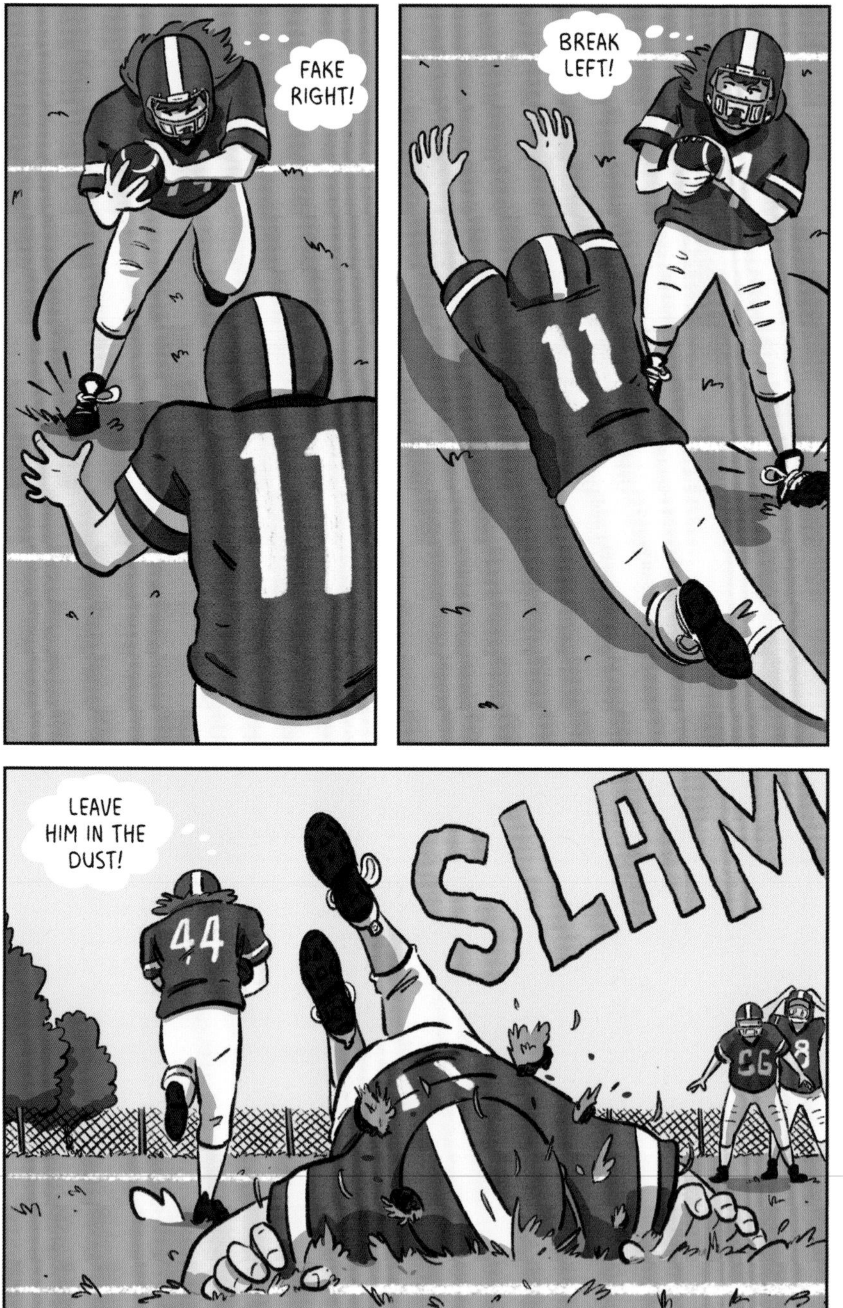
FAKE RIGHT!
11
BREAK LEFT!
11
LEAVE HIM IN THE DUST!
44
SLAM

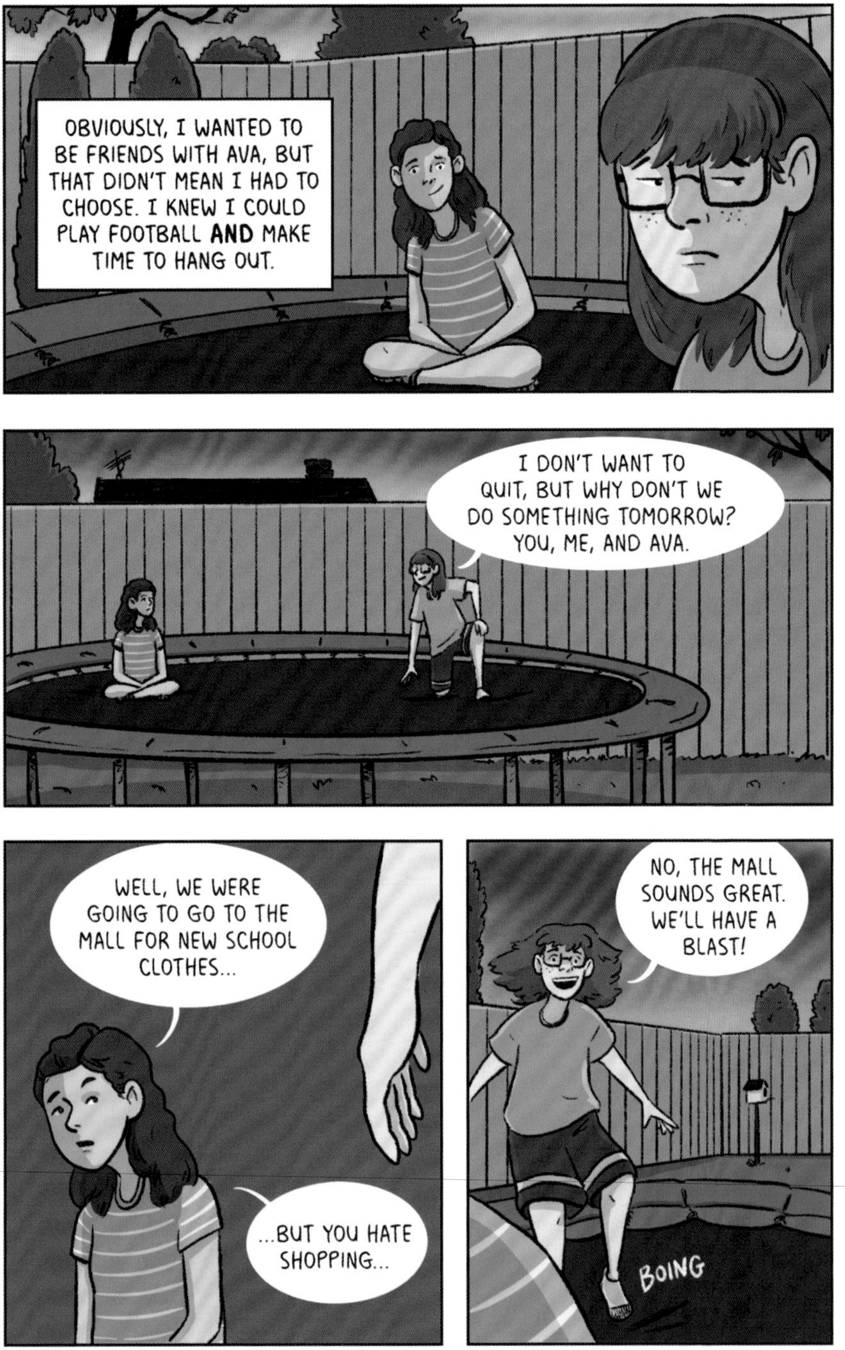
OBVIOUSLY, I WANTED TO BE FRIENDS WITH AVA, BUT THAT DIDN'T MEAN I HAD TO CHOOSE. I KNEW I COULD PLAY FOOTBALL **AND** MAKE TIME TO HANG OUT.
I DON'T WANT TO QUIT, BUT WHY DON'T WE DO SOMETHING TOMORROW? YOU, ME, AND AVA.
WELL, WE WERE GOING TO GO TO THE MALL FOR NEW SCHOOL CLOTHES...
...BUT YOU HATE SHOPPING...
NO, THE MALL SOUNDS GREAT. WE'LL HAVE A BLAST!
BOING

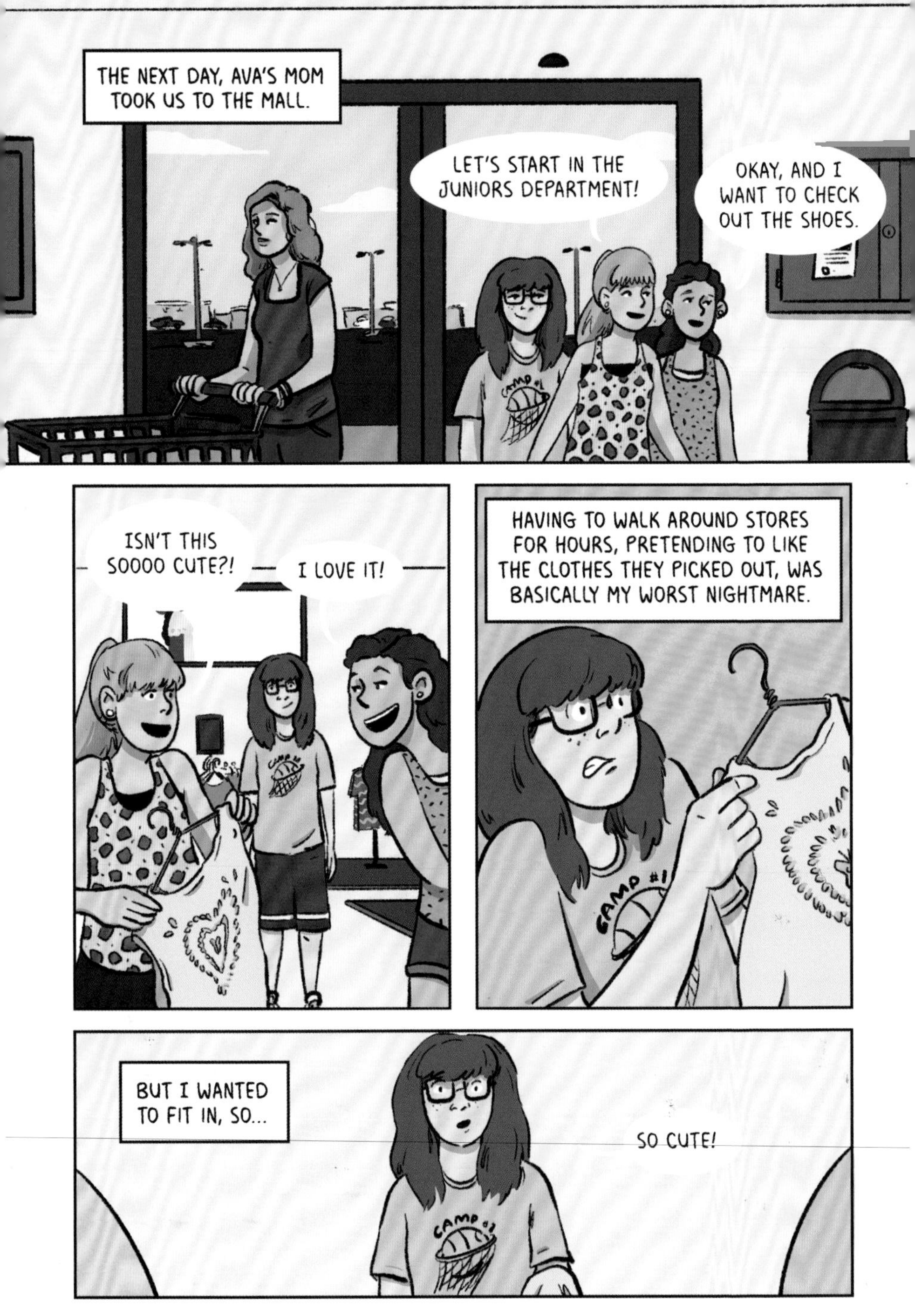
THE NEXT DAY, AVA'S MOM TOOK US TO THE MALL.
LET'S START IN THE JUNIORS DEPARTMENT!
OKAY, AND I WANT TO CHECK OUT THE SHOES.
CAMP #1
ISN'T THIS SOOOO CUTE?!
I LOVE IT!
HAVING TO WALK AROUND STORES FOR HOURS, PRETENDING TO LIKE THE CLOTHES THEY PICKED OUT, WAS BASICALLY MY WORST NIGHTMARE.
BUT I WANTED TO FIT IN, SO...
SO CUTE!

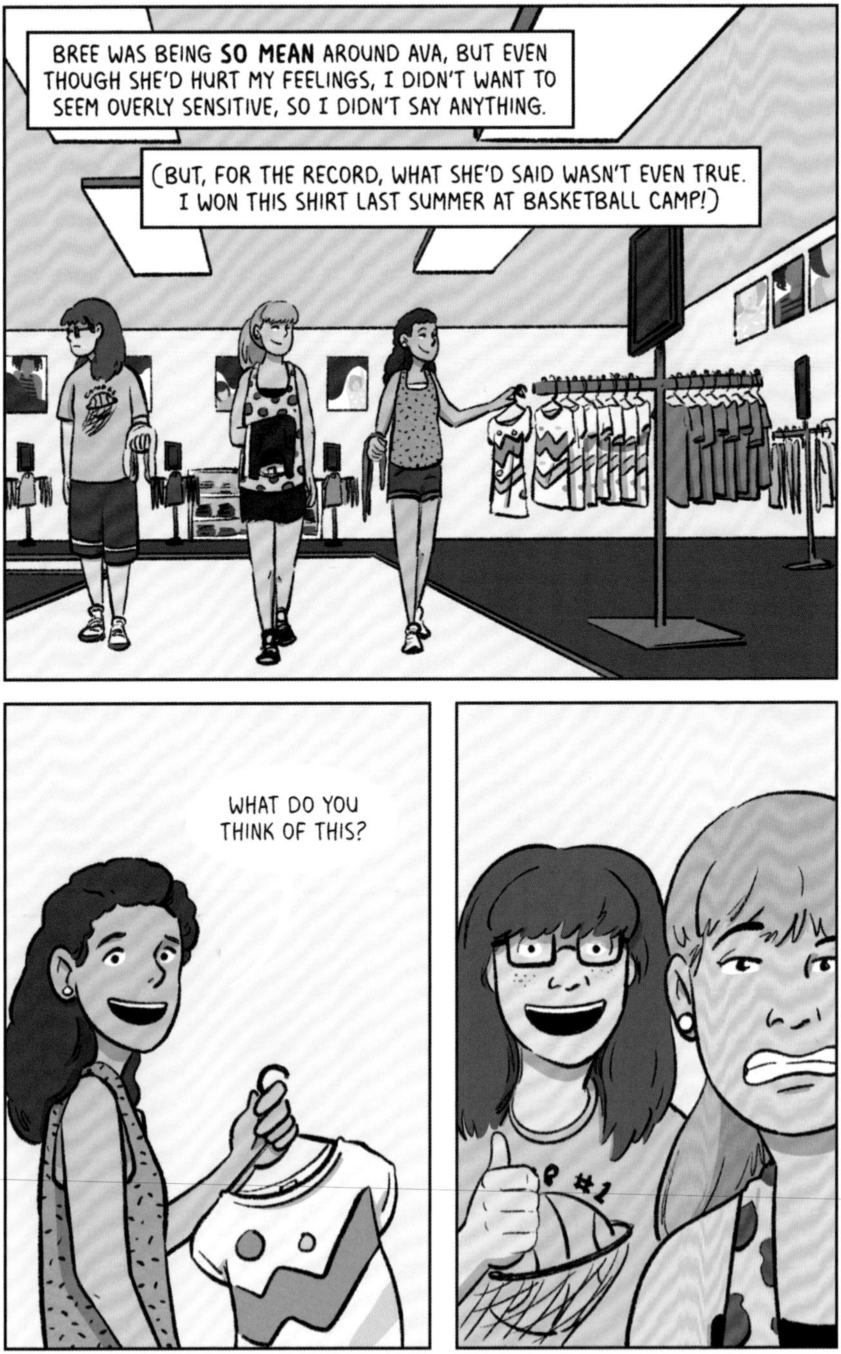
BREE WAS BEING **SO MEAN** AROUND AVA, BUT EVEN THOUGH SHE'D HURT MY FEELINGS, I DIDN'T WANT TO SEEM OVERLY SENSITIVE, SO I DIDN'T SAY ANYTHING.
(BUT, FOR THE RECORD, WHAT SHE'D SAID WASN'T EVEN TRUE. I WON THIS SHIRT LAST SUMMER AT BASKETBALL CAMP!)
WHAT DO YOU THINK OF THIS?

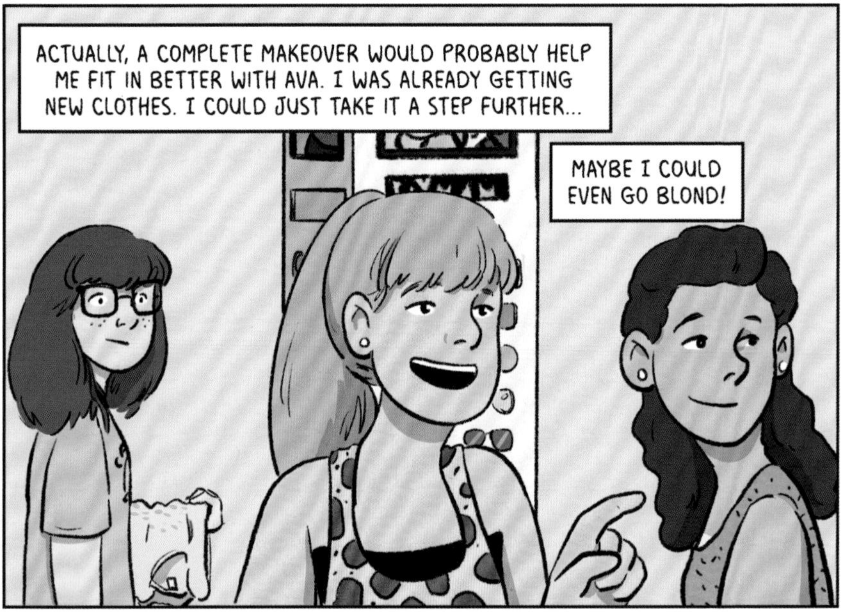
ACTUALLY, A COMPLETE MAKEOVER WOULD PROBABLY HELP ME FIT IN BETTER WITH AVA. I WAS ALREADY GETTING NEW CLOTHES. I COULD JUST TAKE IT A STEP FURTHER...
MAYBE I COULD EVEN GO BLOND!

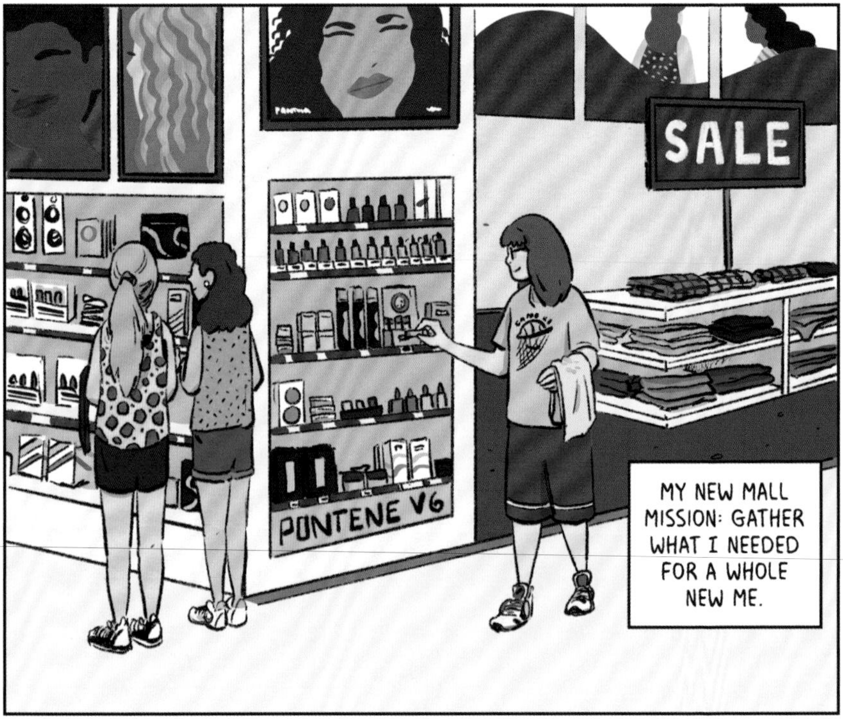
SALE
PONTENE V6
MY NEW MALL MISSION: GATHER WHAT I NEEDED FOR A WHOLE NEW ME.

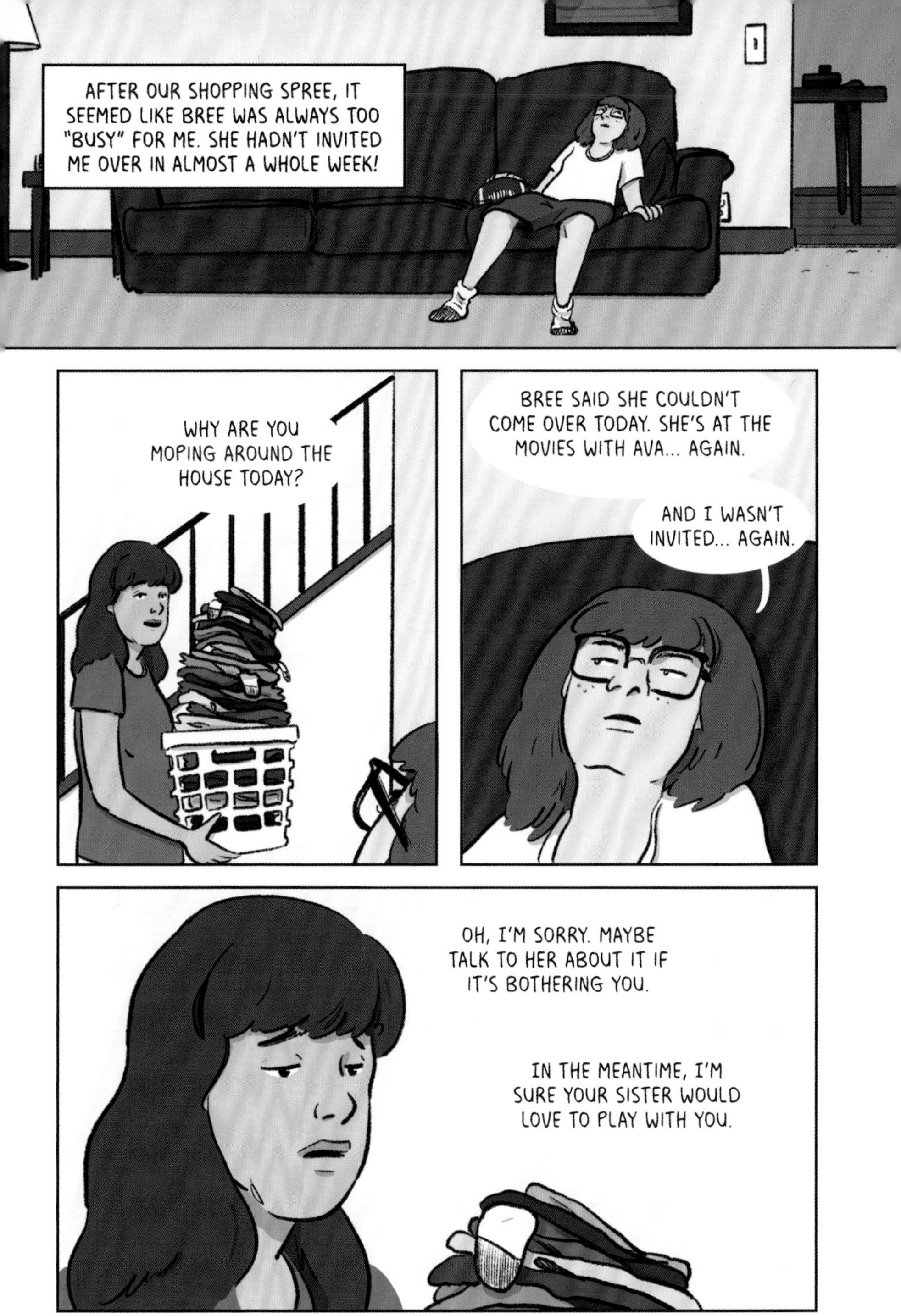
AFTER OUR SHOPPING SPREE, IT SEEMED LIKE BREE WAS ALWAYS TOO "BUSY" FOR ME. SHE HADN'T INVITED ME OVER IN ALMOST A WHOLE WEEK!
WHY ARE YOU MOPING AROUND THE HOUSE TODAY?
BREE SAID SHE COULDN'T COME OVER TODAY. SHE'S AT THE MOVIES WITH AVA... AGAIN.
AND I WASN'T INVITED... AGAIN.
OH, I'M SORRY. MAYBE TALK TO HER ABOUT IT IF IT'S BOTHERING YOU.
IN THE MEANTIME, I'M SURE YOUR SISTER WOULD LOVE TO PLAY WITH YOU.

CHAPTER 4

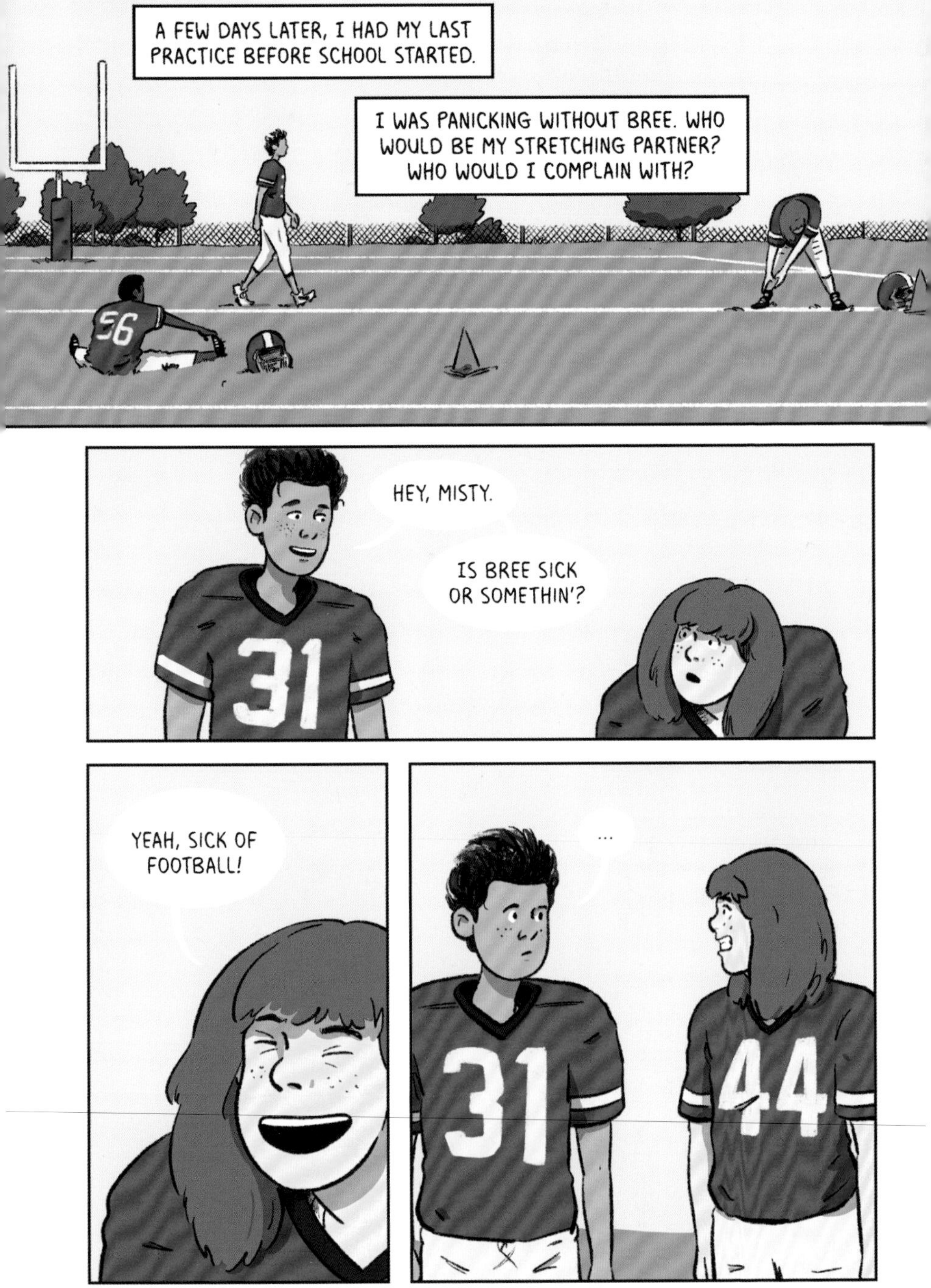

A FEW DAYS LATER, I HAD MY LAST PRACTICE BEFORE SCHOOL STARTED.
I WAS PANICKING WITHOUT BREE. WHO WOULD BE MY STRETCHING PARTNER? WHO WOULD I COMPLAIN WITH?
56
HEY, MISTY.
IS BREE SICK OR SOMETHIN'?
31
YEAH, SICK OF FOOTBALL!
...
31
44

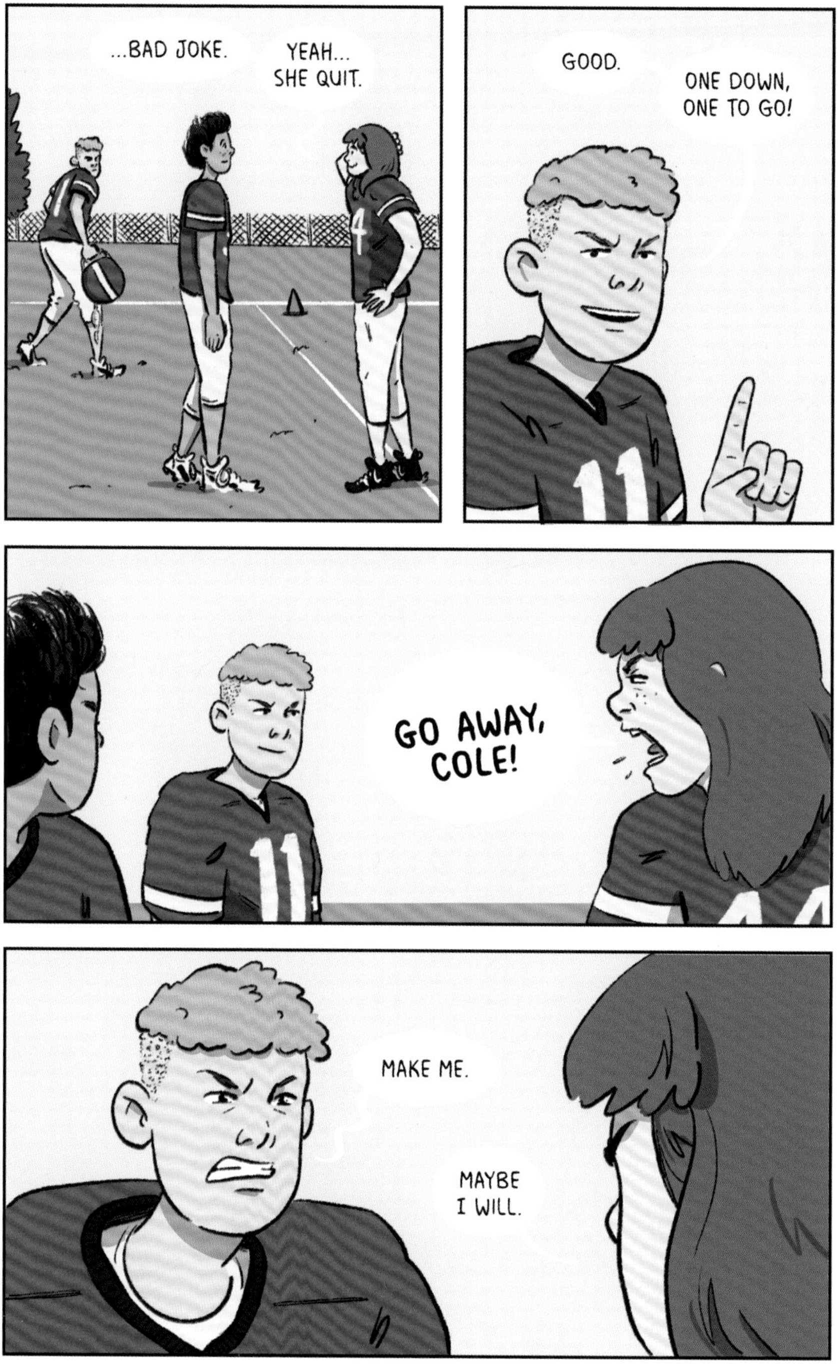
...BAD JOKE.
YEAH... SHE QUIT.
GOOD.
ONE DOWN, ONE TO GO!
GO AWAY, COLE!
MAKE ME.
MAYBE I WILL.

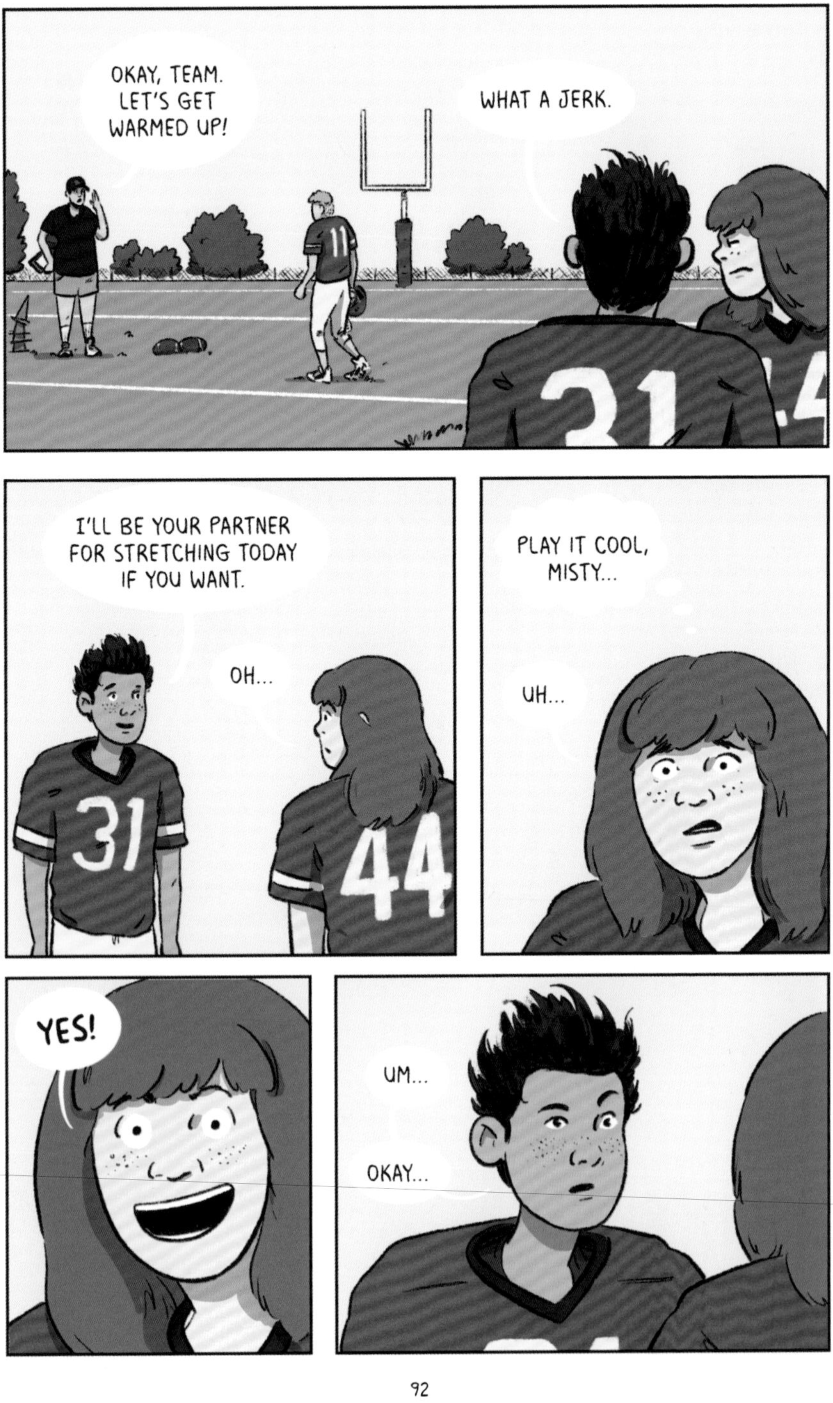
OKAY, TEAM. LET'S GET WARMED UP!
WHAT A JERK.
11
31
I'LL BE YOUR PARTNER FOR STRETCHING TODAY IF YOU WANT.
OH...
31
44
PLAY IT COOL, MISTY...
UH...
YES!
UM...
OKAY...

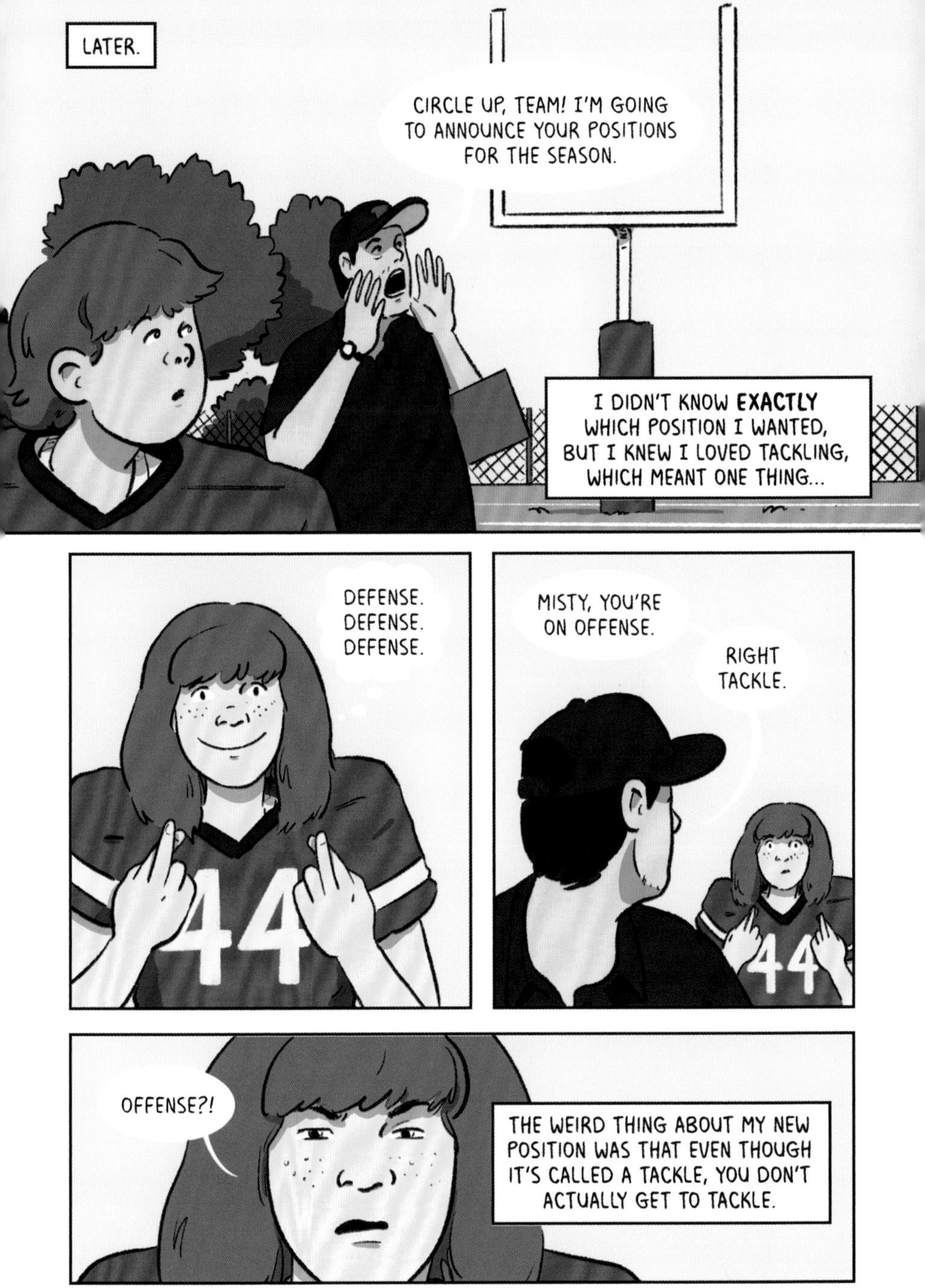
LATER.
CIRCLE UP, TEAM! I'M GOING TO ANNOUNCE YOUR POSITIONS FOR THE SEASON.
I DIDN'T KNOW **EXACTLY** WHICH POSITION I WANTED, BUT I KNEW I LOVED TACKLING, WHICH MEANT ONE THING...
DEFENSE. DEFENSE. DEFENSE.
MISTY, YOU'RE ON OFFENSE.
RIGHT TACKLE.
OFFENSE?!
THE WEIRD THING ABOUT MY NEW POSITION WAS THAT EVEN THOUGH IT'S CALLED A TACKLE, YOU DON'T ACTUALLY GET TO TACKLE.

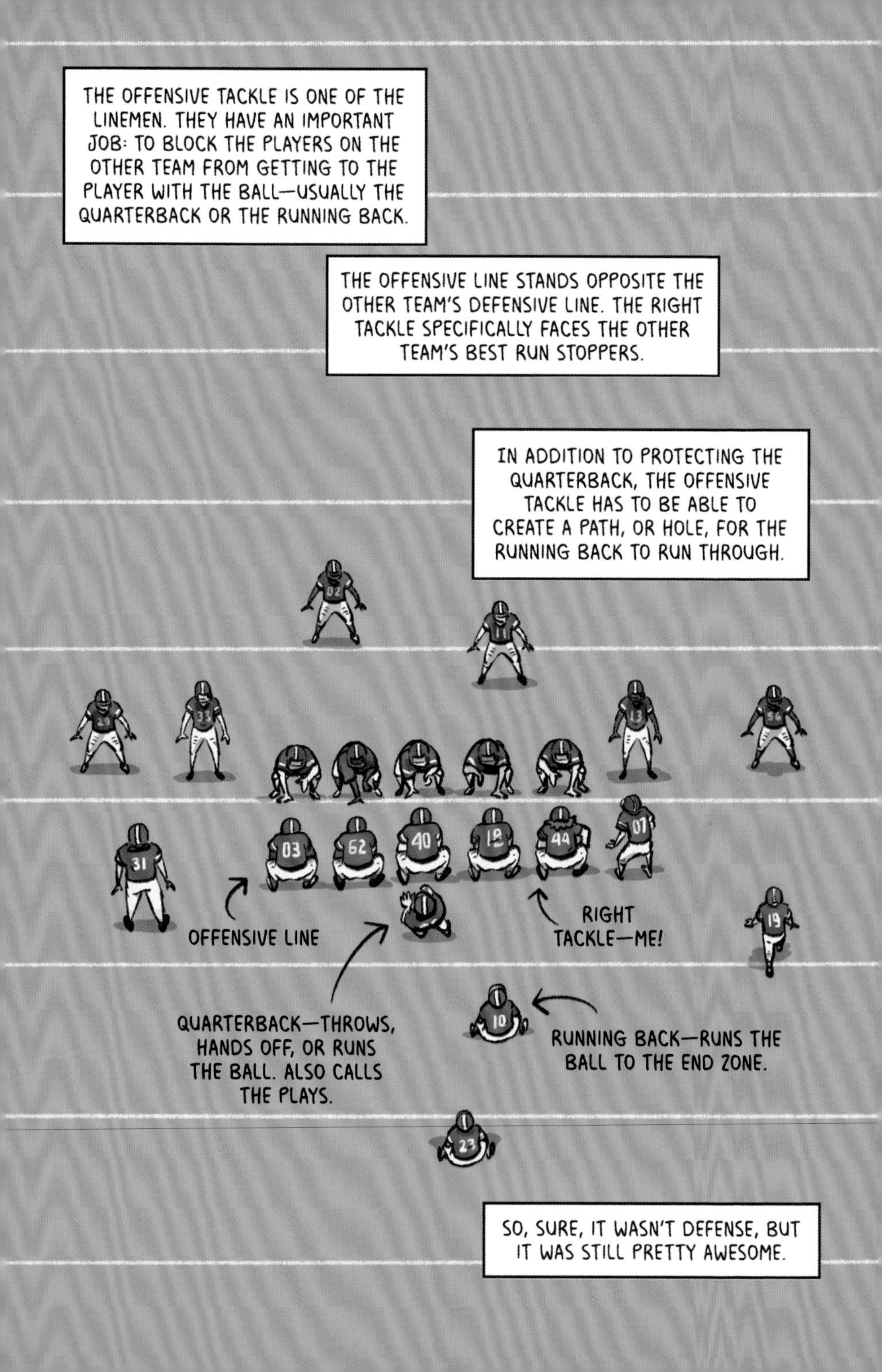
THE OFFENSIVE TACKLE IS ONE OF THE LINEMEN. THEY HAVE AN IMPORTANT JOB: TO BLOCK THE PLAYERS ON THE OTHER TEAM FROM GETTING TO THE PLAYER WITH THE BALL—USUALLY THE QUARTERBACK OR THE RUNNING BACK.
THE OFFENSIVE LINE STANDS OPPOSITE THE OTHER TEAM'S DEFENSIVE LINE. THE RIGHT TACKLE SPECIFICALLY FACES THE OTHER TEAM'S BEST RUN STOPPERS.
IN ADDITION TO PROTECTING THE QUARTERBACK, THE OFFENSIVE TACKLE HAS TO BE ABLE TO CREATE A PATH, OR HOLE, FOR THE RUNNING BACK TO RUN THROUGH.
OFFENSIVE LINE
RIGHT TACKLE—ME!
QUARTERBACK—THROWS, HANDS OFF, OR RUNS THE BALL. ALSO CALLS THE PLAYS.
RUNNING BACK—RUNS THE BALL TO THE END ZONE.
SO, SURE, IT WASN'T DEFENSE, BUT IT WAS STILL PRETTY AWESOME.

95

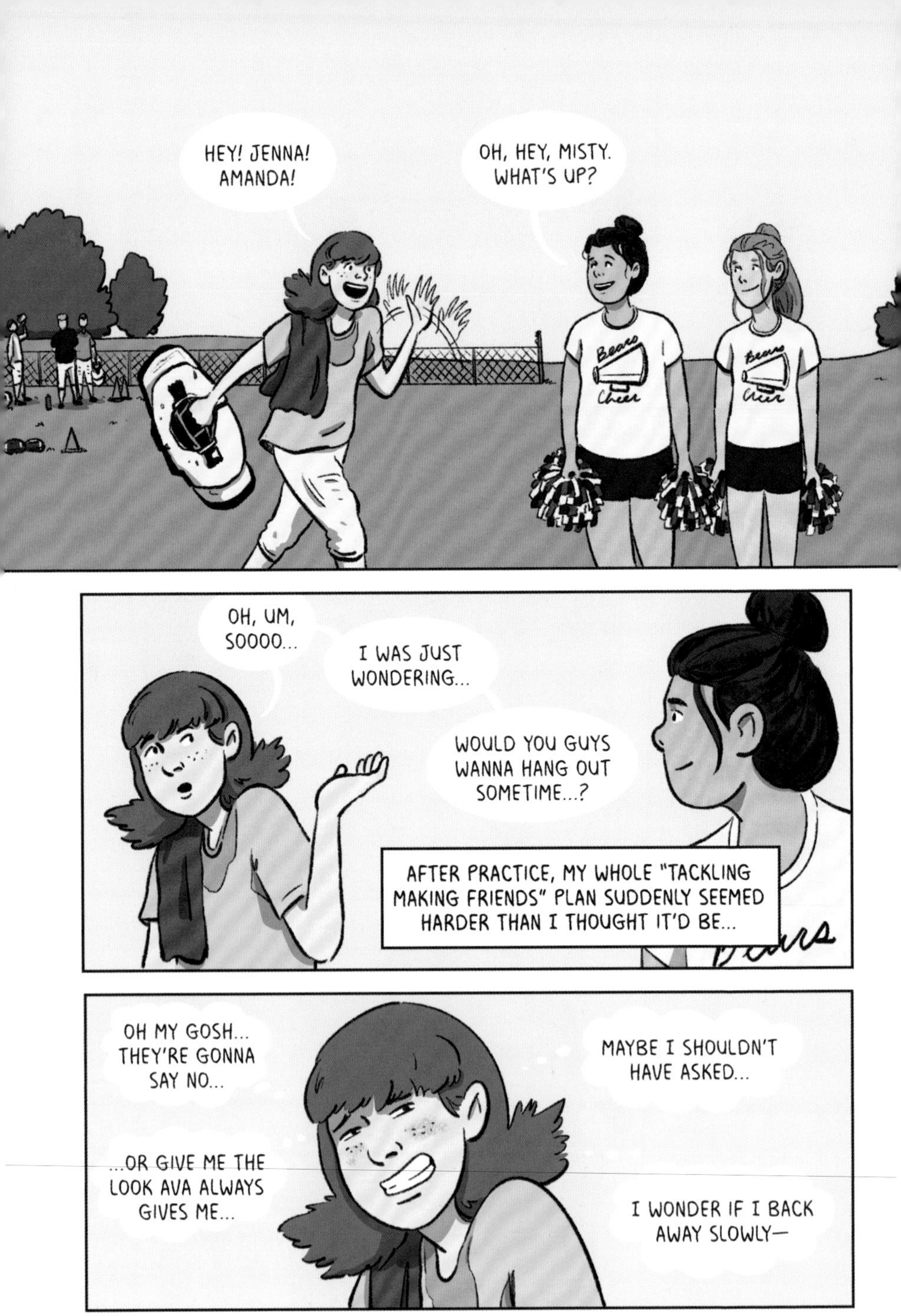
HEY! JENNA! AMANDA!
OH, HEY, MISTY. WHAT'S UP?
OH, UM, SOOOO...
I WAS JUST WONDERING...
WOULD YOU GUYS WANNA HANG OUT SOMETIME...?
AFTER PRACTICE, MY WHOLE "TACKLING MAKING FRIENDS" PLAN SUDDENLY SEEMED HARDER THAN I THOUGHT IT'D BE...
OH MY GOSH... THEY'RE GONNA SAY NO...
MAYBE I SHOULDN'T HAVE ASKED...
...OR GIVE ME THE LOOK AVA ALWAYS GIVES ME...
I WONDER IF I BACK AWAY SLOWLY—

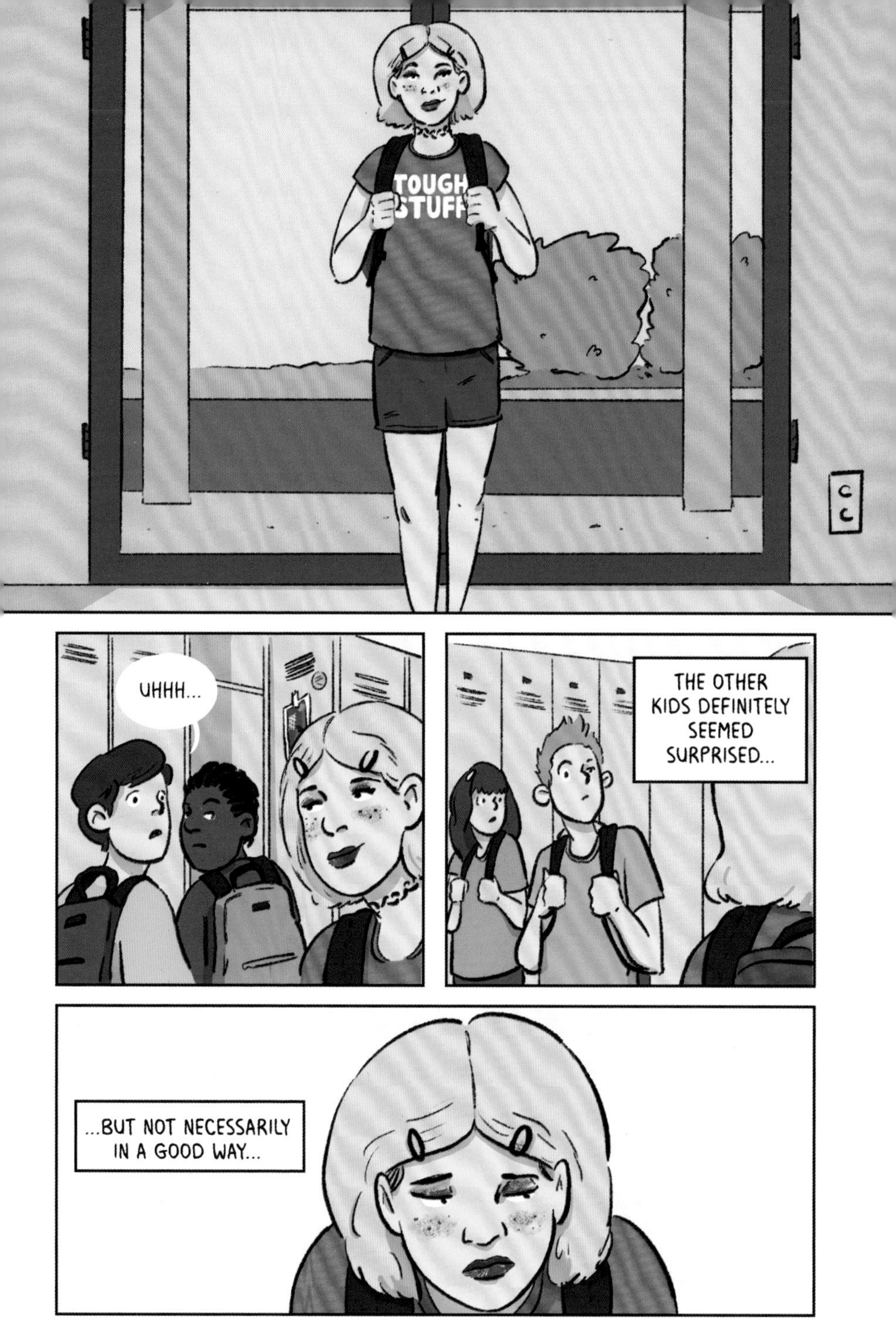
TOUGH STUFF
UHHH...
THE OTHER KIDS DEFINITELY SEEMED SURPRISED...
...BUT NOT NECESSARILY IN A GOOD WAY...

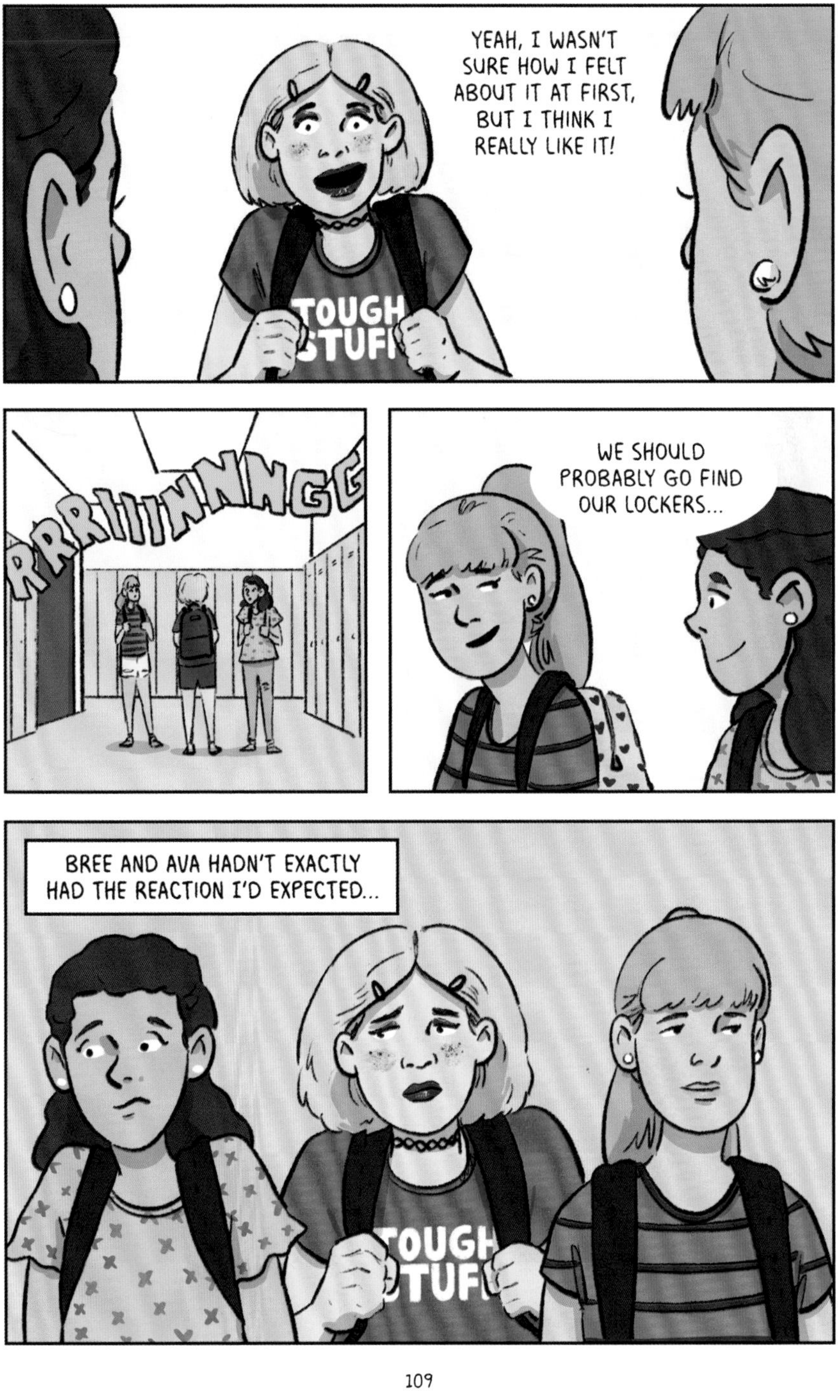
YEAH, I WASN'T SURE HOW I FELT ABOUT IT AT FIRST, BUT I THINK I REALLY LIKE IT!
TOUGH STUFF
RRRIIIINNNNGG
WE SHOULD PROBABLY GO FIND OUR LOCKERS...
BREE AND AVA HADN'T EXACTLY HAD THE REACTION I'D EXPECTED...
TOUGH STUFF

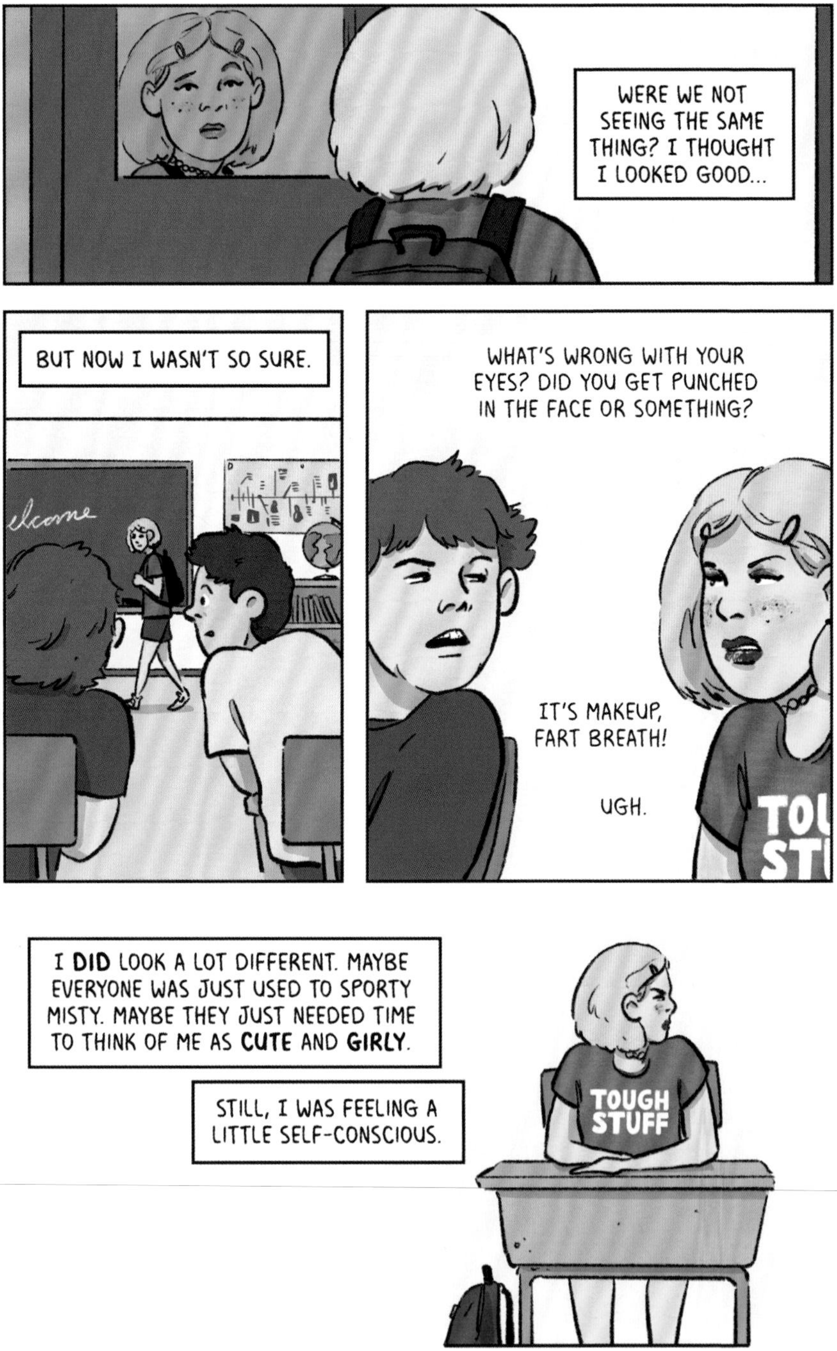
WERE WE NOT SEEING THE SAME THING? I THOUGHT I LOOKED GOOD...
BUT NOW I WASN'T SO SURE.
WHAT'S WRONG WITH YOUR EYES? DID YOU GET PUNCHED IN THE FACE OR SOMETHING?
IT'S MAKEUP, FART BREATH!
UGH.
I **DID** LOOK A LOT DIFFERENT. MAYBE EVERYONE WAS JUST USED TO SPORTY MISTY. MAYBE THEY JUST NEEDED TIME TO THINK OF ME AS **CUTE** AND **GIRLY**.
STILL, I WAS FEELING A LITTLE SELF-CONSCIOUS.
TOUGH STUFF

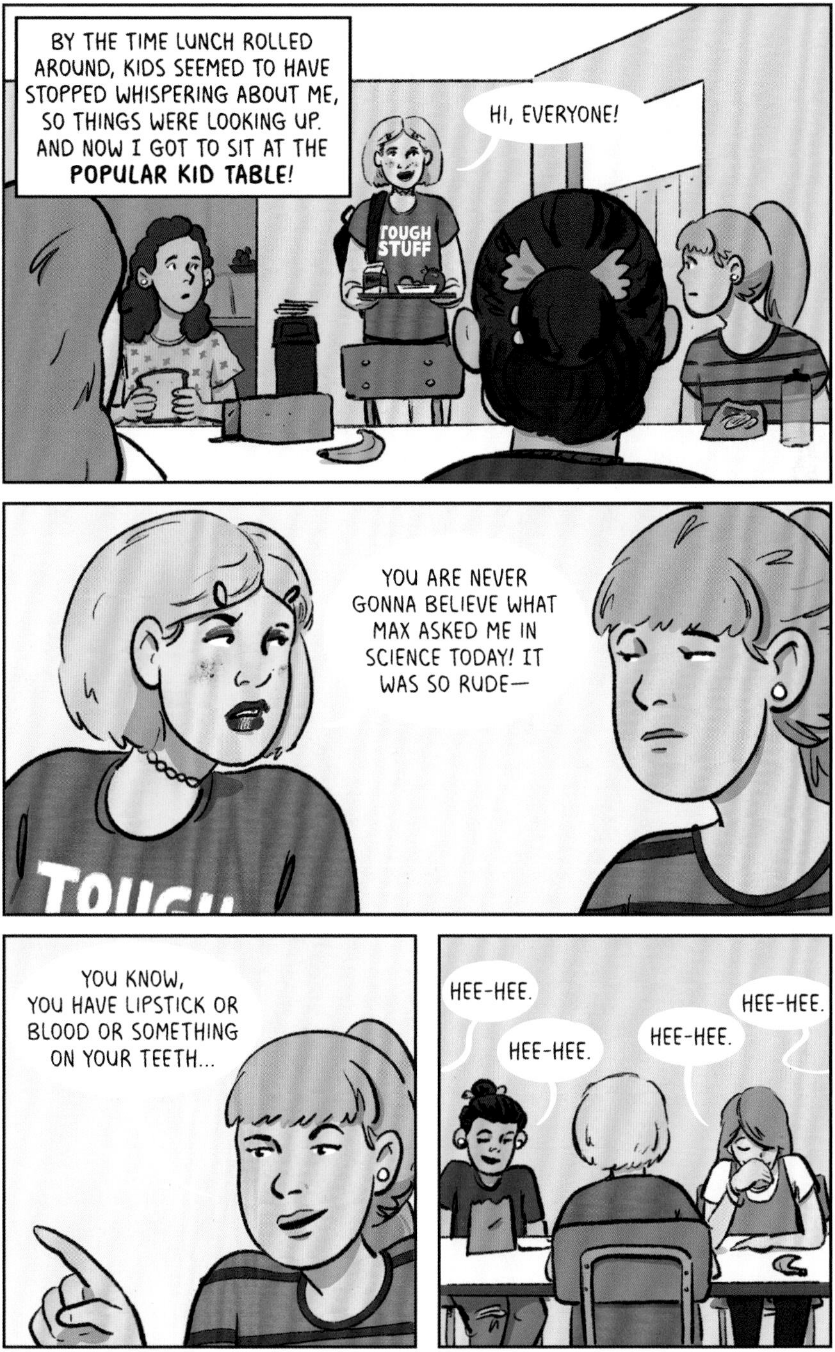
BY THE TIME LUNCH ROLLED AROUND, KIDS SEEMED TO HAVE STOPPED WHISPERING ABOUT ME, SO THINGS WERE LOOKING UP. AND NOW I GOT TO SIT AT THE **POPULAR KID TABLE**!
HI, EVERYONE!
TOUGH STUFF
YOU ARE NEVER GONNA BELIEVE WHAT MAX ASKED ME IN SCIENCE TODAY! IT WAS SO RUDE—
YOU KNOW, YOU HAVE LIPSTICK OR BLOOD OR SOMETHING ON YOUR TEETH...
HEE-HEE.
HEE-HEE.
HEE-HEE.
HEE-HEE.

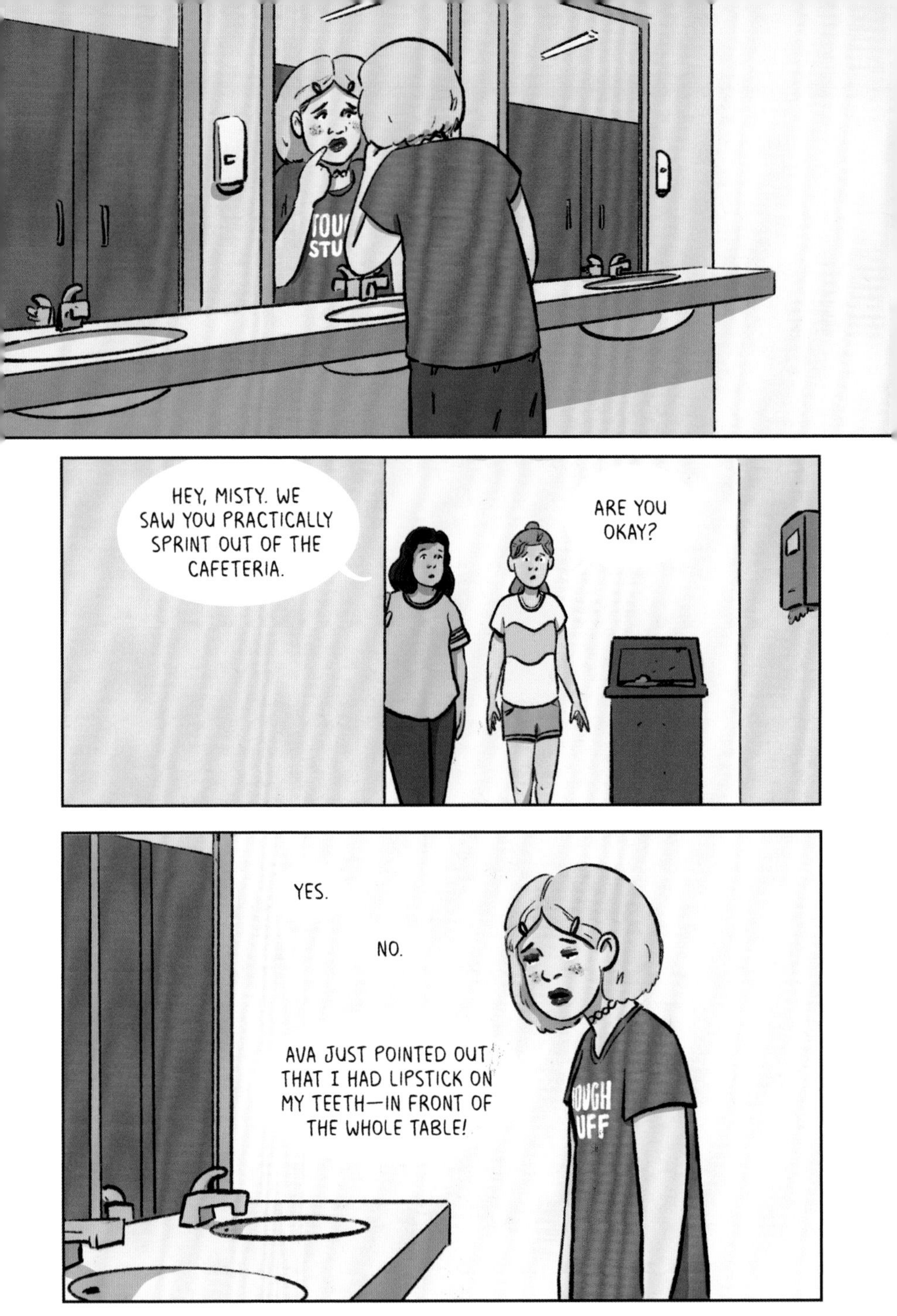
HEY, MISTY. WE SAW YOU PRACTICALLY SPRINT OUT OF THE CAFETERIA.
ARE YOU OKAY?
YES.
NO.
AVA JUST POINTED OUT THAT I HAD LIPSTICK ON MY TEETH—IN FRONT OF THE WHOLE TABLE!

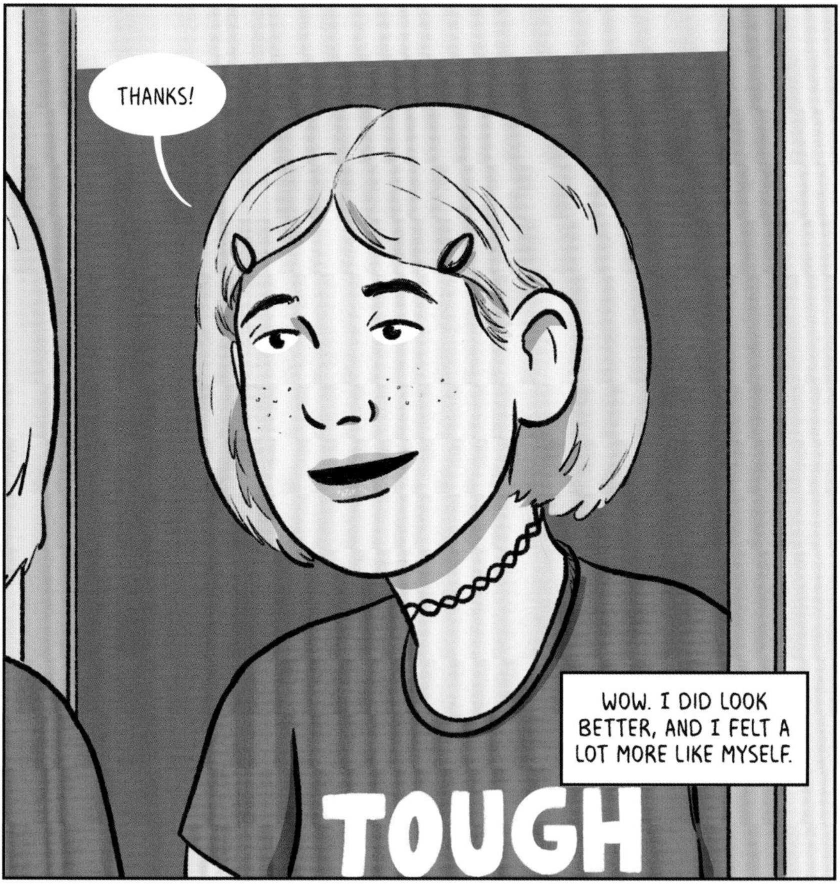
THANKS!
WOW. I DID LOOK BETTER, AND I FELT A LOT MORE LIKE MYSELF.
TOUGH

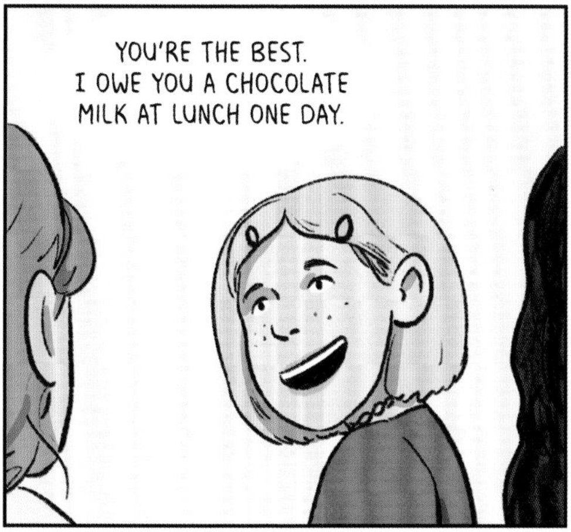
YOU'RE THE BEST. I OWE YOU A CHOCOLATE MILK AT LUNCH ONE DAY.

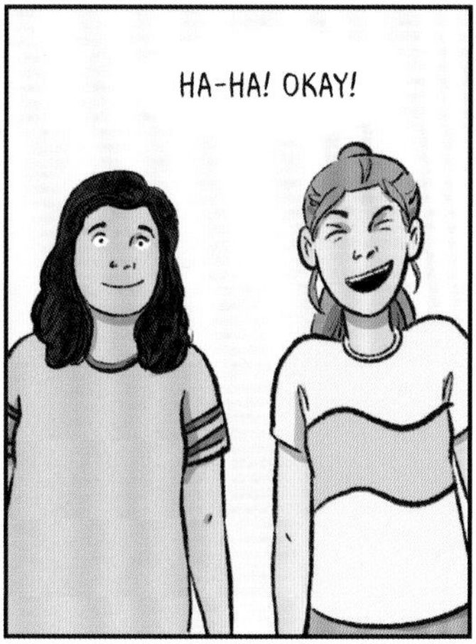
HA-HA! OKAY!

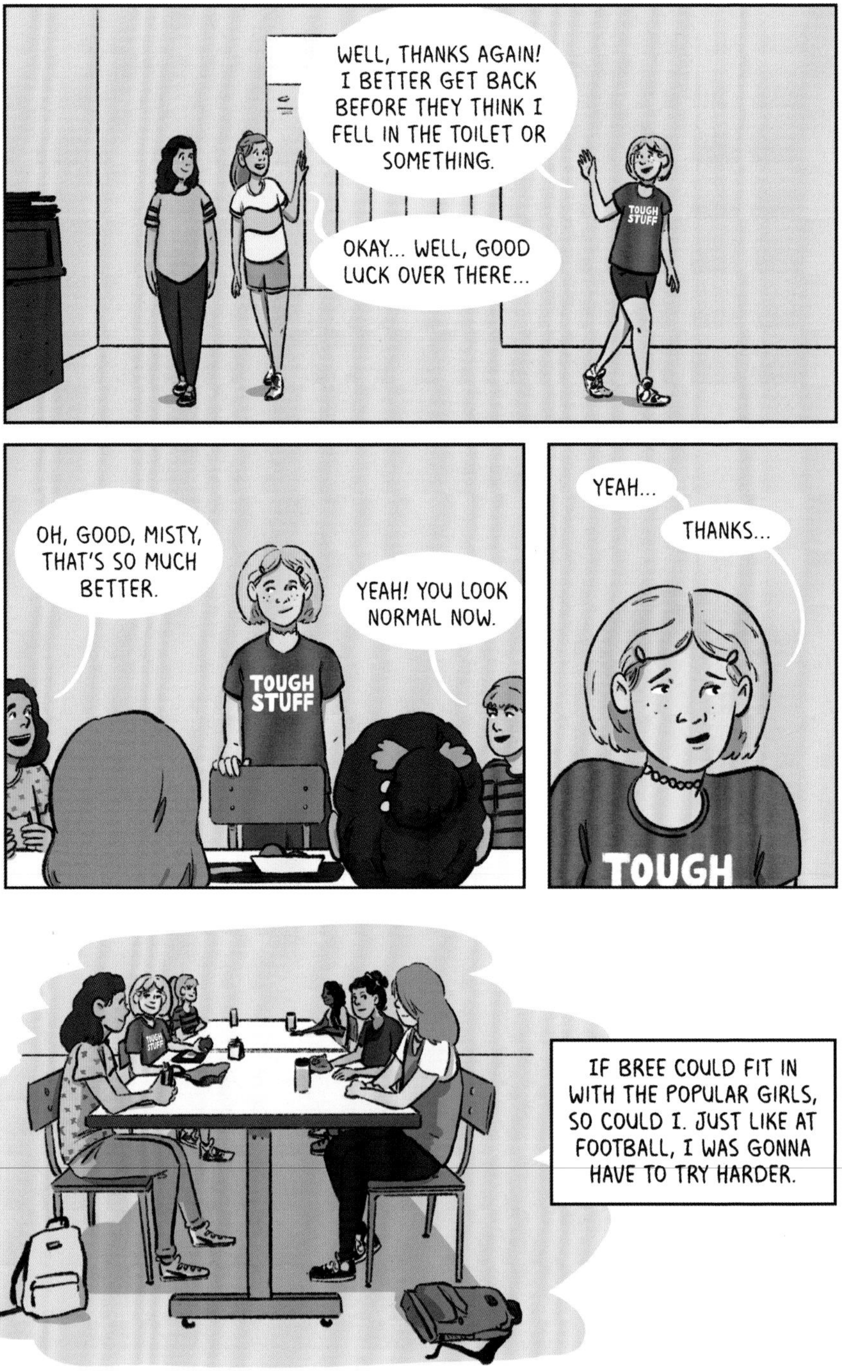
WELL, THANKS AGAIN! I BETTER GET BACK BEFORE THEY THINK I FELL IN THE TOILET OR SOMETHING.
TOUGH STUFF
OKAY... WELL, GOOD LUCK OVER THERE...
OH, GOOD, MISTY, THAT'S SO MUCH BETTER.
YEAH! YOU LOOK NORMAL NOW.
TOUGH STUFF
YEAH...
THANKS...
TOUGH
TOUGH STUFF
IF BREE COULD FIT IN WITH THE POPULAR GIRLS, SO COULD I. JUST LIKE AT FOOTBALL, I WAS GONNA HAVE TO TRY HARDER.

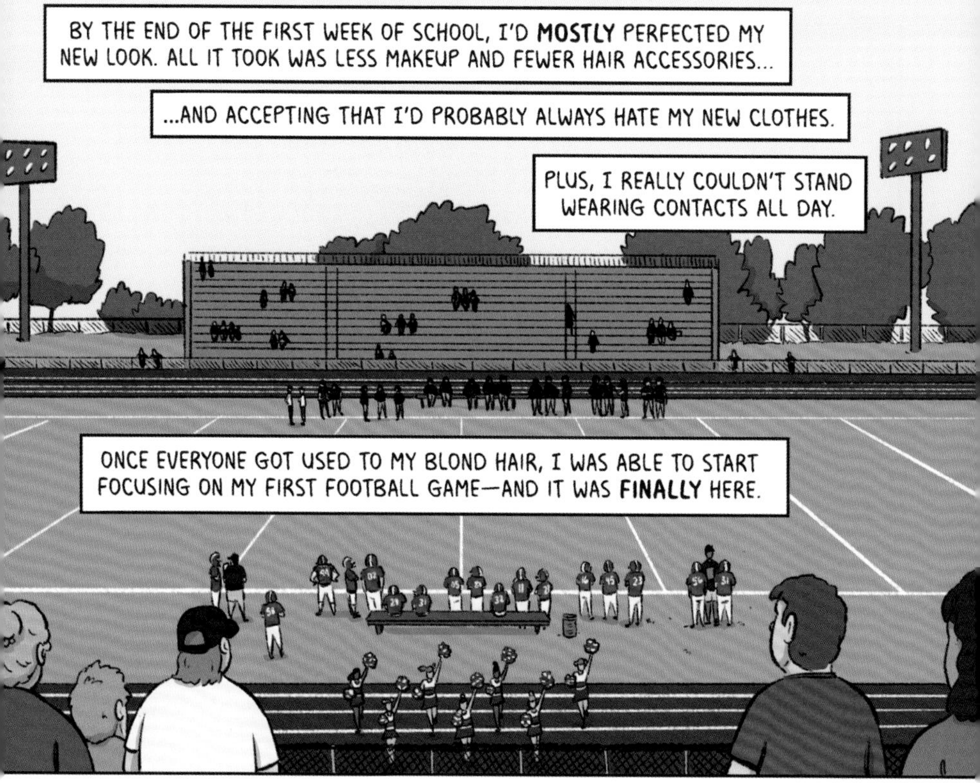
BY THE END OF THE FIRST WEEK OF SCHOOL, I'D **MOSTLY** PERFECTED MY NEW LOOK. ALL IT TOOK WAS LESS MAKEUP AND FEWER HAIR ACCESSORIES...
...AND ACCEPTING THAT I'D PROBABLY ALWAYS HATE MY NEW CLOTHES.
PLUS, I REALLY COULDN'T STAND WEARING CONTACTS ALL DAY.
ONCE EVERYONE GOT USED TO MY BLOND HAIR, I WAS ABLE TO START FOCUSING ON MY FIRST FOOTBALL GAME—AND IT WAS **FINALLY** HERE.

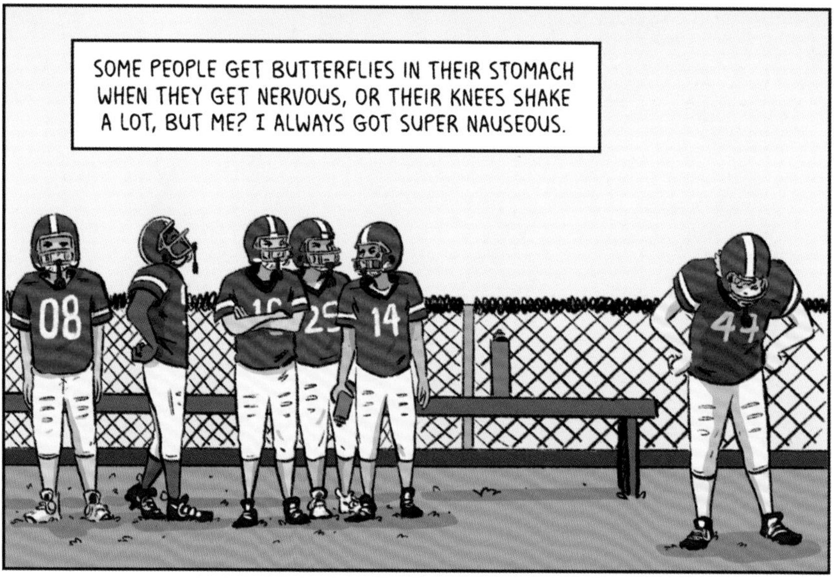
SOME PEOPLE GET BUTTERFLIES IN THEIR STOMACH WHEN THEY GET NERVOUS, OR THEIR KNEES SHAKE A LOT, BUT ME? I ALWAYS GOT SUPER NAUSEOUS.
08
14
44

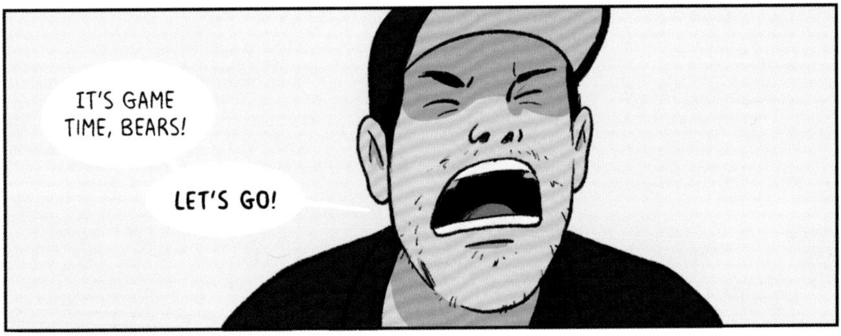
IT'S GAME TIME, BEARS!
LET'S GO!

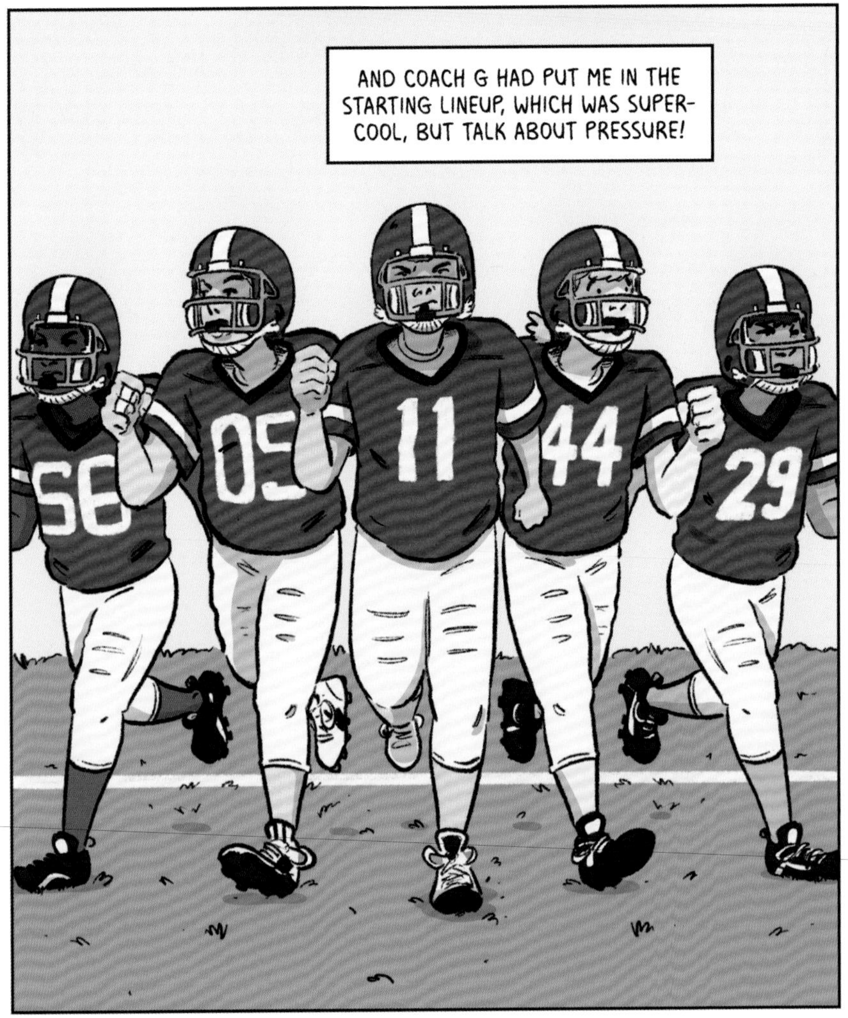
AND COACH G HAD PUT ME IN THE STARTING LINEUP, WHICH WAS SUPER-COOL, BUT TALK ABOUT PRESSURE!
05
11
44
29

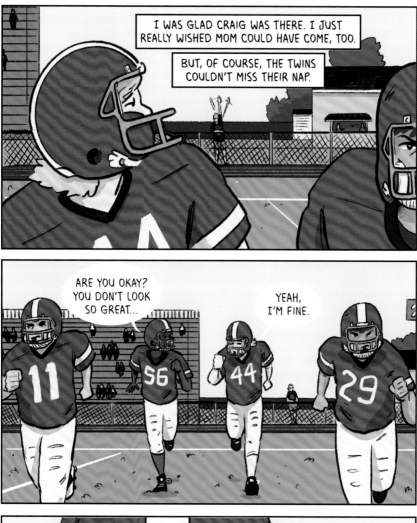

119

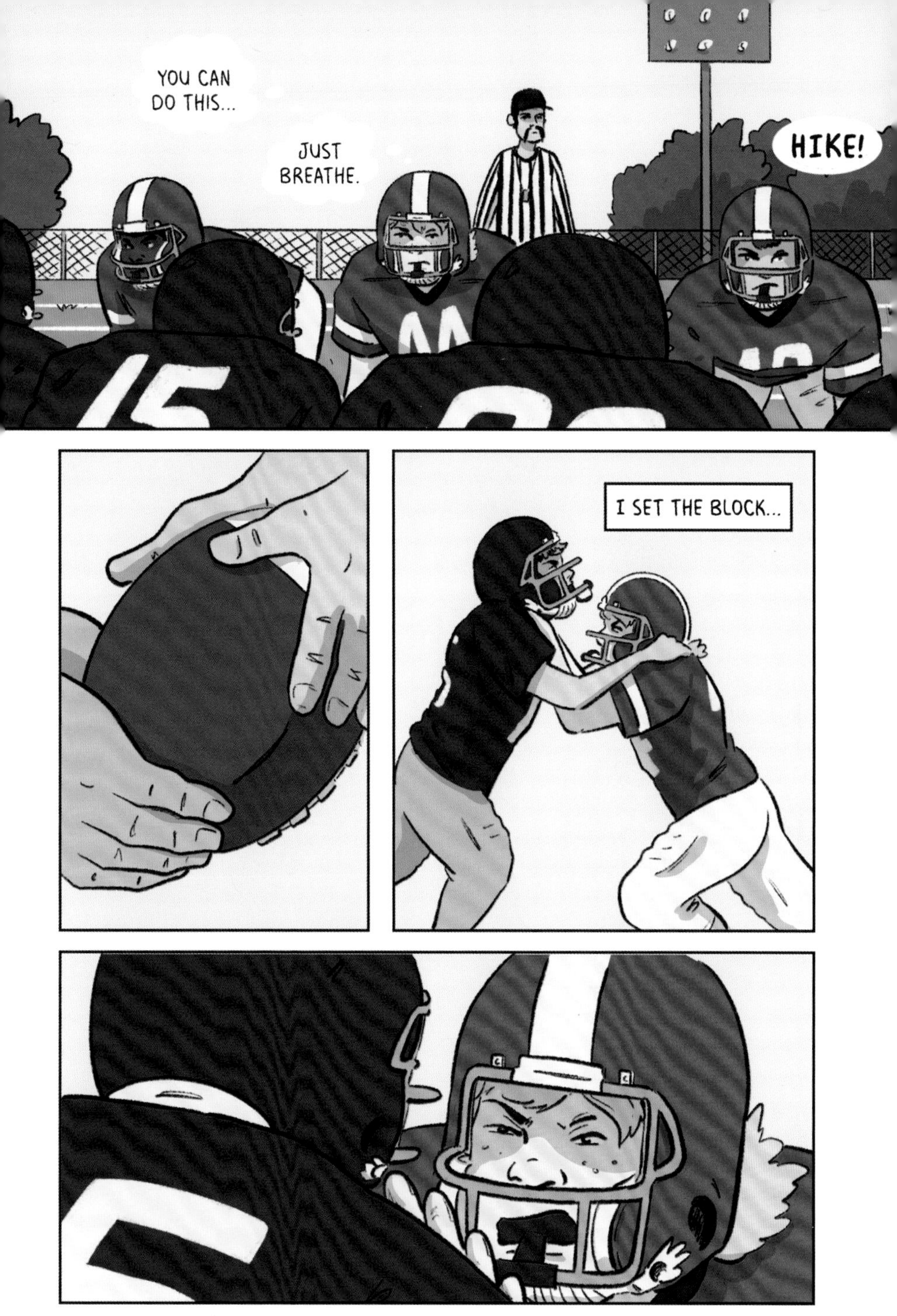
YOU CAN DO THIS...
JUST BREATHE.
HIKE!
I SET THE BLOCK...

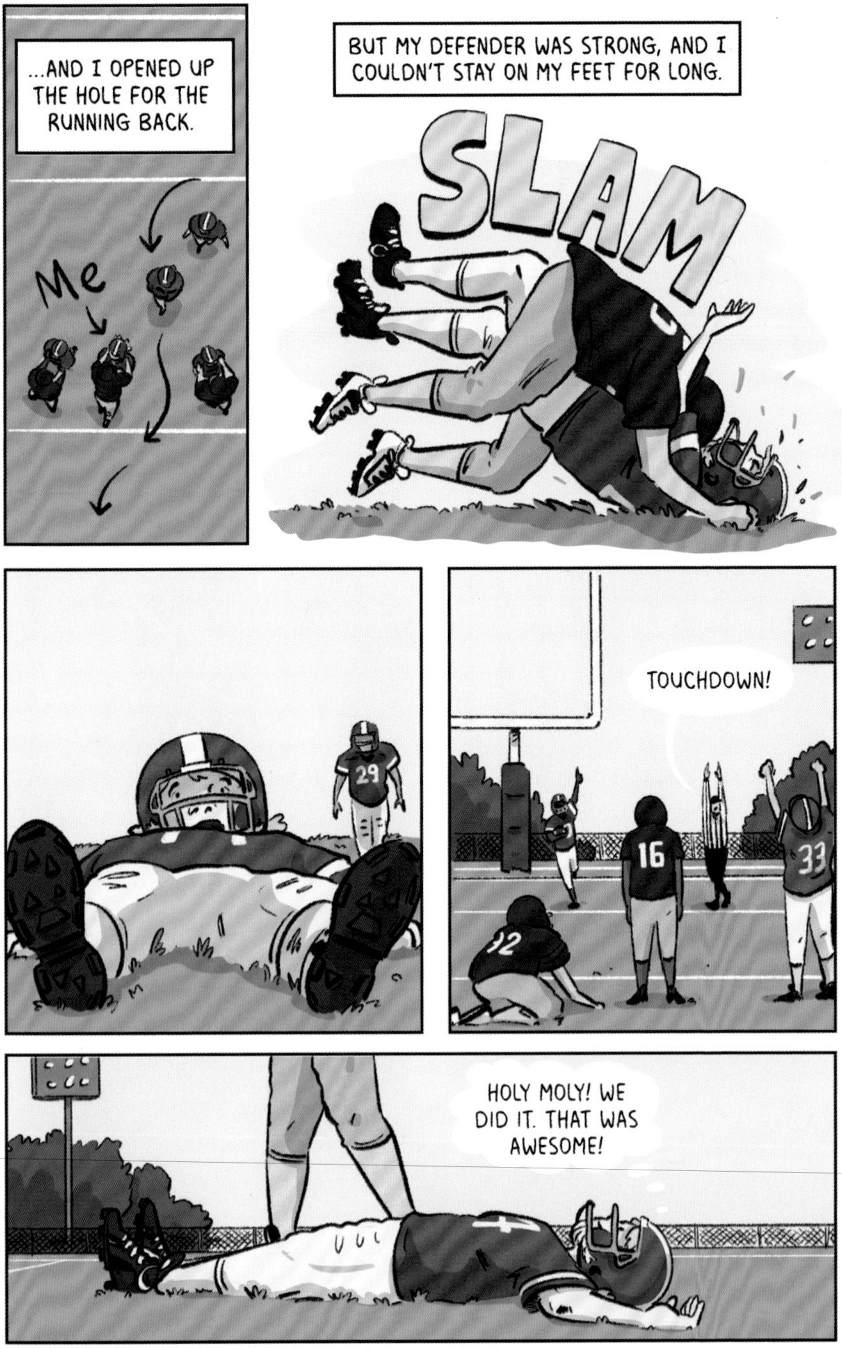
...AND I OPENED UP THE HOLE FOR THE RUNNING BACK.
Me
BUT MY DEFENDER WAS STRONG, AND I COULDN'T STAY ON MY FEET FOR LONG.
SLAM
TOUCHDOWN!
HOLY MOLY! WE DID IT. THAT WAS AWESOME!

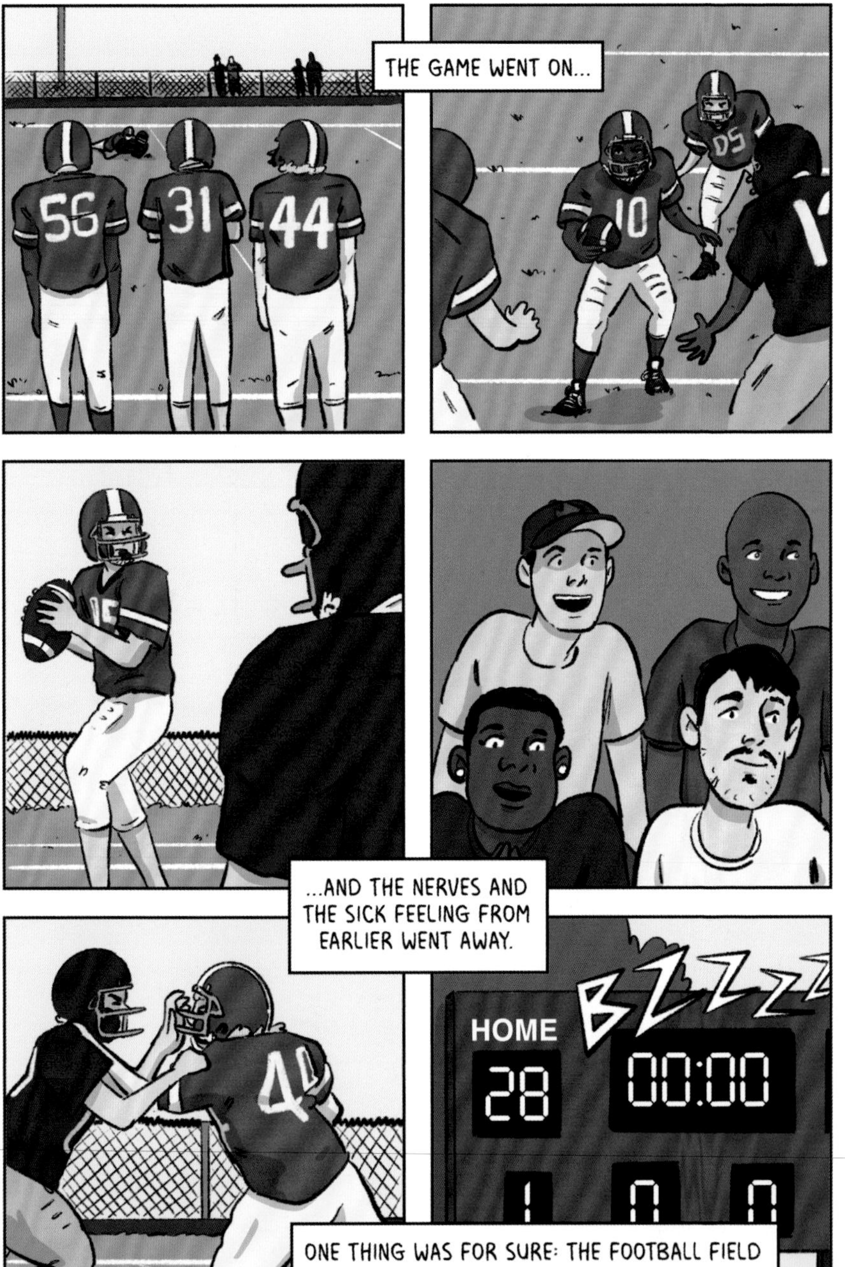
56
31
44
THE GAME WENT ON...
DS
10
...AND THE NERVES AND THE SICK FEELING FROM EARLIER WENT AWAY.
40
BZZZZ
HOME
28
00:00
ONE THING WAS FOR SURE: THE FOOTBALL FIELD WAS **EXACTLY** WHERE I WAS MEANT TO BE.

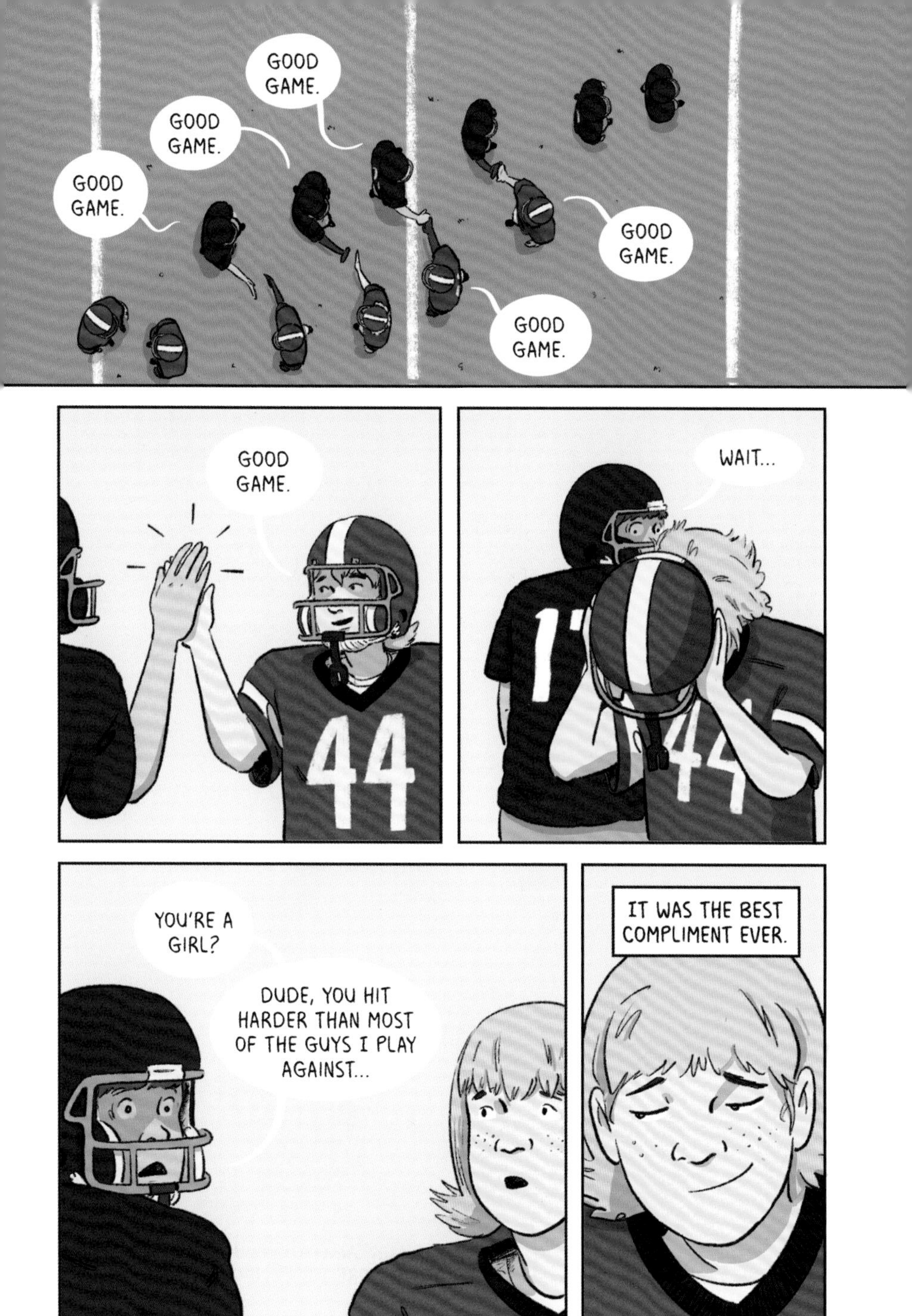
GOOD GAME.
GOOD GAME.
GOOD GAME.
GOOD GAME.
GOOD GAME.
GOOD GAME.
WAIT...
YOU'RE A GIRL?
DUDE, YOU HIT HARDER THAN MOST OF THE GUYS I PLAY AGAINST...
IT WAS THE BEST COMPLIMENT EVER.

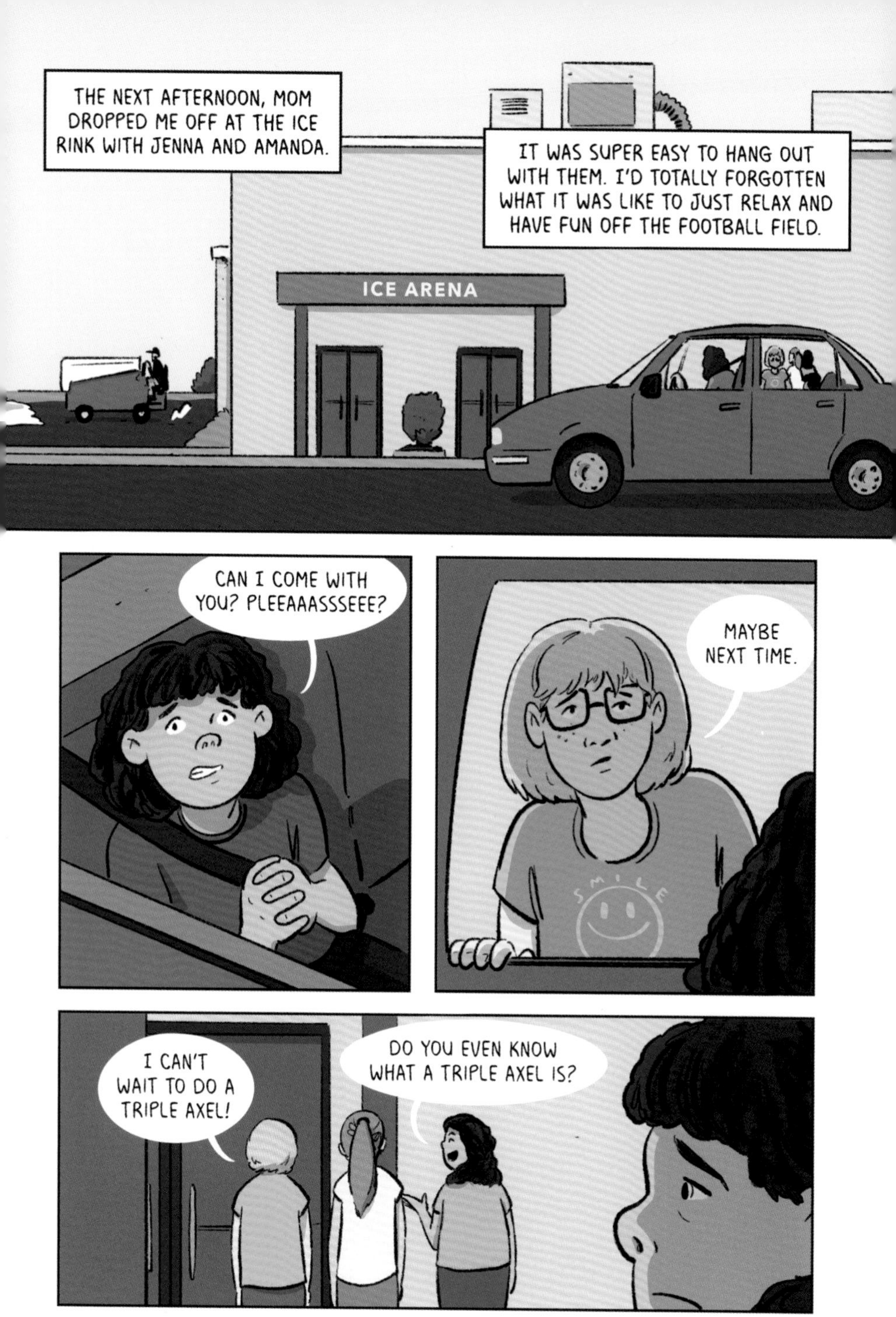
THE NEXT AFTERNOON, MOM DROPPED ME OFF AT THE ICE RINK WITH JENNA AND AMANDA.
IT WAS SUPER EASY TO HANG OUT WITH THEM. I'D TOTALLY FORGOTTEN WHAT IT WAS LIKE TO JUST RELAX AND HAVE FUN OFF THE FOOTBALL FIELD.
ICE ARENA
CAN I COME WITH YOU? PLEEAAASSSEEE?
MAYBE NEXT TIME.
SMILE
I CAN'T WAIT TO DO A TRIPLE AXEL!
DO YOU EVEN KNOW WHAT A TRIPLE AXEL IS?

CHAPTER 6

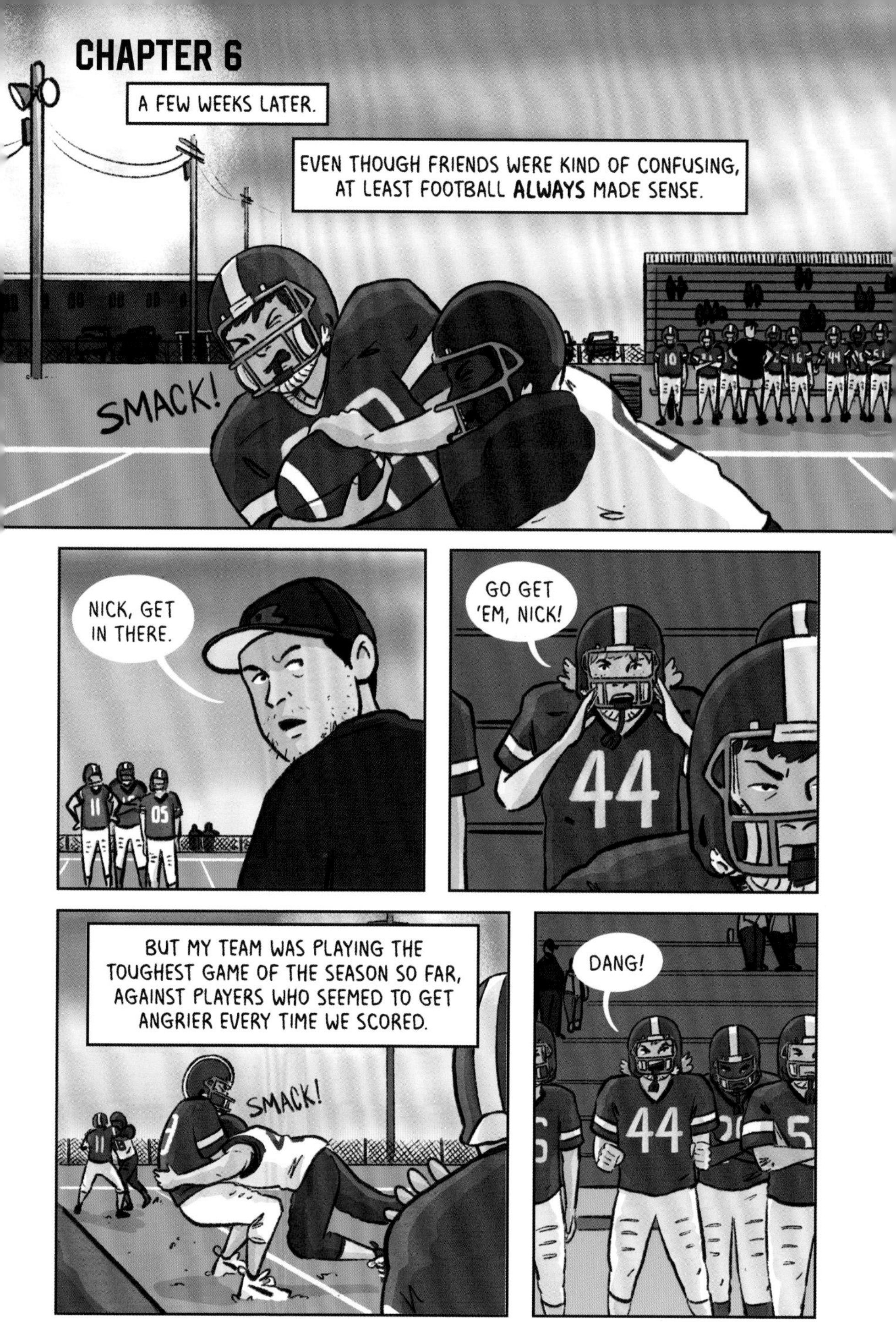

A FEW WEEKS LATER.
EVEN THOUGH FRIENDS WERE KIND OF CONFUSING, AT LEAST FOOTBALL **ALWAYS** MADE SENSE.
SMACK!
NICK, GET IN THERE.
GO GET 'EM, NICK!
BUT MY TEAM WAS PLAYING THE TOUGHEST GAME OF THE SEASON SO FAR, AGAINST PLAYERS WHO SEEMED TO GET ANGRIER EVERY TIME WE SCORED.
SMACK!
DANG!

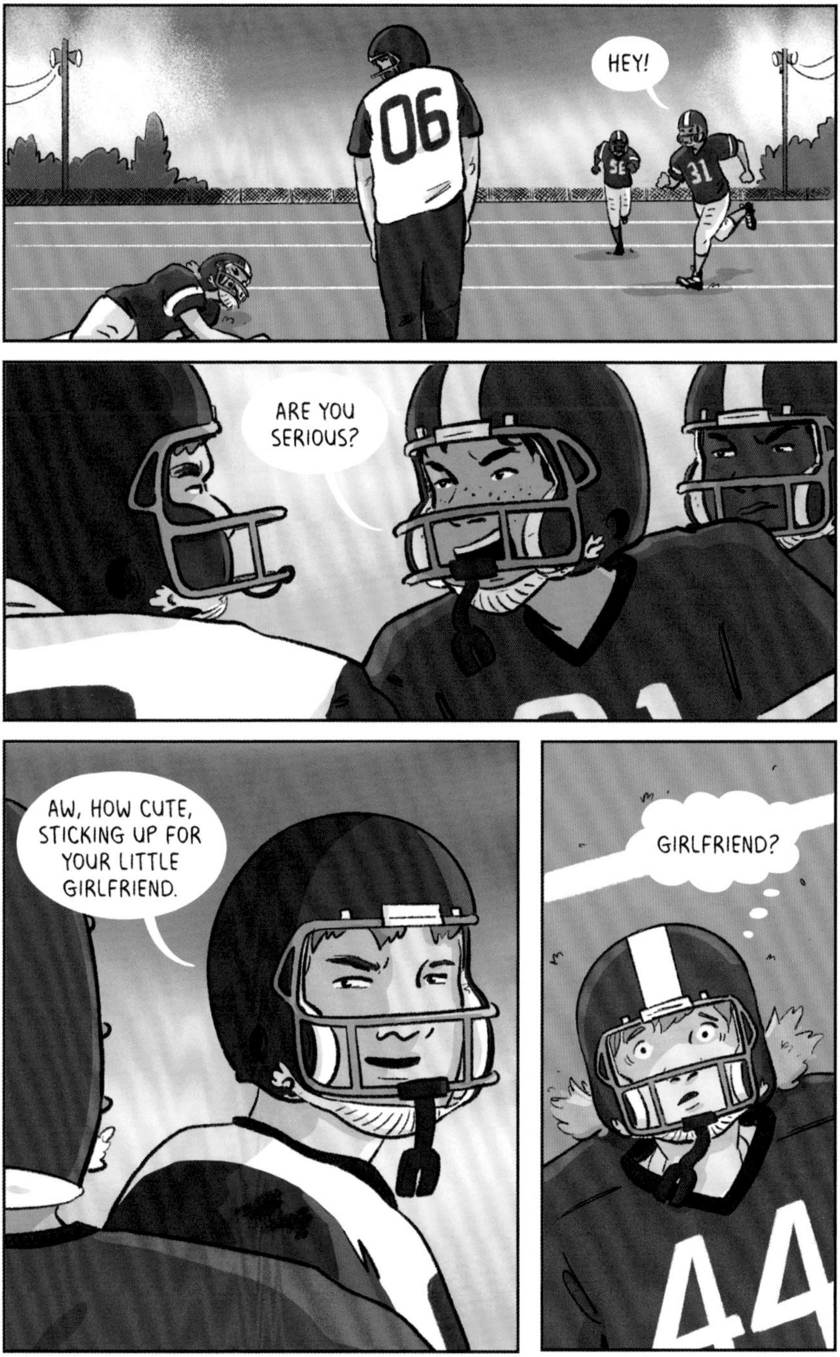
HEY!
ARE YOU SERIOUS?
AW, HOW CUTE, STICKING UP FOR YOUR LITTLE GIRLFRIEND.
GIRLFRIEND?

138

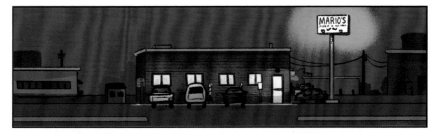

OH, YOU'RE COMING THIS TIME, MISTY?

YEP...

THAT'S COOL.

IT IS?

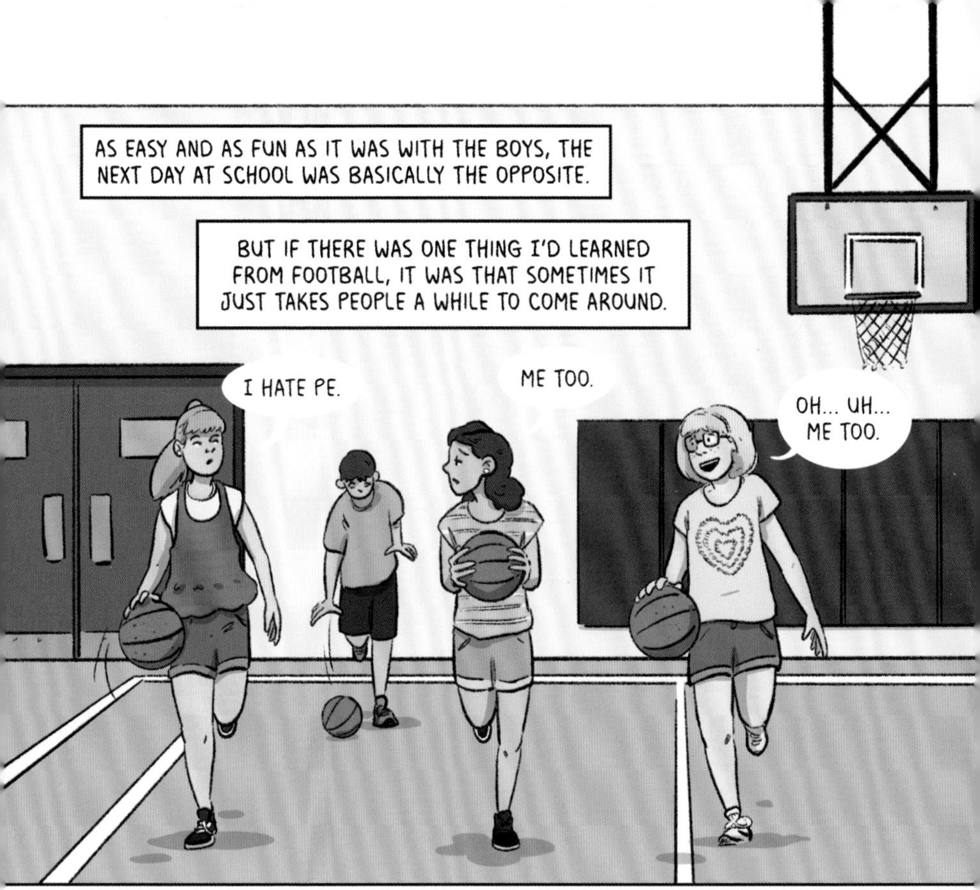
AS EASY AND AS FUN AS IT WAS WITH THE BOYS, THE NEXT DAY AT SCHOOL WAS BASICALLY THE OPPOSITE.
BUT IF THERE WAS ONE THING I'D LEARNED FROM FOOTBALL, IT WAS THAT SOMETIMES IT JUST TAKES PEOPLE A WHILE TO COME AROUND.
I HATE PE.
ME TOO.
OH... UH... ME TOO.

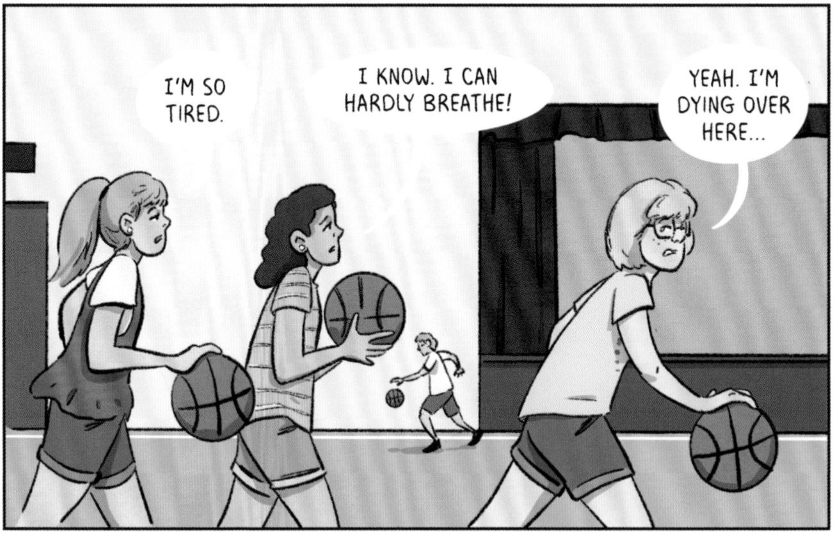
I'M SO TIRED.
I KNOW. I CAN HARDLY BREATHE!
YEAH. I'M DYING OVER HERE...

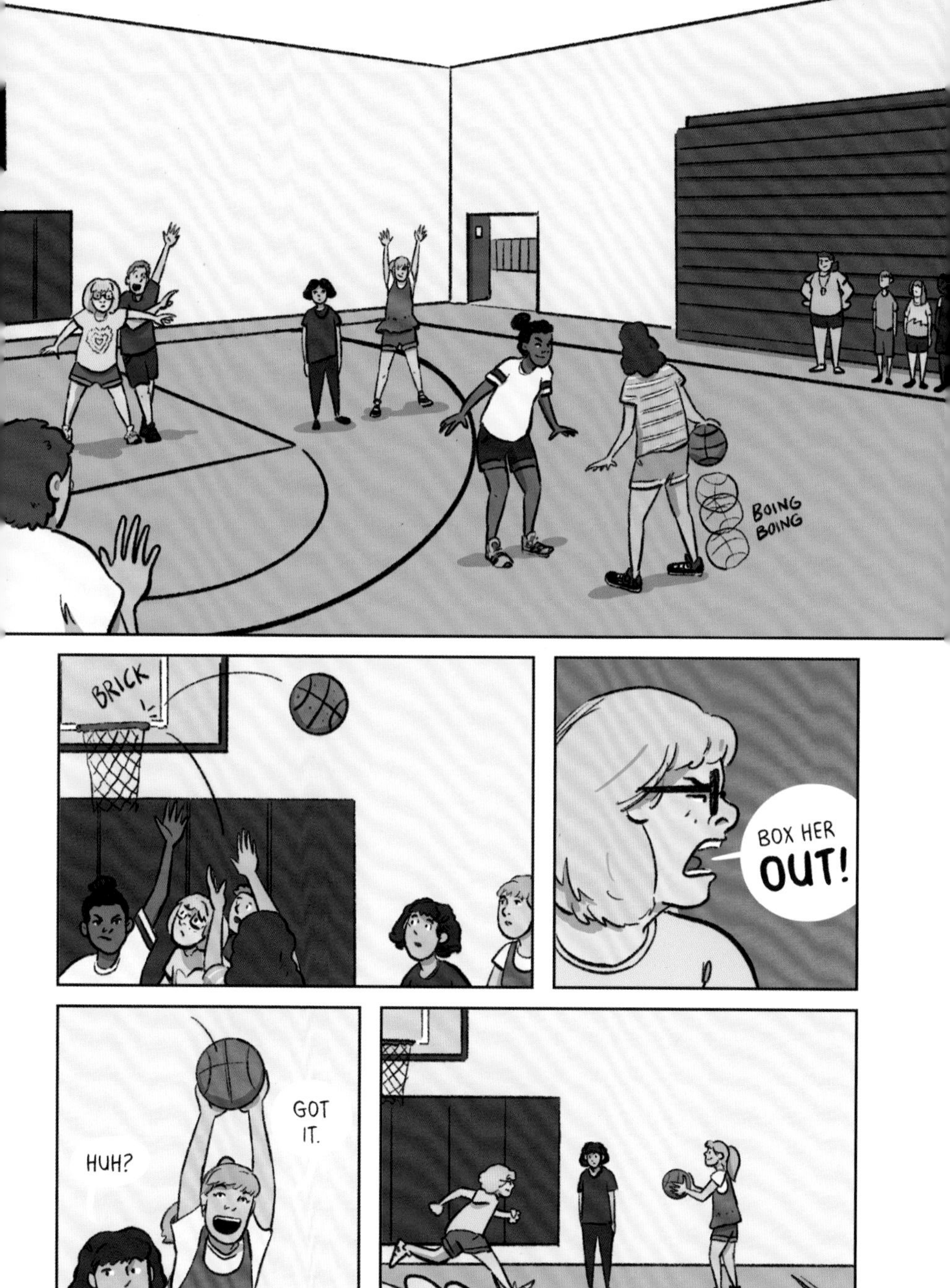
BOING
BOING
BRICK
BOX HER OUT!
GOT IT.
HUH?

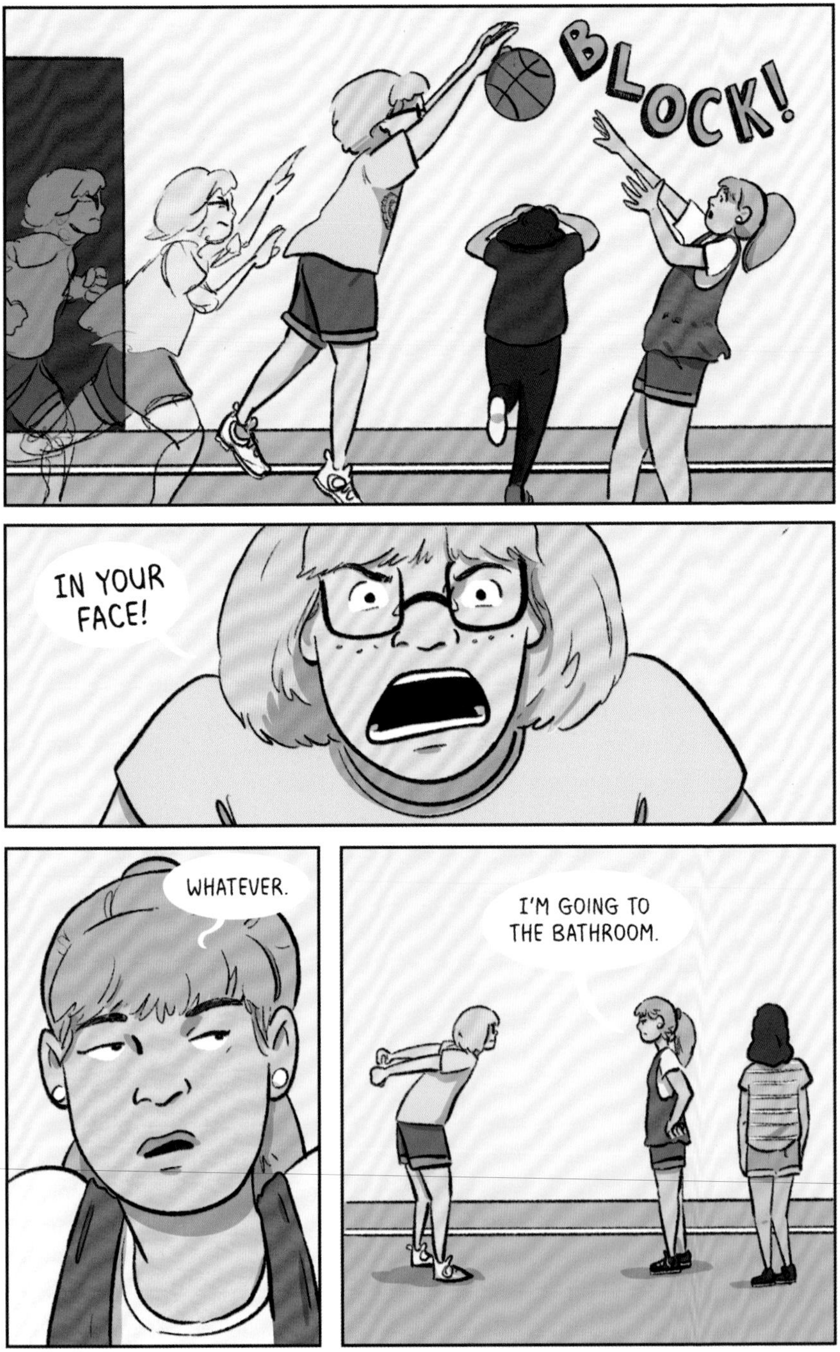
BLOCK!
IN YOUR FACE!
WHATEVER.
I'M GOING TO THE BATHROOM.

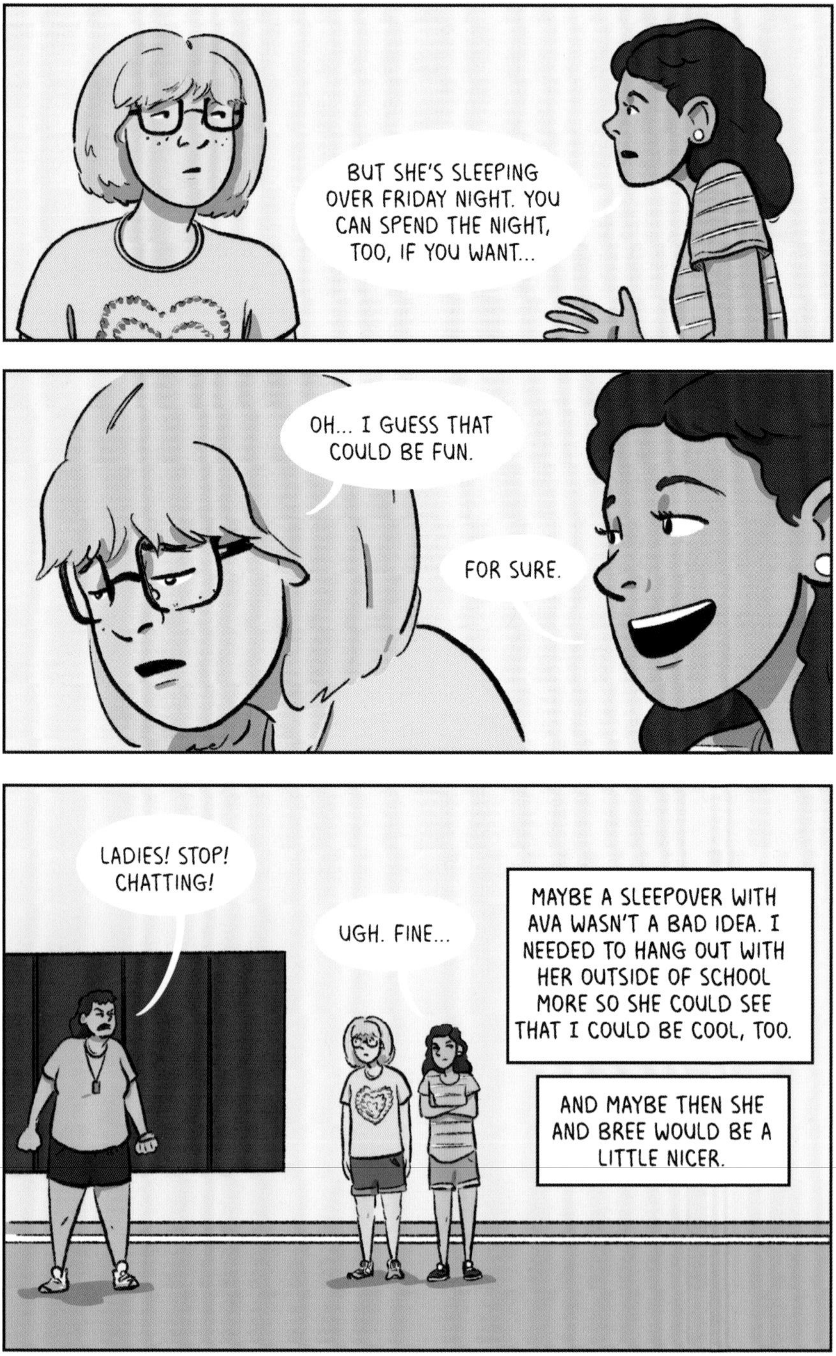
BUT SHE'S SLEEPING OVER FRIDAY NIGHT. YOU CAN SPEND THE NIGHT, TOO, IF YOU WANT...
OH... I GUESS THAT COULD BE FUN.
FOR SURE.
LADIES! STOP! CHATTING!
UGH. FINE...
MAYBE A SLEEPOVER WITH AVA WASN'T A BAD IDEA. I NEEDED TO HANG OUT WITH HER OUTSIDE OF SCHOOL MORE SO SHE COULD SEE THAT I COULD BE COOL, TOO.
AND MAYBE THEN SHE AND BREE WOULD BE A LITTLE NICER.

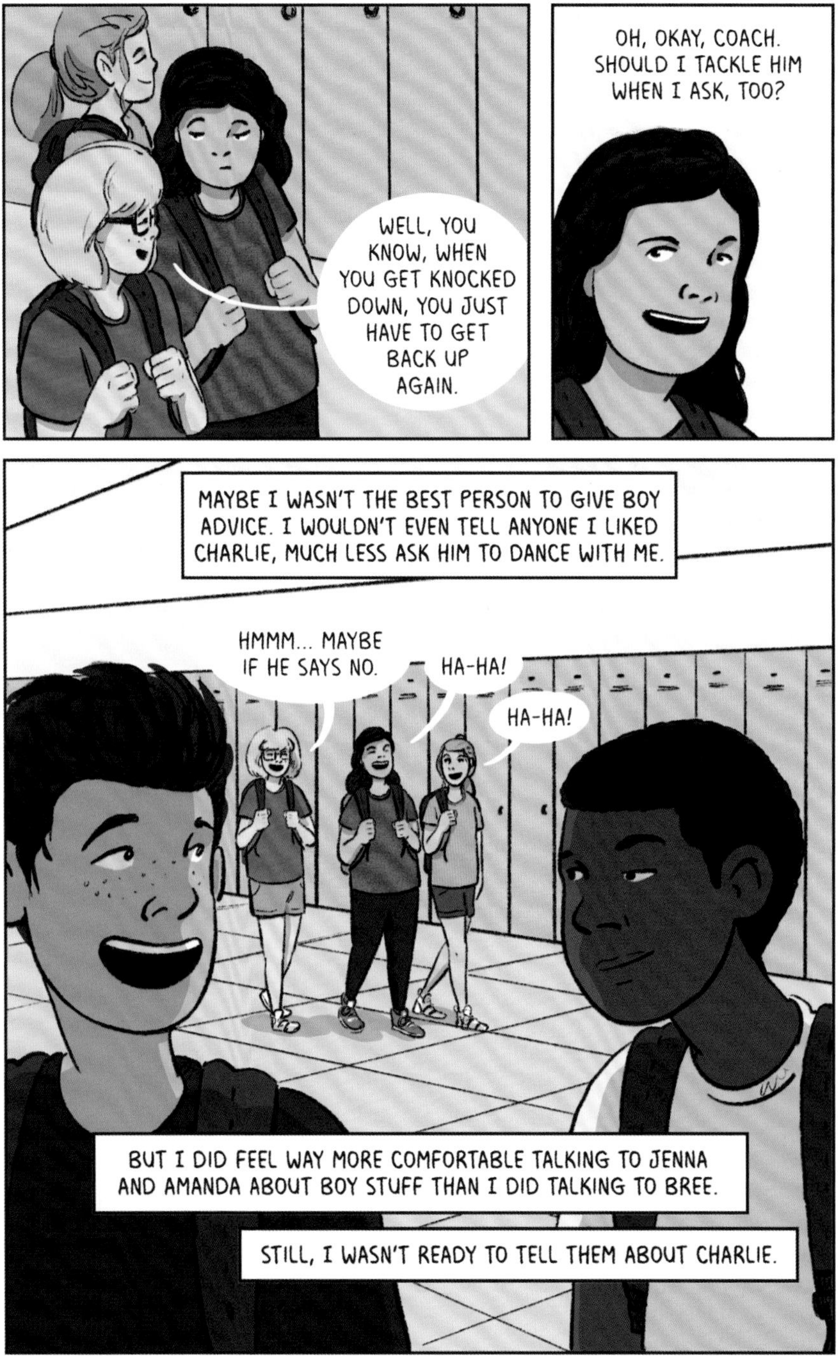
WELL, YOU KNOW, WHEN YOU GET KNOCKED DOWN, YOU JUST HAVE TO GET BACK UP AGAIN.
OH, OKAY, COACH. SHOULD I TACKLE HIM WHEN I ASK, TOO?
MAYBE I WASN'T THE BEST PERSON TO GIVE BOY ADVICE. I WOULDN'T EVEN TELL ANYONE I LIKED CHARLIE, MUCH LESS ASK HIM TO DANCE WITH ME.
HMMM... MAYBE IF HE SAYS NO.
HA-HA!
HA-HA!
BUT I DID FEEL WAY MORE COMFORTABLE TALKING TO JENNA AND AMANDA ABOUT BOY STUFF THAN I DID TALKING TO BREE.
STILL, I WASN'T READY TO TELL THEM ABOUT CHARLIE.

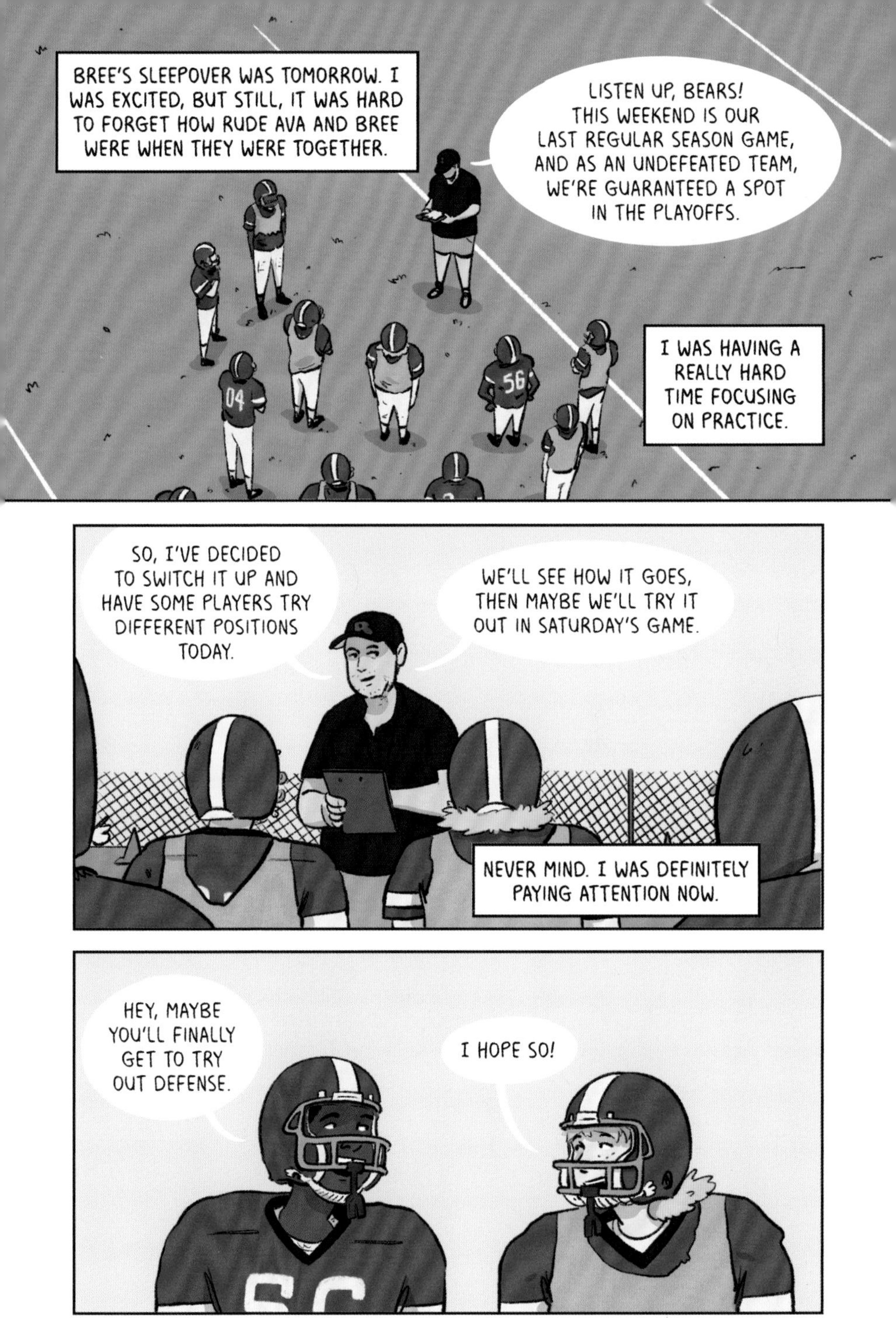
BREE'S SLEEPOVER WAS TOMORROW. I WAS EXCITED, BUT STILL, IT WAS HARD TO FORGET HOW RUDE AVA AND BREE WERE WHEN THEY WERE TOGETHER.
LISTEN UP, BEARS! THIS WEEKEND IS OUR LAST REGULAR SEASON GAME, AND AS AN UNDEFEATED TEAM, WE'RE GUARANTEED A SPOT IN THE PLAYOFFS.
I WAS HAVING A REALLY HARD TIME FOCUSING ON PRACTICE.
SO, I'VE DECIDED TO SWITCH IT UP AND HAVE SOME PLAYERS TRY DIFFERENT POSITIONS TODAY.
WE'LL SEE HOW IT GOES, THEN MAYBE WE'LL TRY IT OUT IN SATURDAY'S GAME.
NEVER MIND. I WAS DEFINITELY PAYING ATTENTION NOW.
HEY, MAYBE YOU'LL FINALLY GET TO TRY OUT DEFENSE.
I HOPE SO!

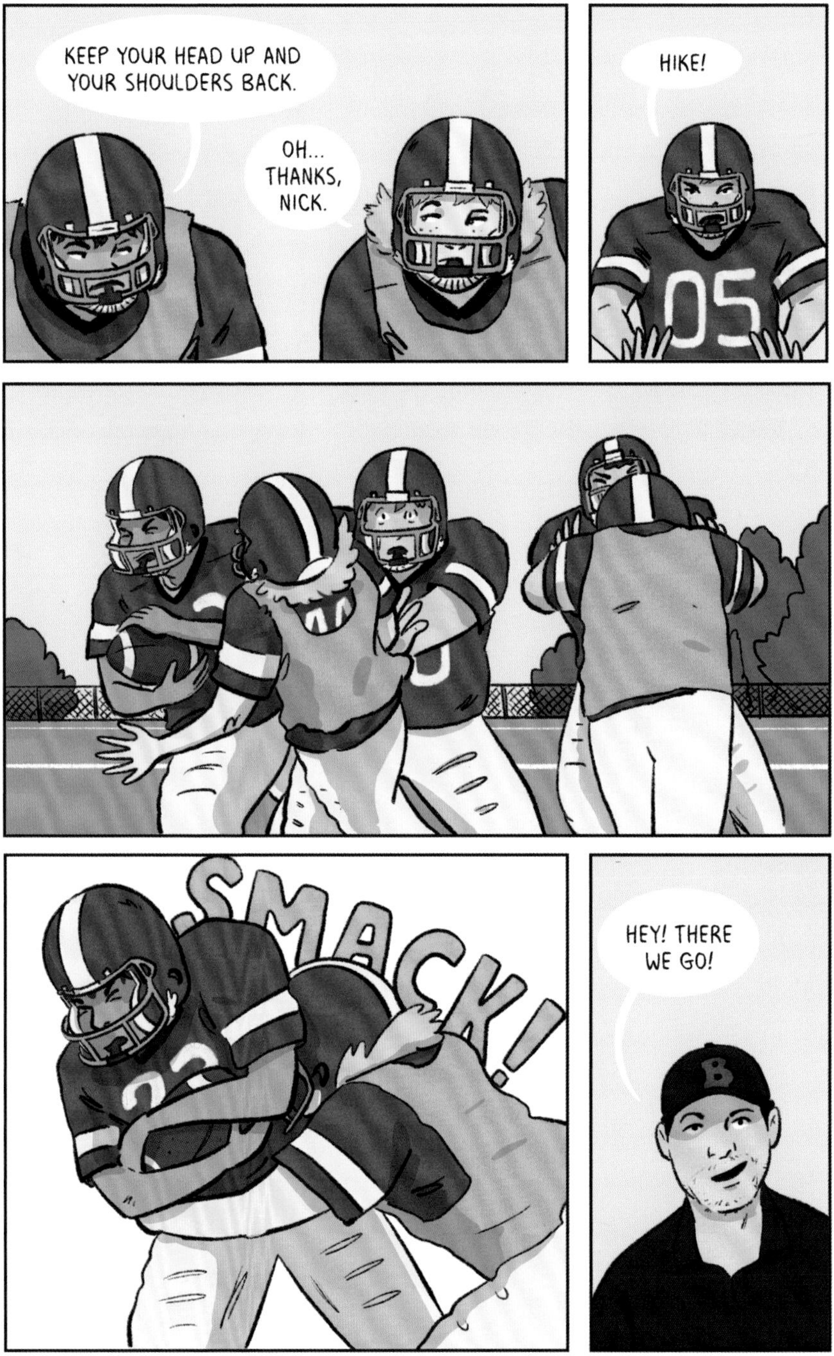
KEEP YOUR HEAD UP AND YOUR SHOULDERS BACK.
OH... THANKS, NICK.
HIKE!
05
SMACK!
HEY! THERE WE GO!

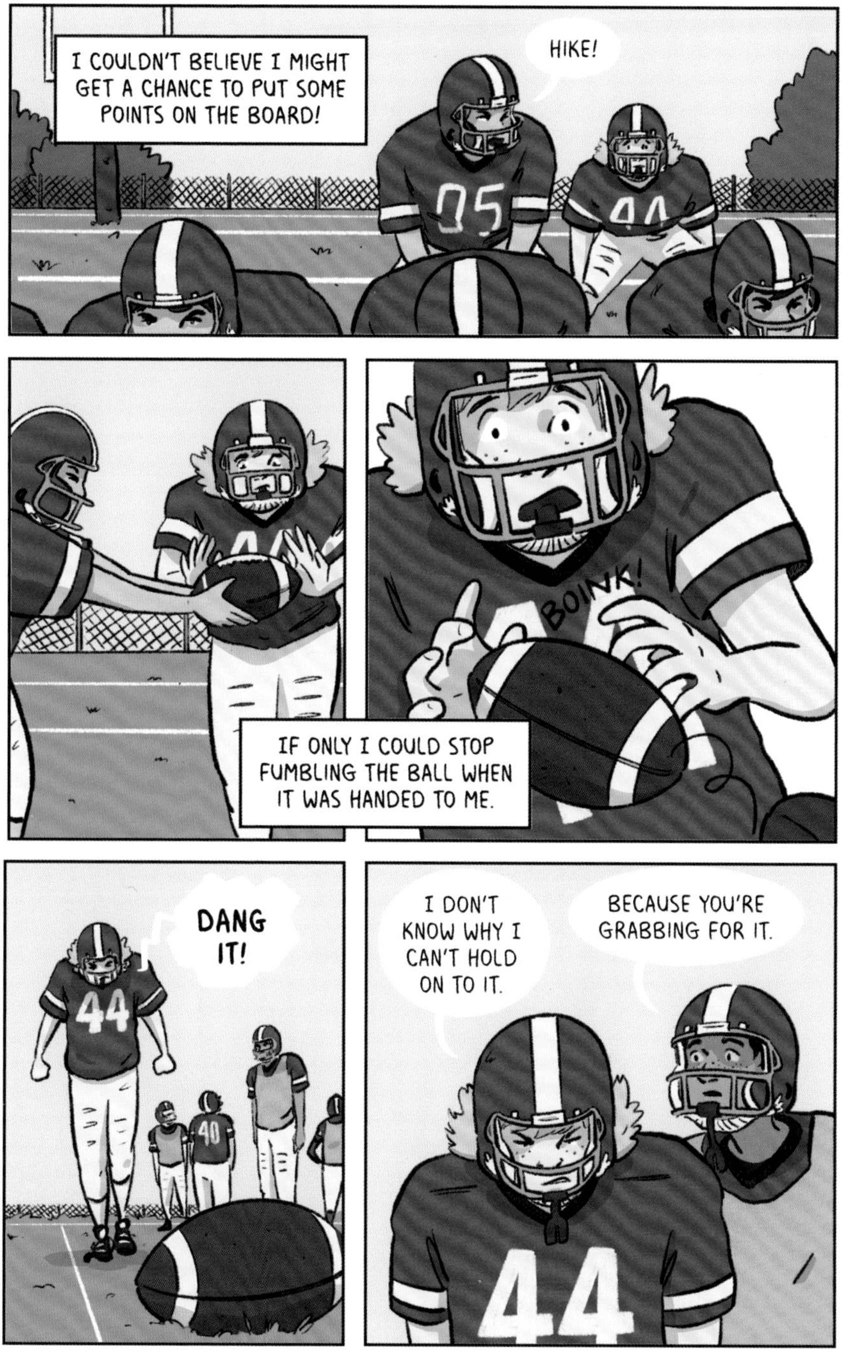
I COULDN'T BELIEVE I MIGHT GET A CHANCE TO PUT SOME POINTS ON THE BOARD!
HIKE!
BOINK!
IF ONLY I COULD STOP FUMBLING THE BALL WHEN IT WAS HANDED TO ME.
DANG IT!
I DON'T KNOW WHY I CAN'T HOLD ON TO IT.
BECAUSE YOU'RE GRABBING FOR IT.

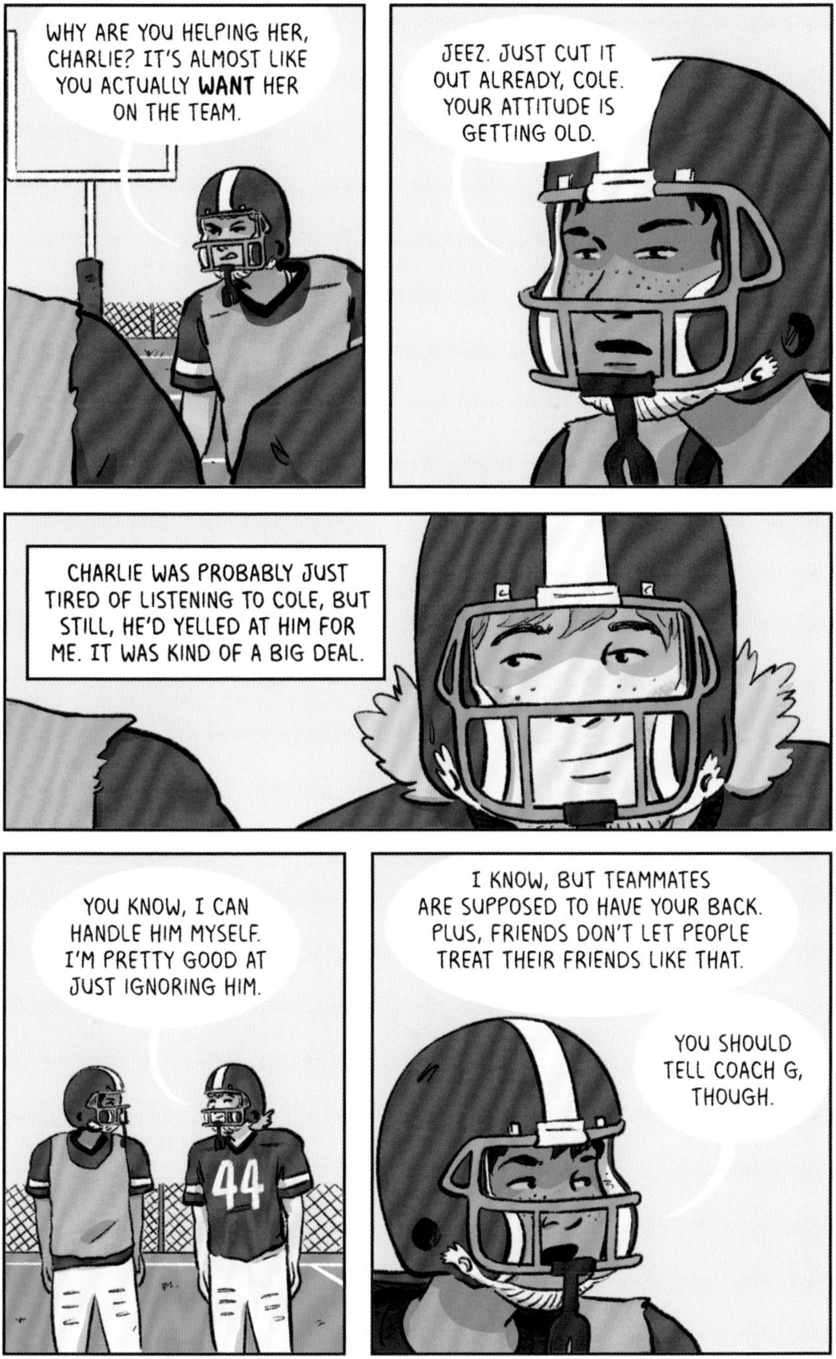
WHY ARE YOU HELPING HER, CHARLIE? IT'S ALMOST LIKE YOU ACTUALLY **WANT** HER ON THE TEAM.
JEEZ. JUST CUT IT OUT ALREADY, COLE. YOUR ATTITUDE IS GETTING OLD.
CHARLIE WAS PROBABLY JUST TIRED OF LISTENING TO COLE, BUT STILL, HE'D YELLED AT HIM FOR ME. IT WAS KIND OF A BIG DEAL.
YOU KNOW, I CAN HANDLE HIM MYSELF. I'M PRETTY GOOD AT JUST IGNORING HIM.
44
I KNOW, BUT TEAMMATES ARE SUPPOSED TO HAVE YOUR BACK. PLUS, FRIENDS DON'T LET PEOPLE TREAT THEIR FRIENDS LIKE THAT.
YOU SHOULD TELL COACH G, THOUGH.

CHAPTER 7

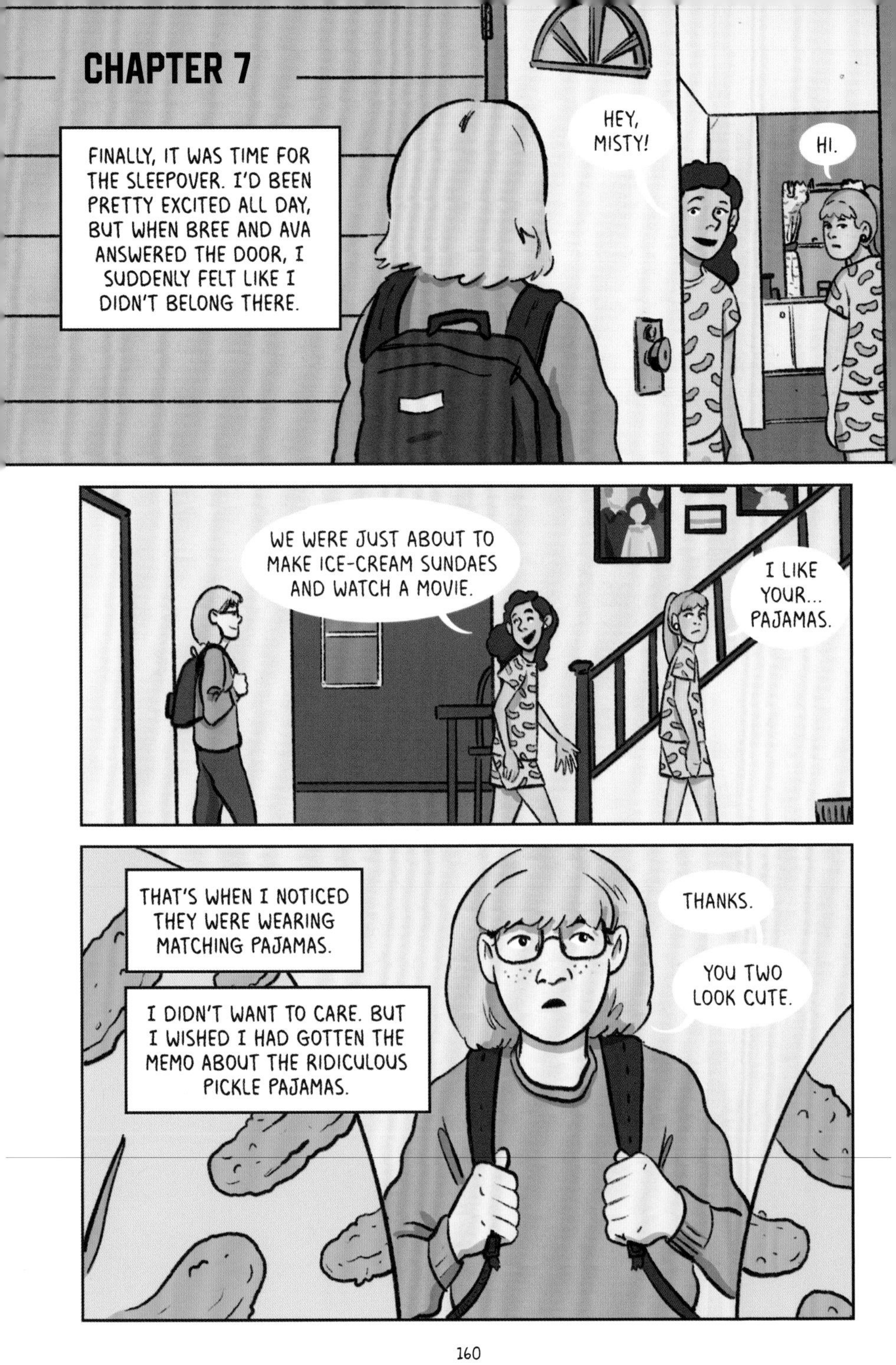
FINALLY, IT WAS TIME FOR THE SLEEPOVER. I'D BEEN PRETTY EXCITED ALL DAY, BUT WHEN BREE AND AVA ANSWERED THE DOOR, I SUDDENLY FELT LIKE I DIDN'T BELONG THERE.
HEY, MISTY!
HI.
WE WERE JUST ABOUT TO MAKE ICE-CREAM SUNDAES AND WATCH A MOVIE.
I LIKE YOUR... PAJAMAS.
THAT'S WHEN I NOTICED THEY WERE WEARING MATCHING PAJAMAS.
I DIDN'T WANT TO CARE. BUT I WISHED I HAD GOTTEN THE MEMO ABOUT THE RIDICULOUS PICKLE PAJAMAS.
THANKS.
YOU TWO LOOK CUTE.

161

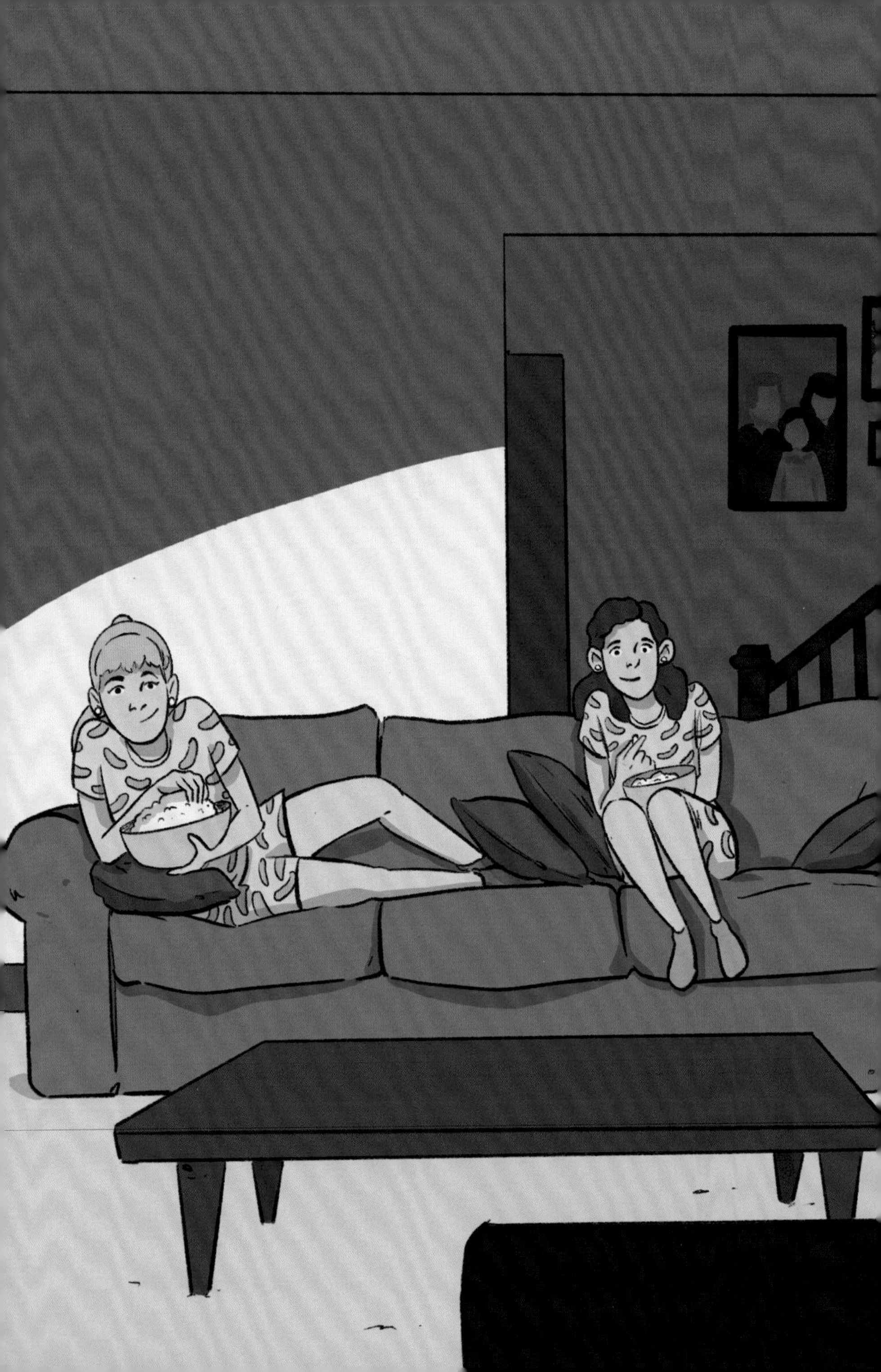

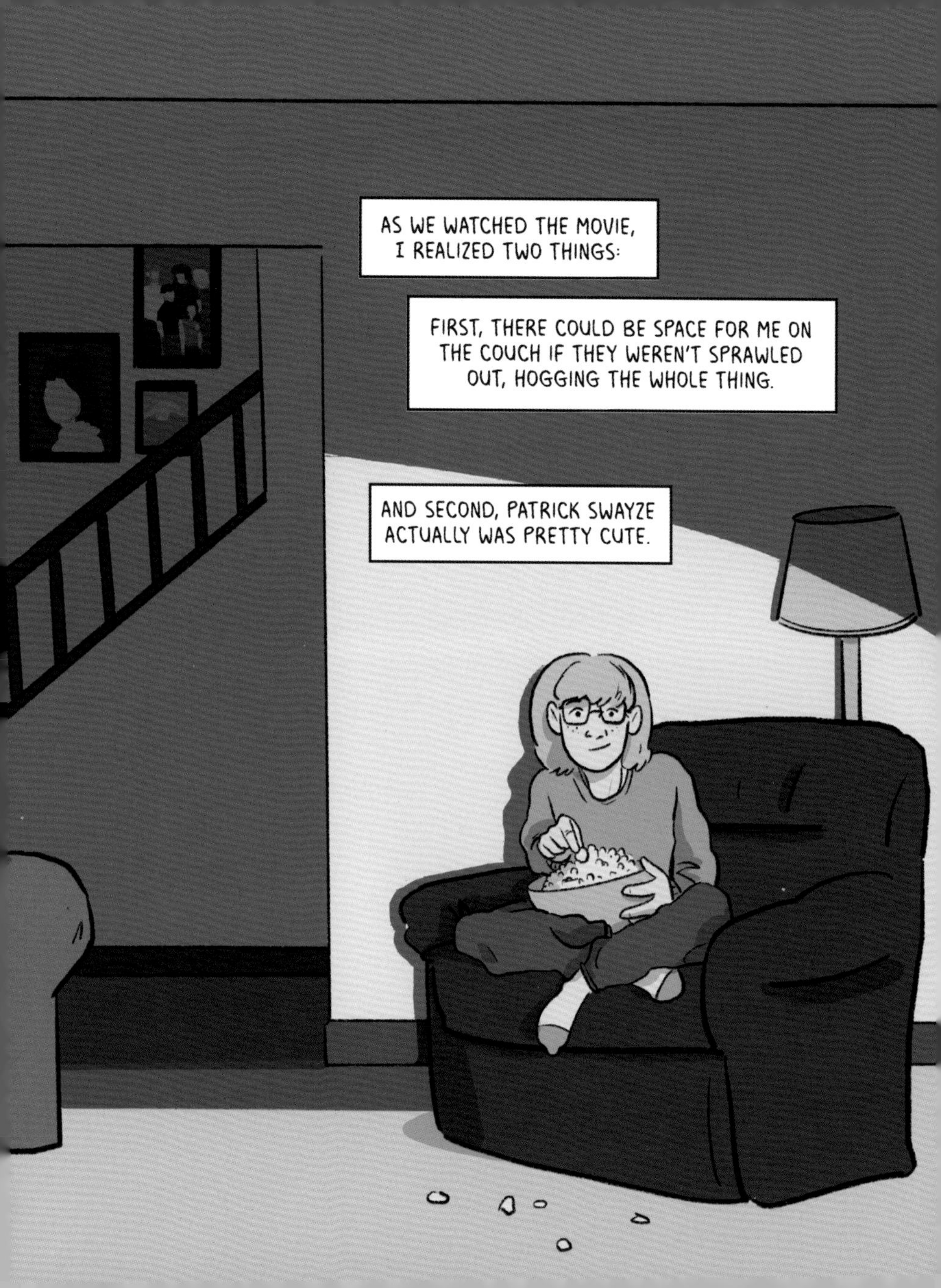
AS WE WATCHED THE MOVIE, I REALIZED TWO THINGS:
FIRST, THERE COULD BE SPACE FOR ME ON THE COUCH IF THEY WEREN'T SPRAWLED OUT, HOGGING THE WHOLE THING.
AND SECOND, PATRICK SWAYZE ACTUALLY WAS PRETTY CUTE.

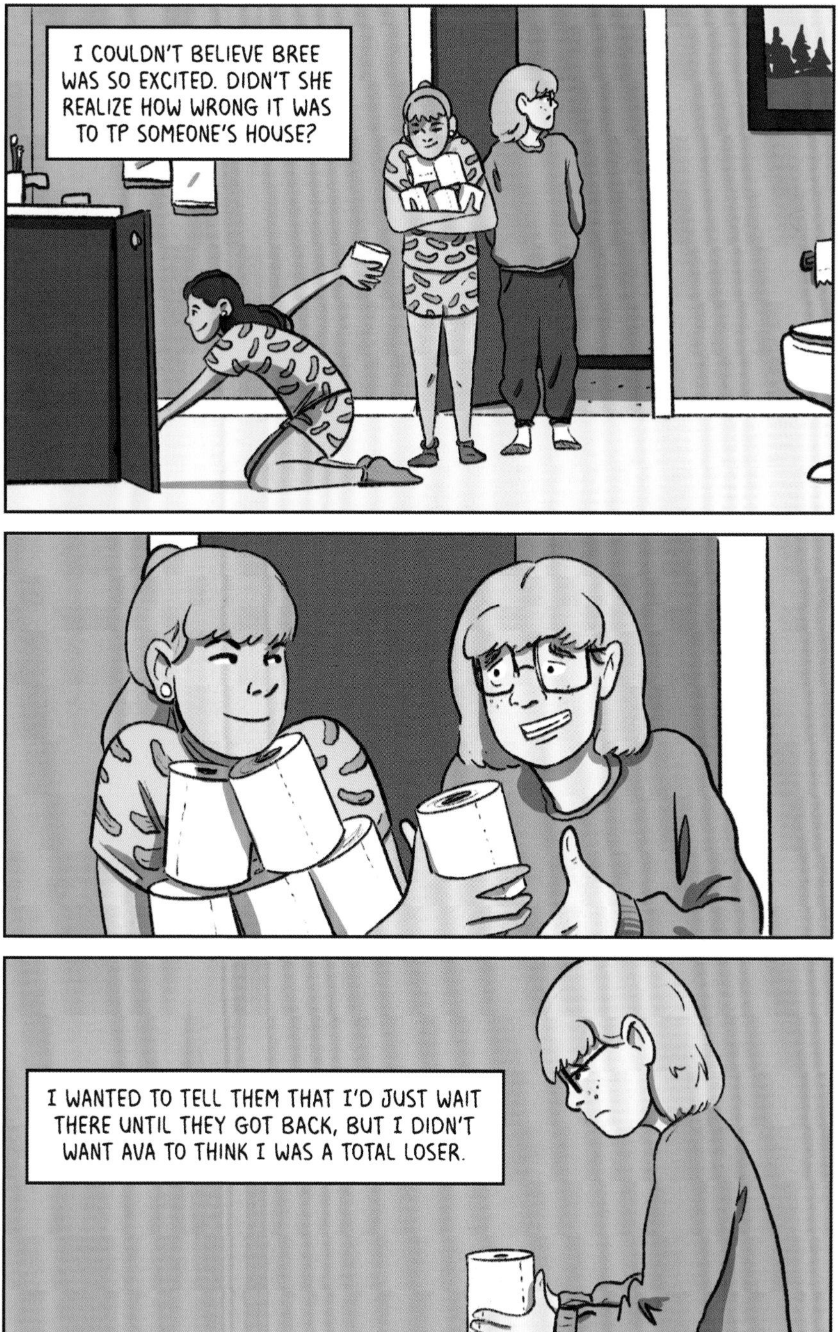
I COULDN'T BELIEVE BREE WAS SO EXCITED. DIDN'T SHE REALIZE HOW WRONG IT WAS TO TP SOMEONE'S HOUSE?
I WANTED TO TELL THEM THAT I'D JUST WAIT THERE UNTIL THEY GOT BACK, BUT I DIDN'T WANT AVA TO THINK I WAS A TOTAL LOSER.

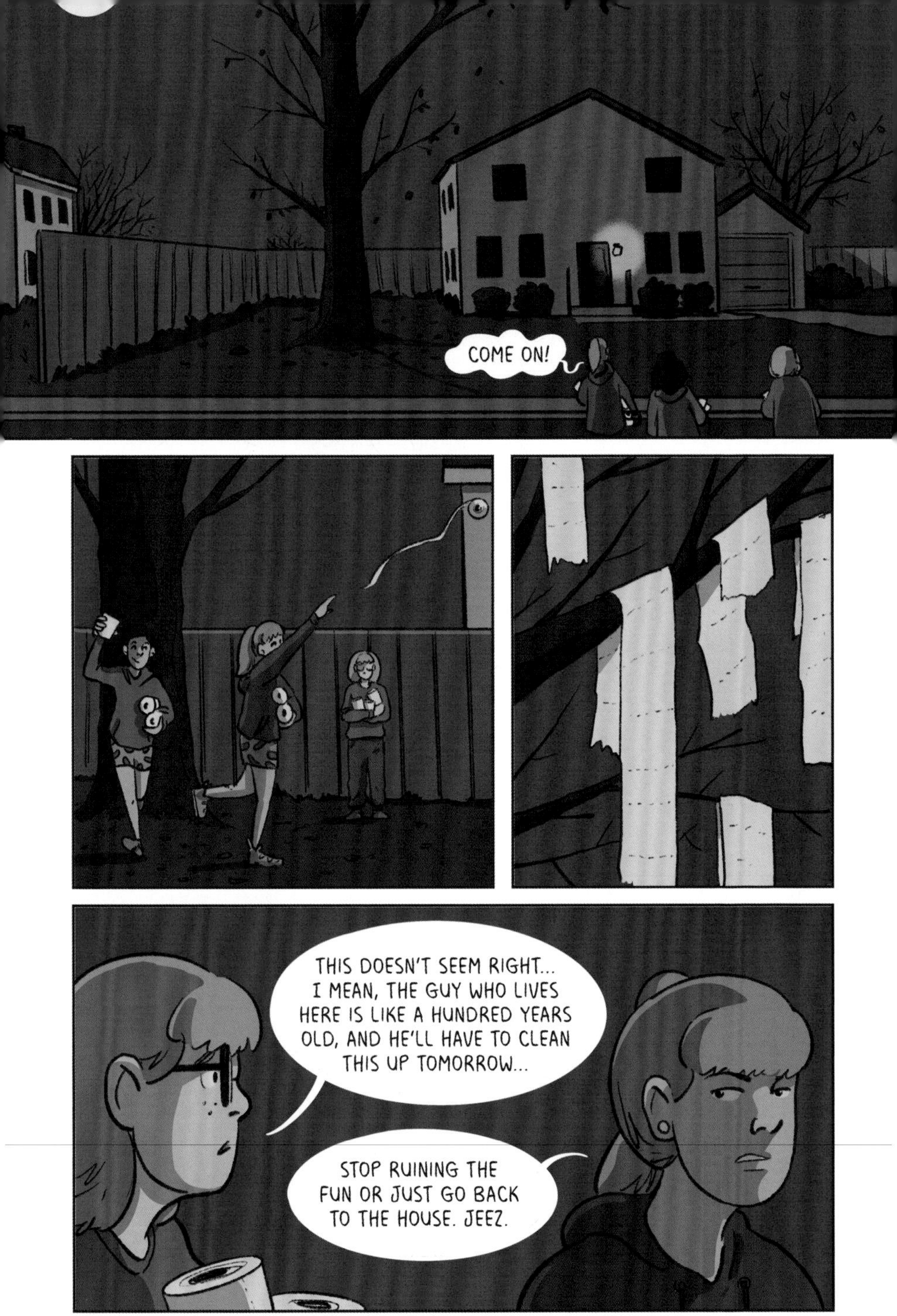
COME ON!
THIS DOESN'T SEEM RIGHT... I MEAN, THE GUY WHO LIVES HERE IS LIKE A HUNDRED YEARS OLD, AND HE'LL HAVE TO CLEAN THIS UP TOMORROW...
STOP RUINING THE FUN OR JUST GO BACK TO THE HOUSE. JEEZ.

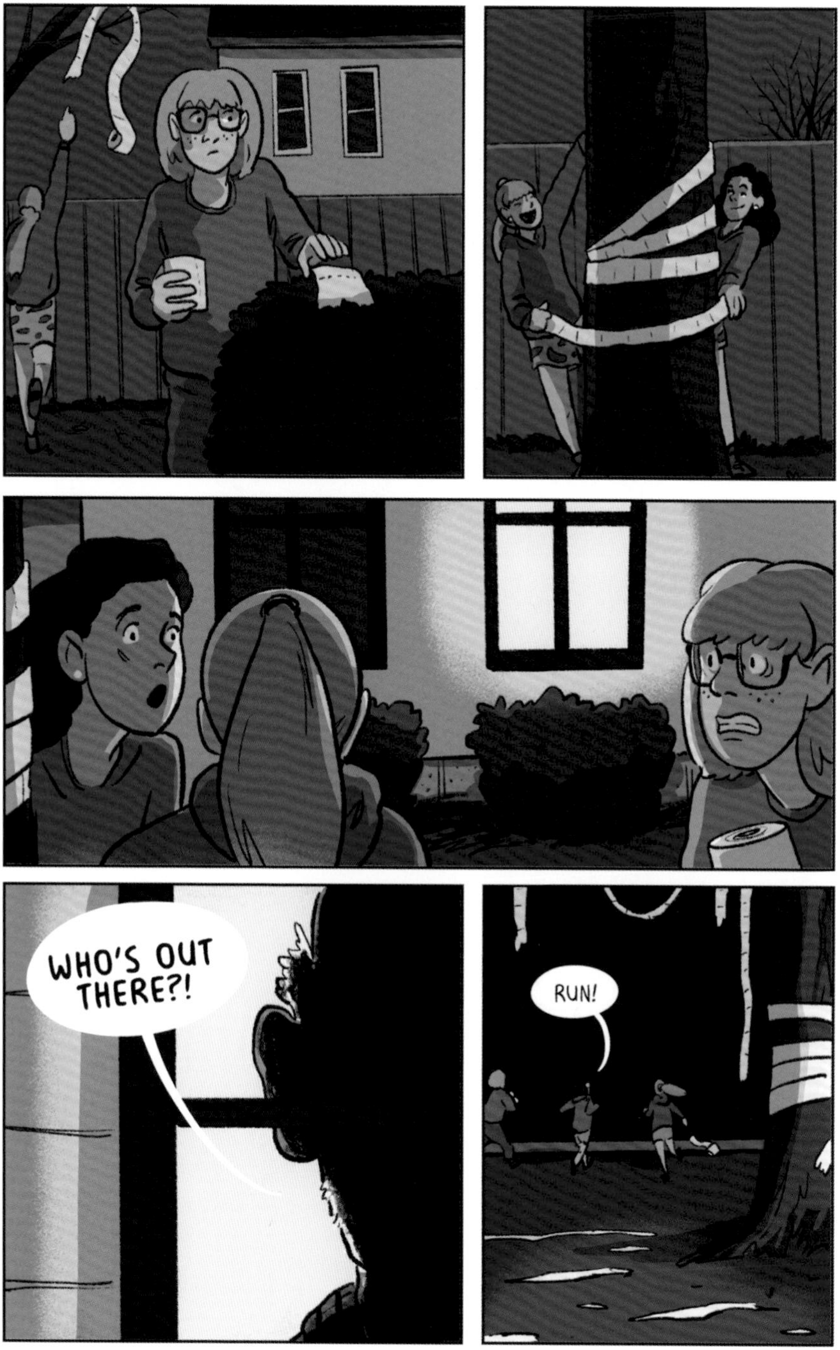
WHO'S OUT THERE?!
RUN!

169

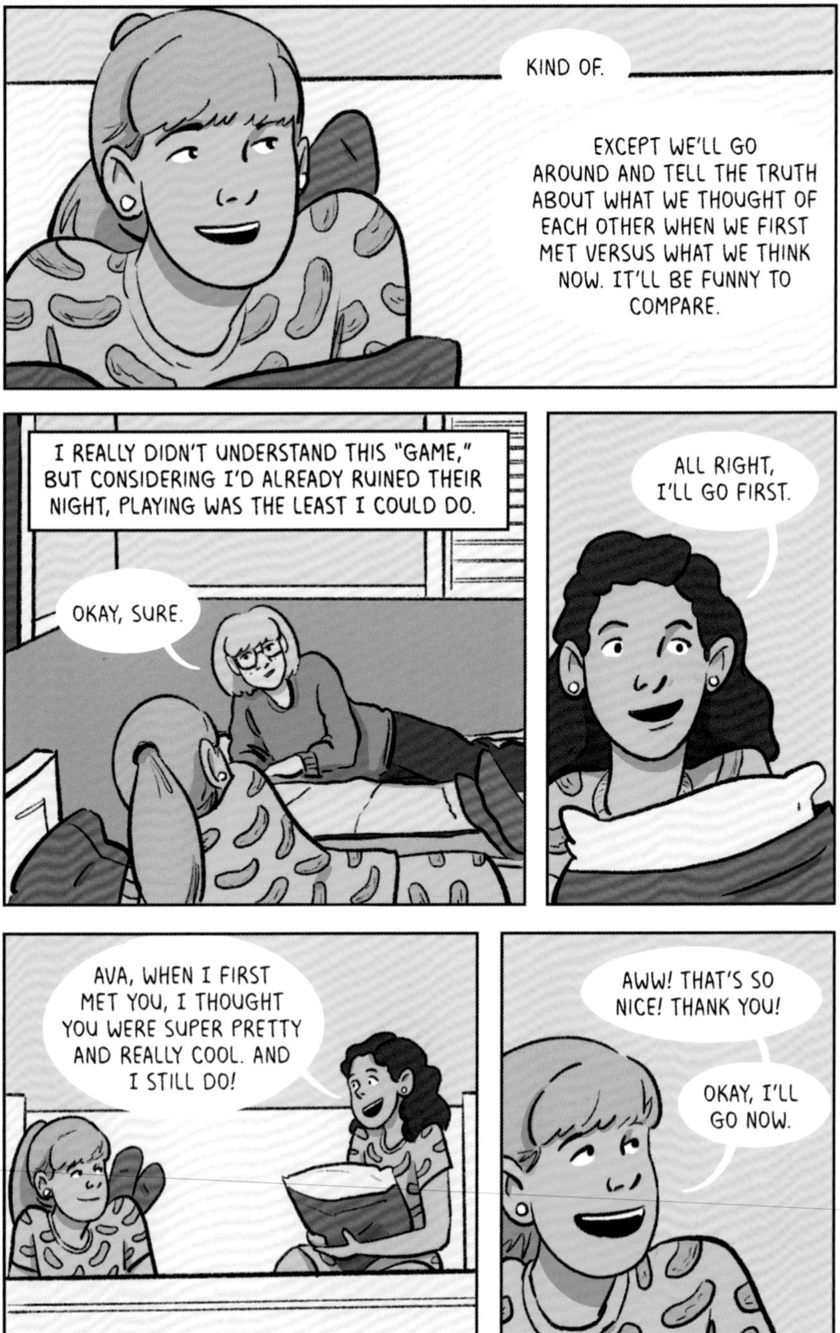
KIND OF.
EXCEPT WE'LL GO AROUND AND TELL THE TRUTH ABOUT WHAT WE THOUGHT OF EACH OTHER WHEN WE FIRST MET VERSUS WHAT WE THINK NOW. IT'LL BE FUNNY TO COMPARE.
I REALLY DIDN'T UNDERSTAND THIS "GAME," BUT CONSIDERING I'D ALREADY RUINED THEIR NIGHT, PLAYING WAS THE LEAST I COULD DO.
OKAY, SURE.
ALL RIGHT, I'LL GO FIRST.
AVA, WHEN I FIRST MET YOU, I THOUGHT YOU WERE SUPER PRETTY AND REALLY COOL. AND I STILL DO!
AWW! THAT'S SO NICE! THANK YOU!
OKAY, I'LL GO NOW.

173

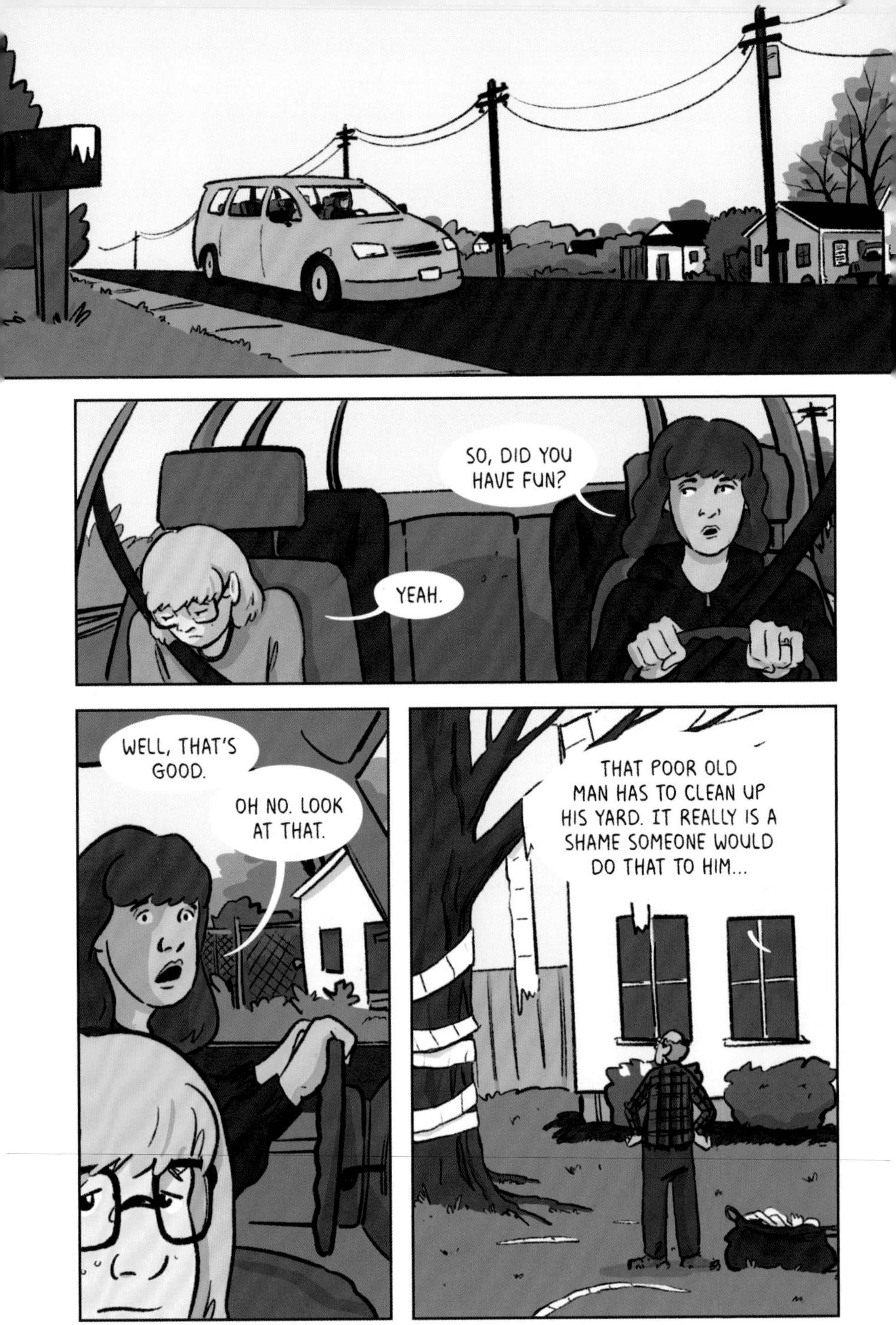
SO, DID YOU HAVE FUN?
YEAH.
WELL, THAT'S GOOD.
OH NO. LOOK AT THAT.
THAT POOR OLD MAN HAS TO CLEAN UP HIS YARD. IT REALLY IS A SHAME SOMEONE WOULD DO THAT TO HIM...

CHAPTER 8

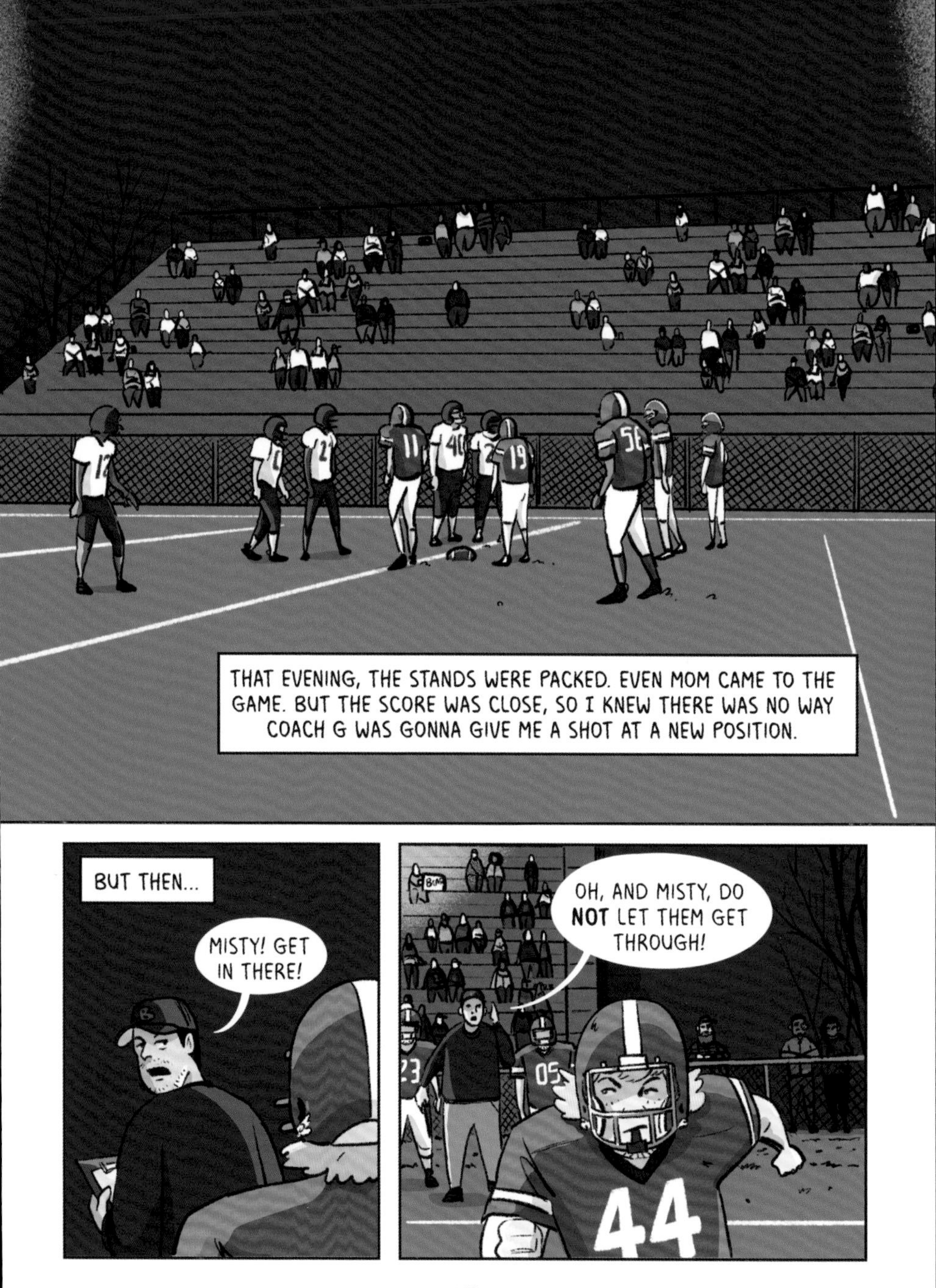
THAT EVENING, THE STANDS WERE PACKED. EVEN MOM CAME TO THE GAME. BUT THE SCORE WAS CLOSE, SO I KNEW THERE WAS NO WAY COACH G WAS GONNA GIVE ME A SHOT AT A NEW POSITION.
BUT THEN...
MISTY! GET IN THERE!
OH, AND MISTY, DO **NOT** LET THEM GET THROUGH!

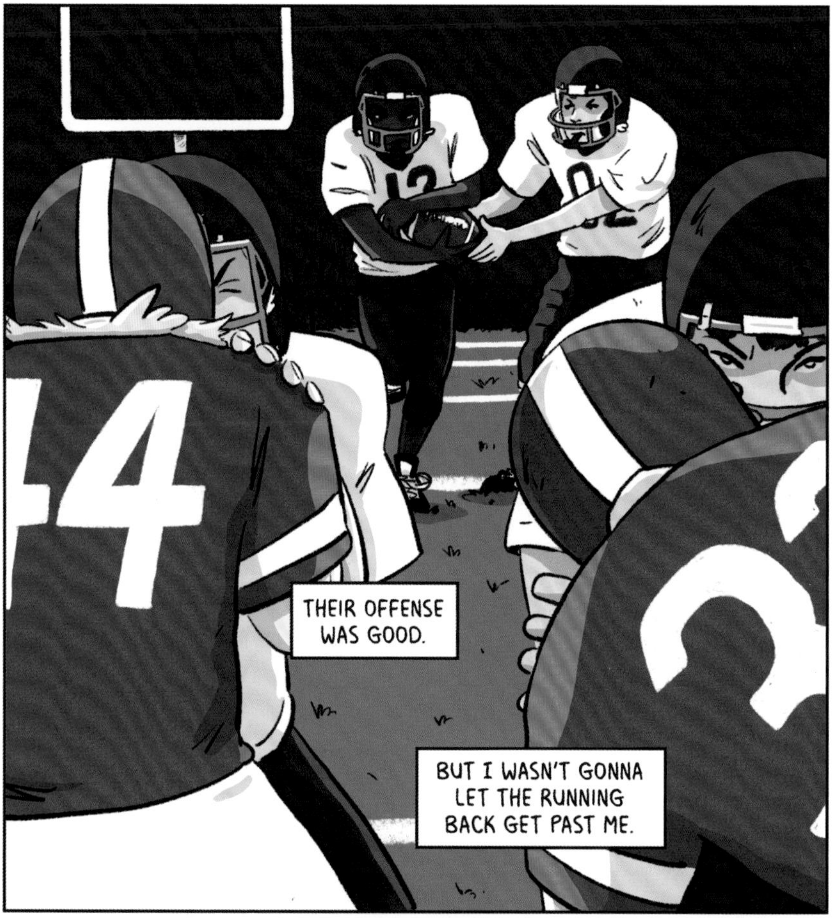
THEIR OFFENSE WAS GOOD.
BUT I WASN'T GONNA LET THE RUNNING BACK GET PAST ME.

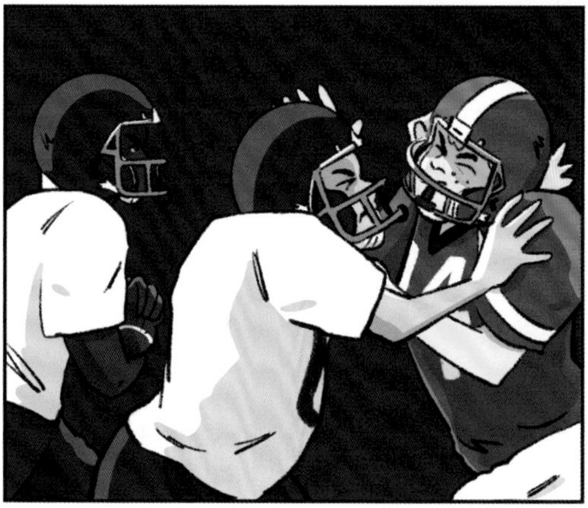

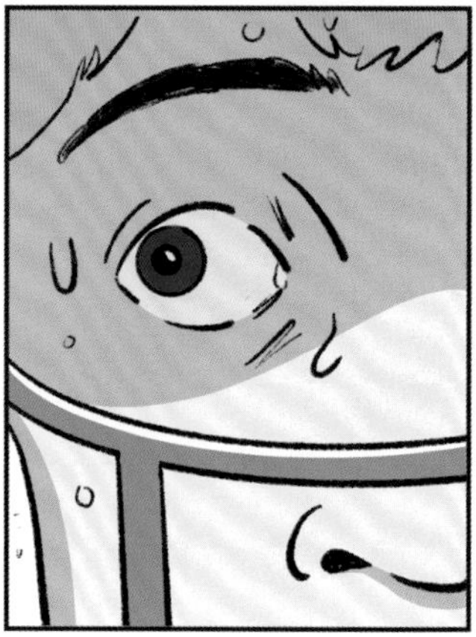

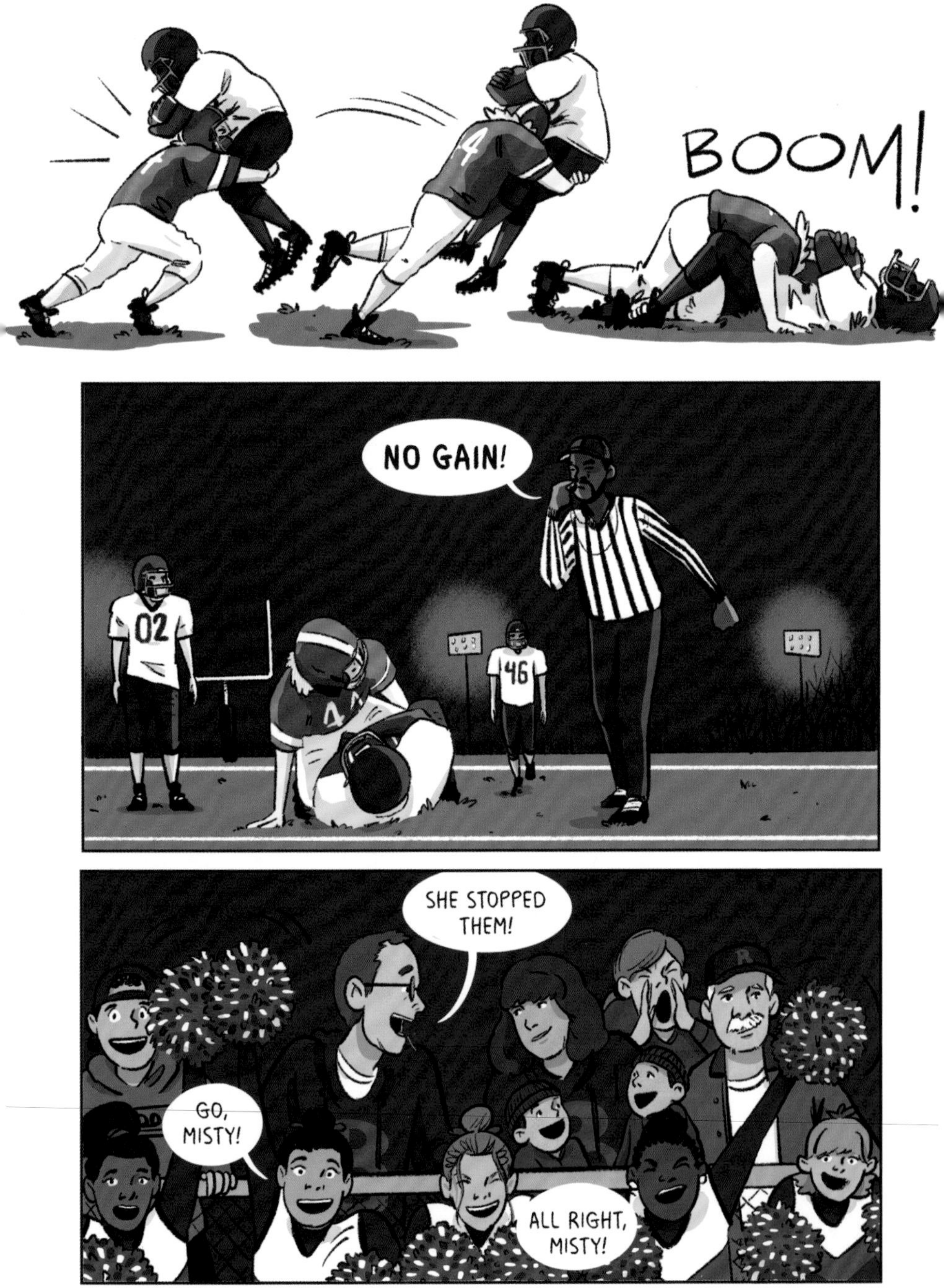
BOOM!
NO GAIN!
SHE STOPPED THEM!
GO, MISTY!
ALL RIGHT, MISTY!

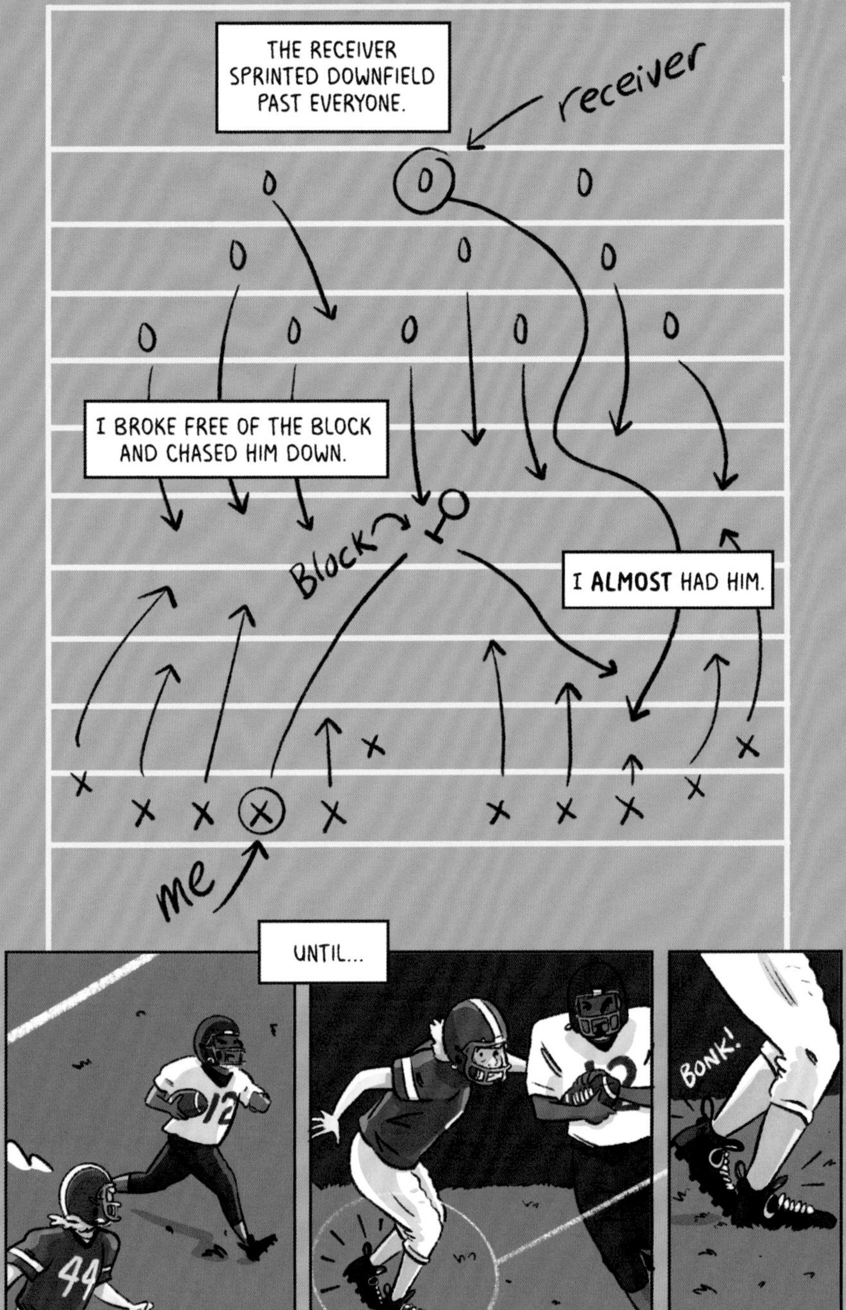
THE RECEIVER SPRINTED DOWNFIELD PAST EVERYONE.
receiver
I BROKE FREE OF THE BLOCK AND CHASED HIM DOWN.
Block
I ALMOST HAD HIM.
me
UNTIL...
BONK!

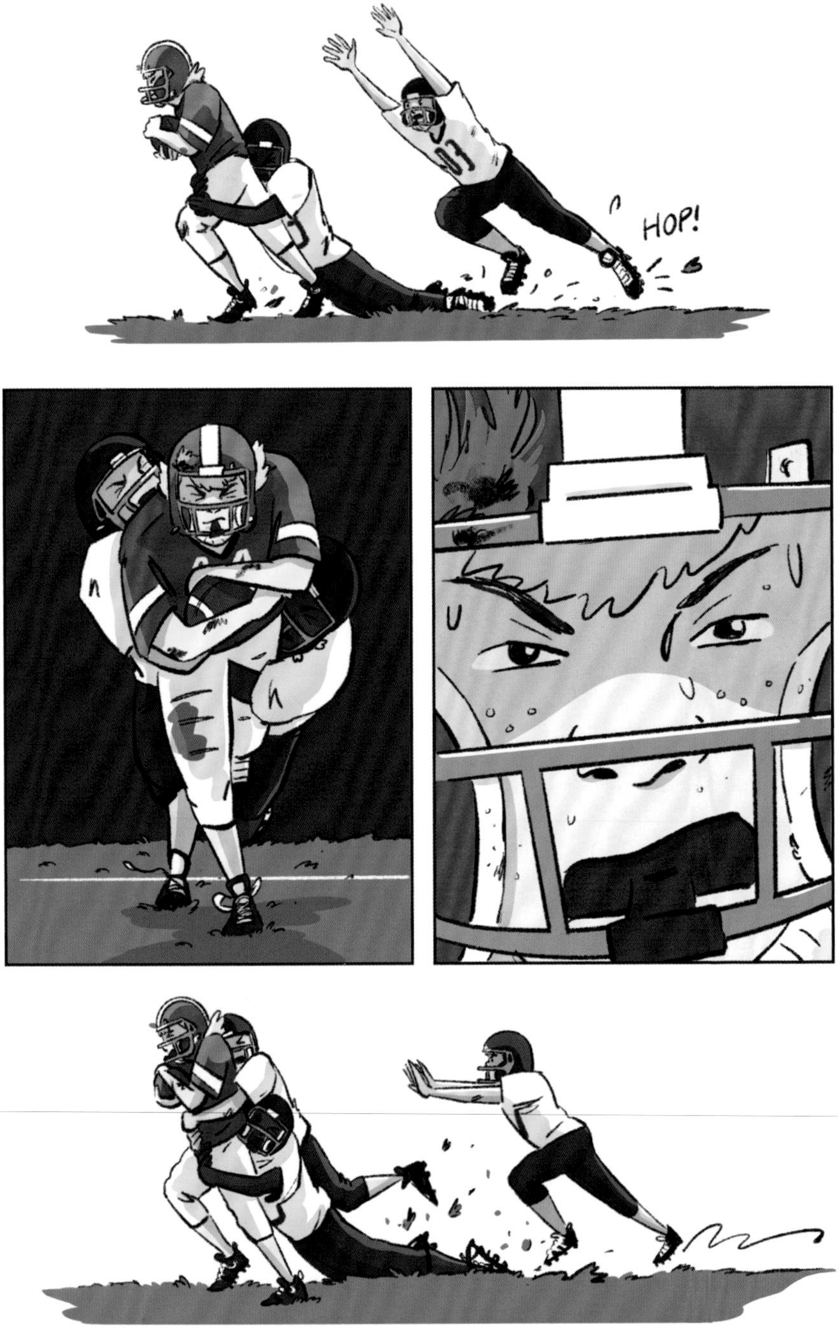
HOP!

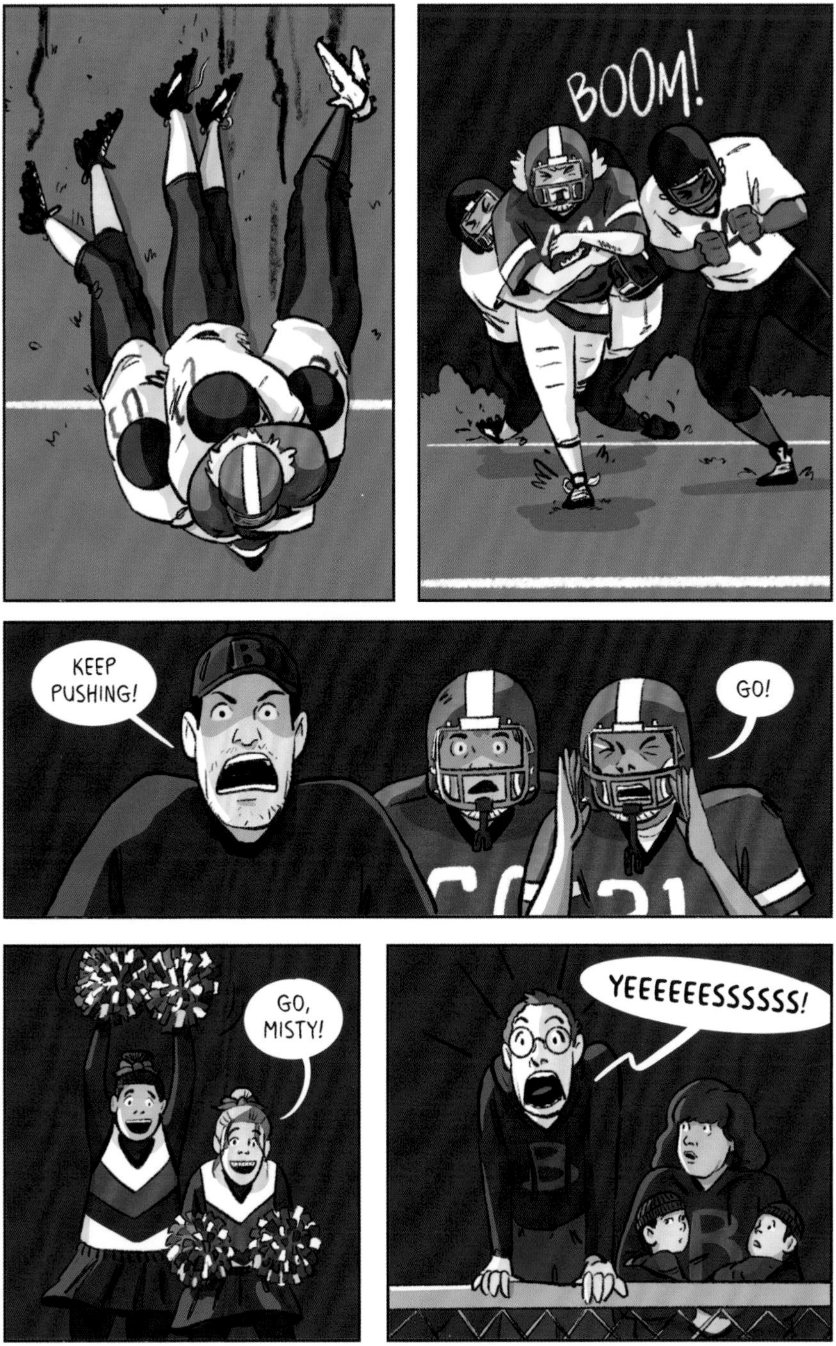
BOOM!
KEEP PUSHING!
GO!
GO, MISTY!
YEEEEEESSSSSS!

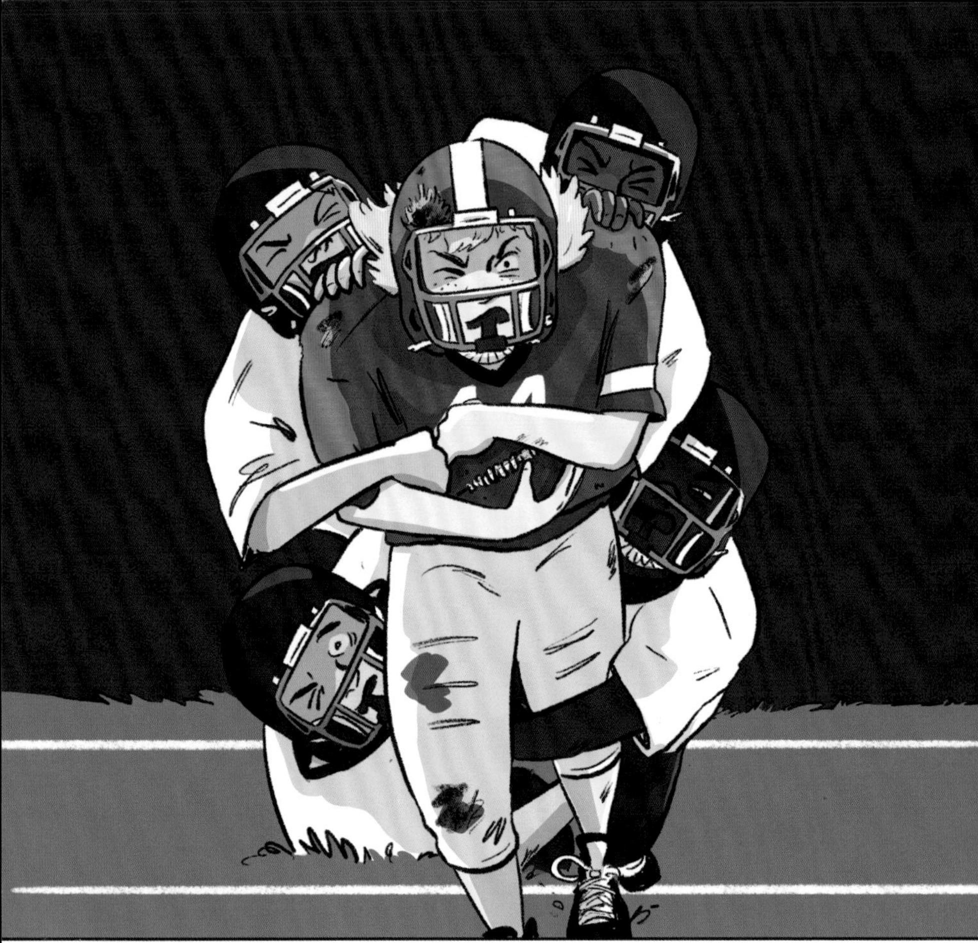

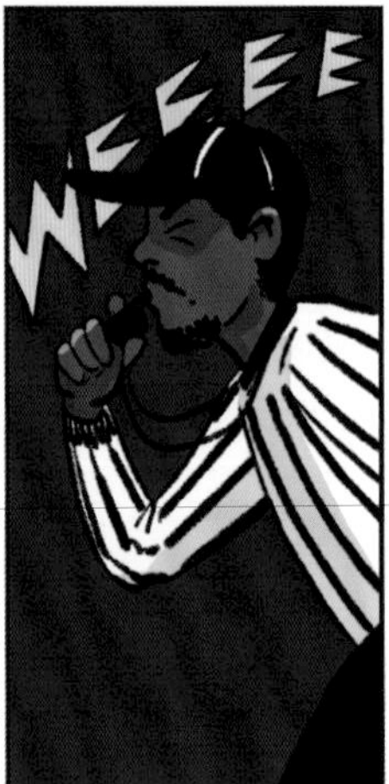
WEEEE

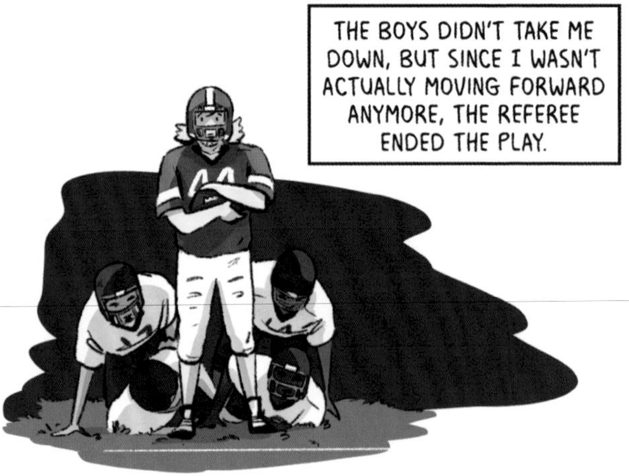
THE BOYS DIDN'T TAKE ME DOWN, BUT SINCE I WASN'T ACTUALLY MOVING FORWARD ANYMORE, THE REFEREE ENDED THE PLAY.

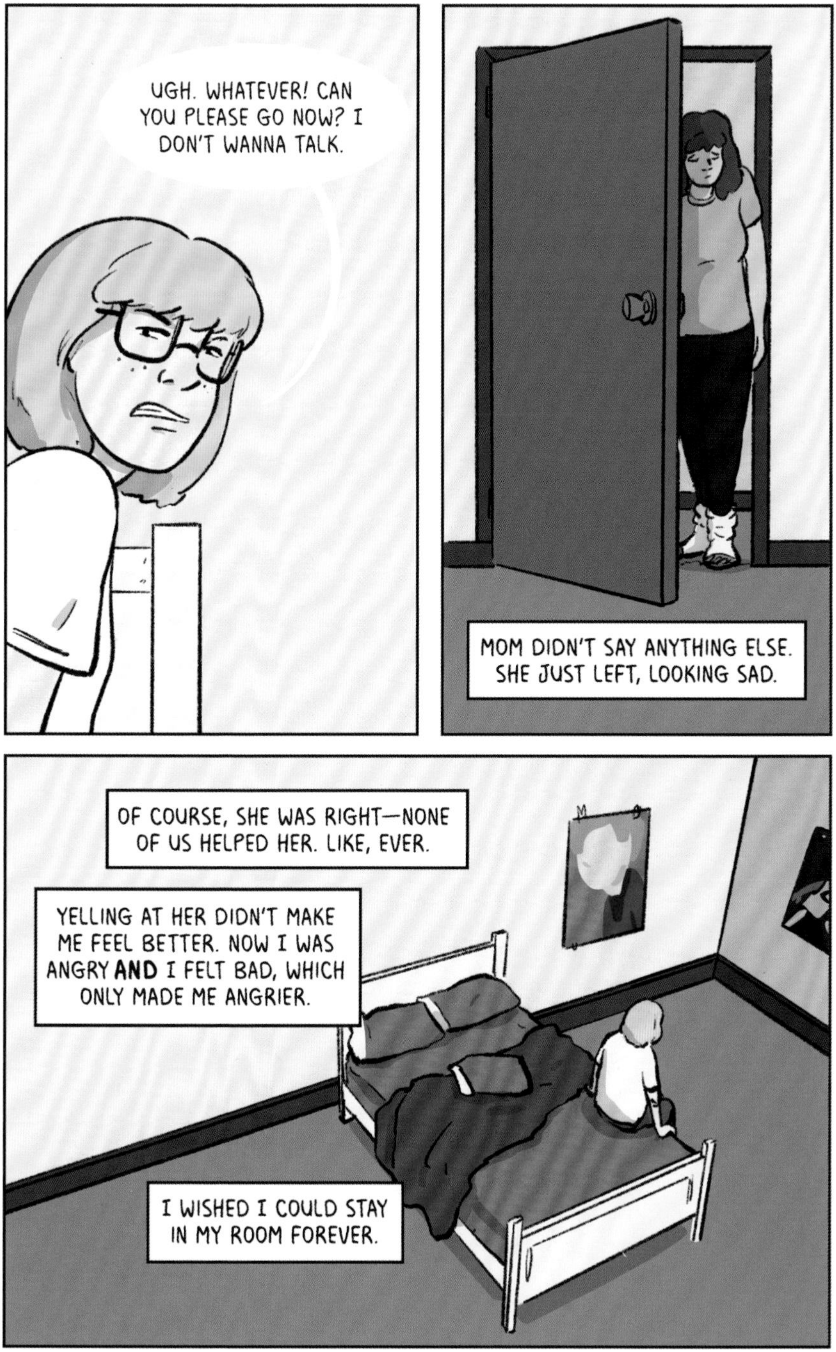
UGH. WHATEVER! CAN YOU PLEASE GO NOW? I DON'T WANNA TALK.
MOM DIDN'T SAY ANYTHING ELSE. SHE JUST LEFT, LOOKING SAD.
OF COURSE, SHE WAS RIGHT—NONE OF US HELPED HER. LIKE, EVER.
YELLING AT HER DIDN'T MAKE ME FEEL BETTER. NOW I WAS ANGRY AND I FELT BAD, WHICH ONLY MADE ME ANGRIER.
I WISHED I COULD STAY IN MY ROOM FOREVER.

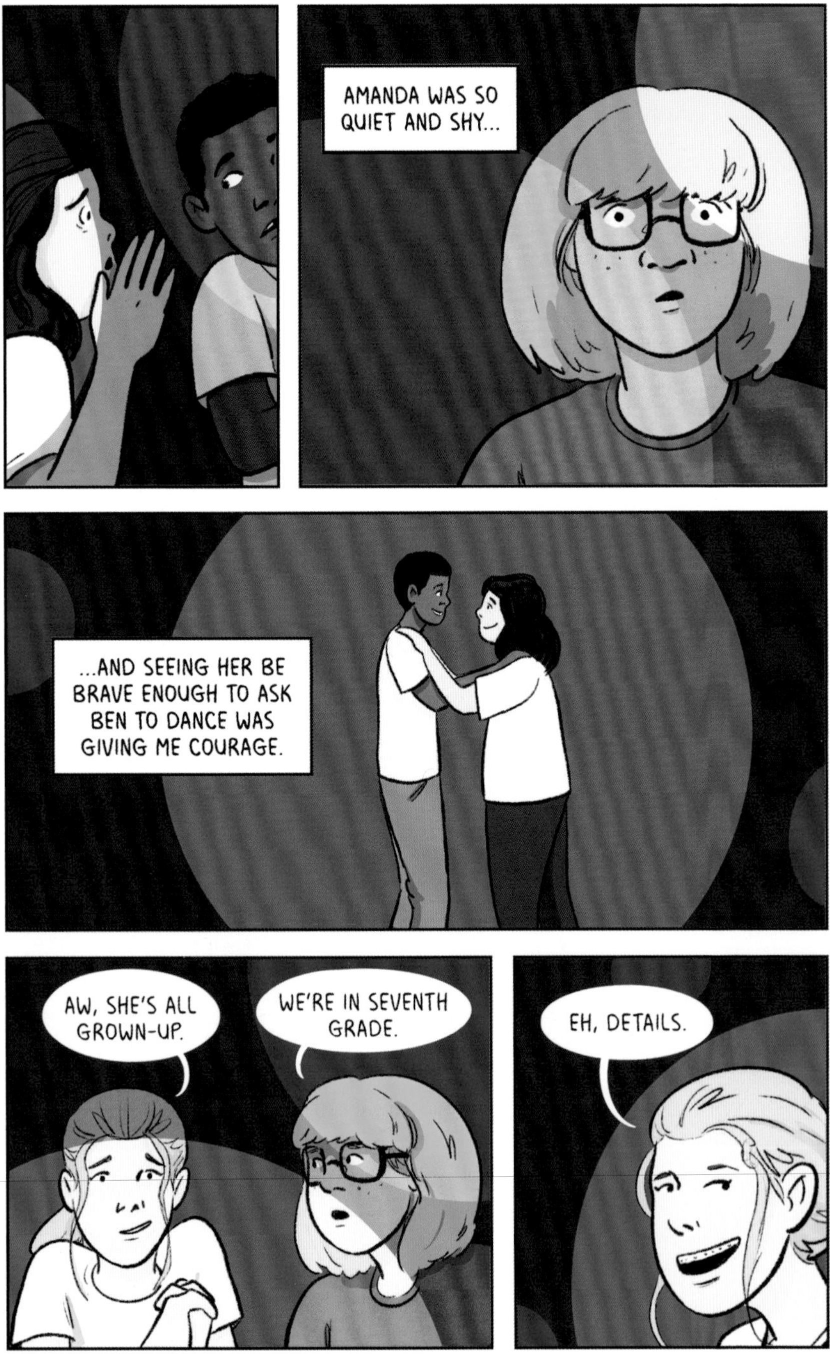
AMANDA WAS SO QUIET AND SHY...
...AND SEEING HER BE BRAVE ENOUGH TO ASK BEN TO DANCE WAS GIVING ME COURAGE.
AW, SHE'S ALL GROWN-UP.
WE'RE IN SEVENTH GRADE.
EH, DETAILS.

207

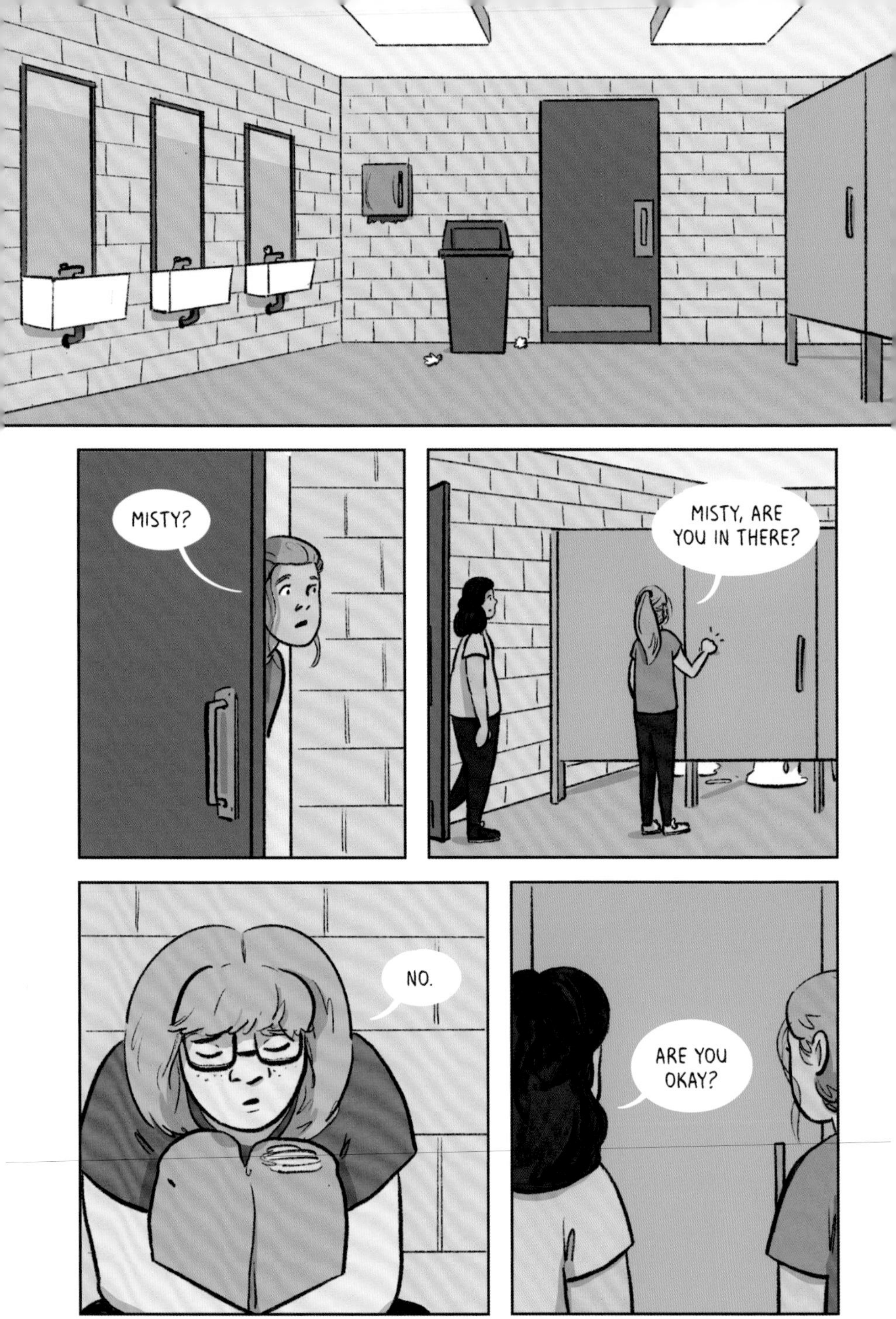
MISTY?
MISTY, ARE YOU IN THERE?
NO.
ARE YOU OKAY?

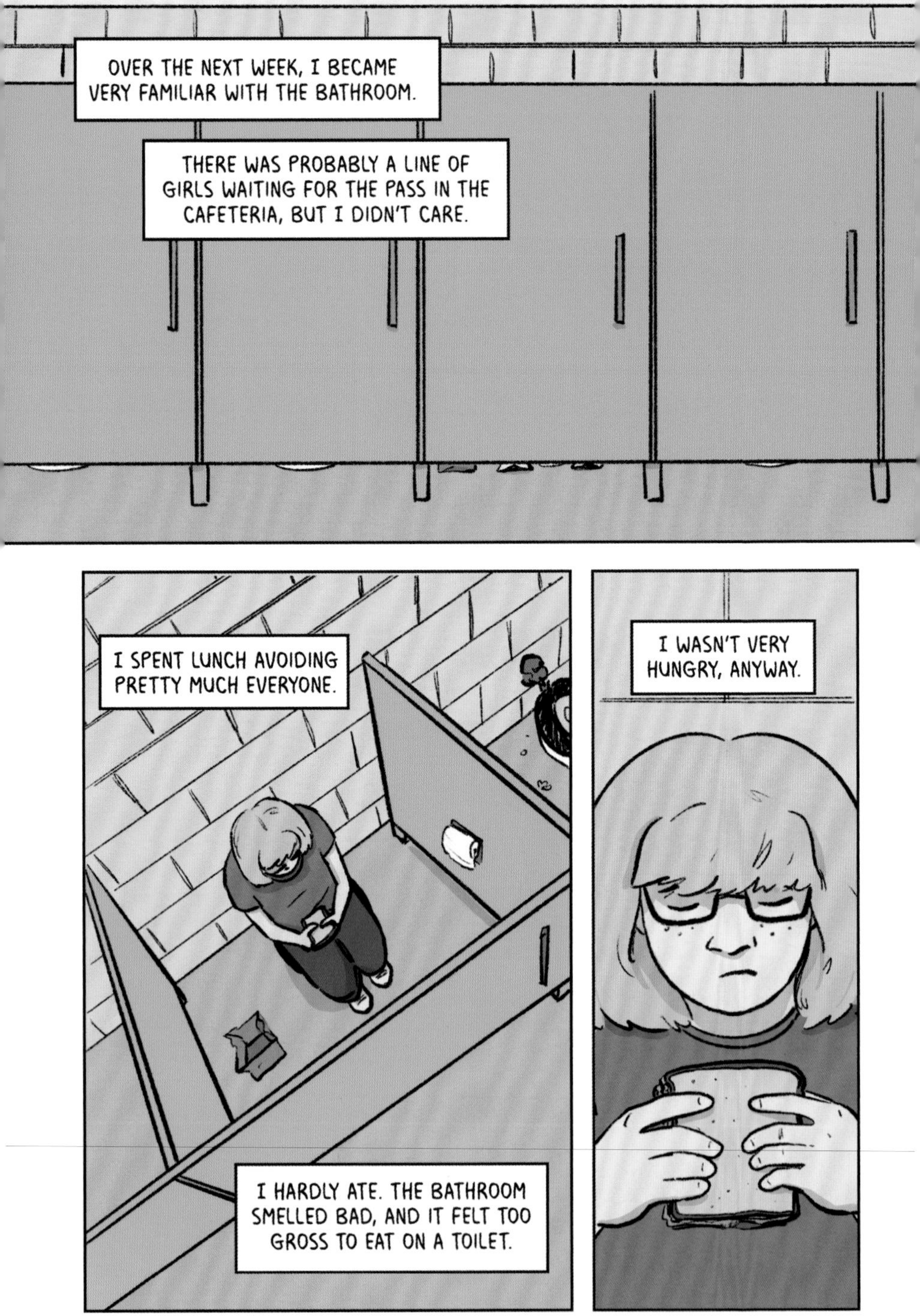
OVER THE NEXT WEEK, I BECAME VERY FAMILIAR WITH THE BATHROOM.
THERE WAS PROBABLY A LINE OF GIRLS WAITING FOR THE PASS IN THE CAFETERIA, BUT I DIDN'T CARE.
I SPENT LUNCH AVOIDING PRETTY MUCH EVERYONE.
I HARDLY ATE. THE BATHROOM SMELLED BAD, AND IT FELT TOO GROSS TO EAT ON A TOILET.
I WASN'T VERY HUNGRY, ANYWAY.

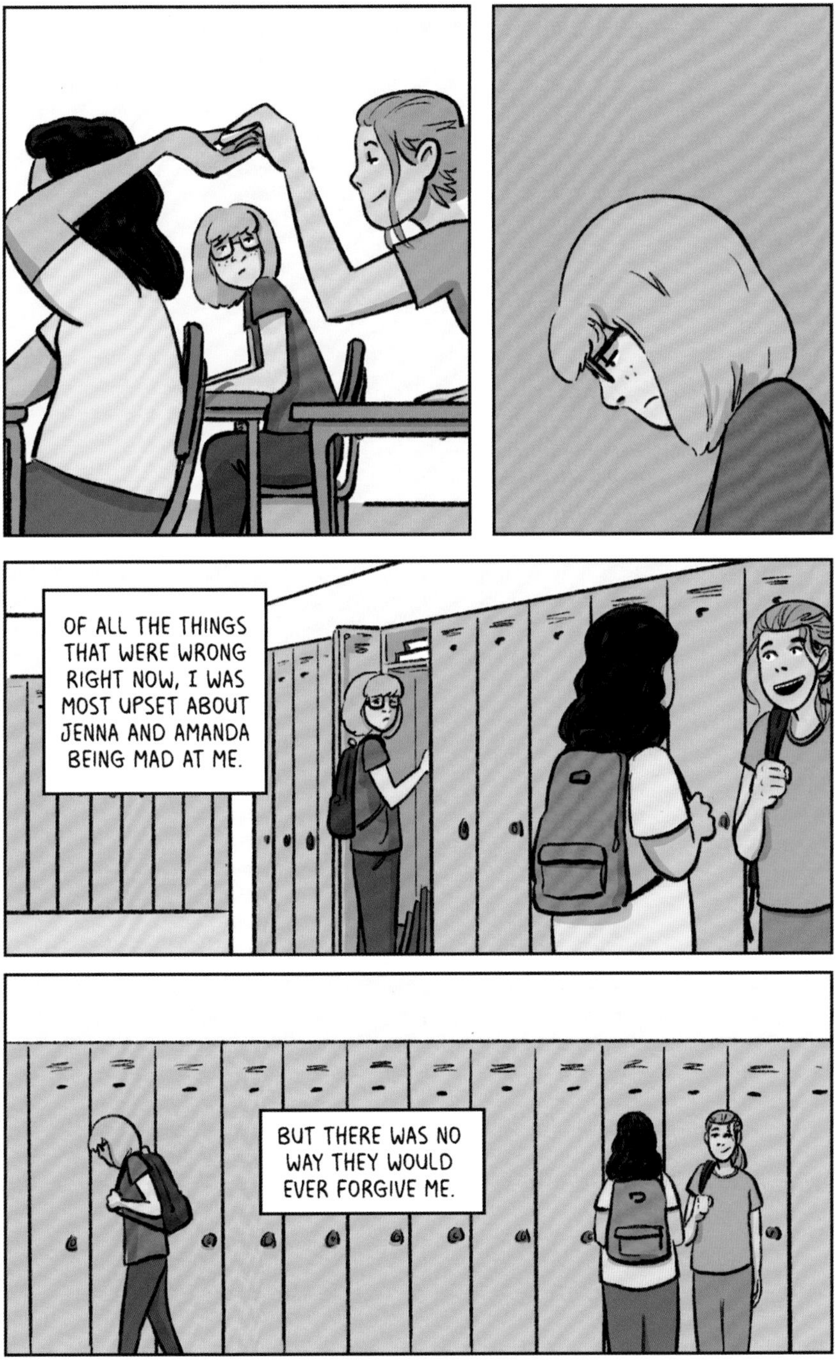

OF ALL THE THINGS THAT WERE WRONG RIGHT NOW, I WAS MOST UPSET ABOUT JENNA AND AMANDA BEING MAD AT ME.
BUT THERE WAS NO WAY THEY WOULD EVER FORGIVE ME.

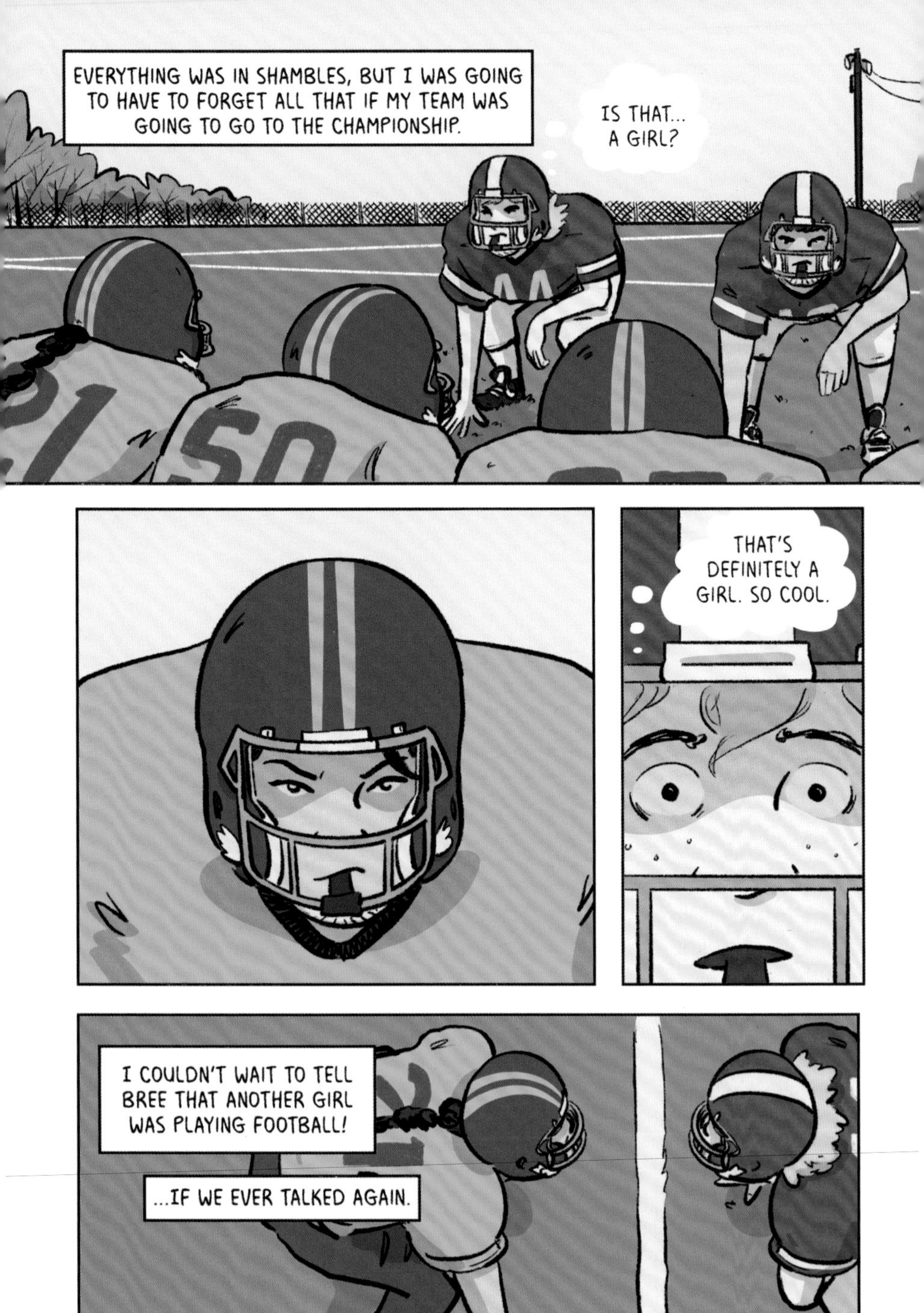
EVERYTHING WAS IN SHAMBLES, BUT I WAS GOING TO HAVE TO FORGET ALL THAT IF MY TEAM WAS GOING TO GO TO THE CHAMPIONSHIP.
IS THAT... A GIRL?
THAT'S DEFINITELY A GIRL. SO COOL.
I COULDN'T WAIT TO TELL BREE THAT ANOTHER GIRL WAS PLAYING FOOTBALL!
...IF WE EVER TALKED AGAIN.

215

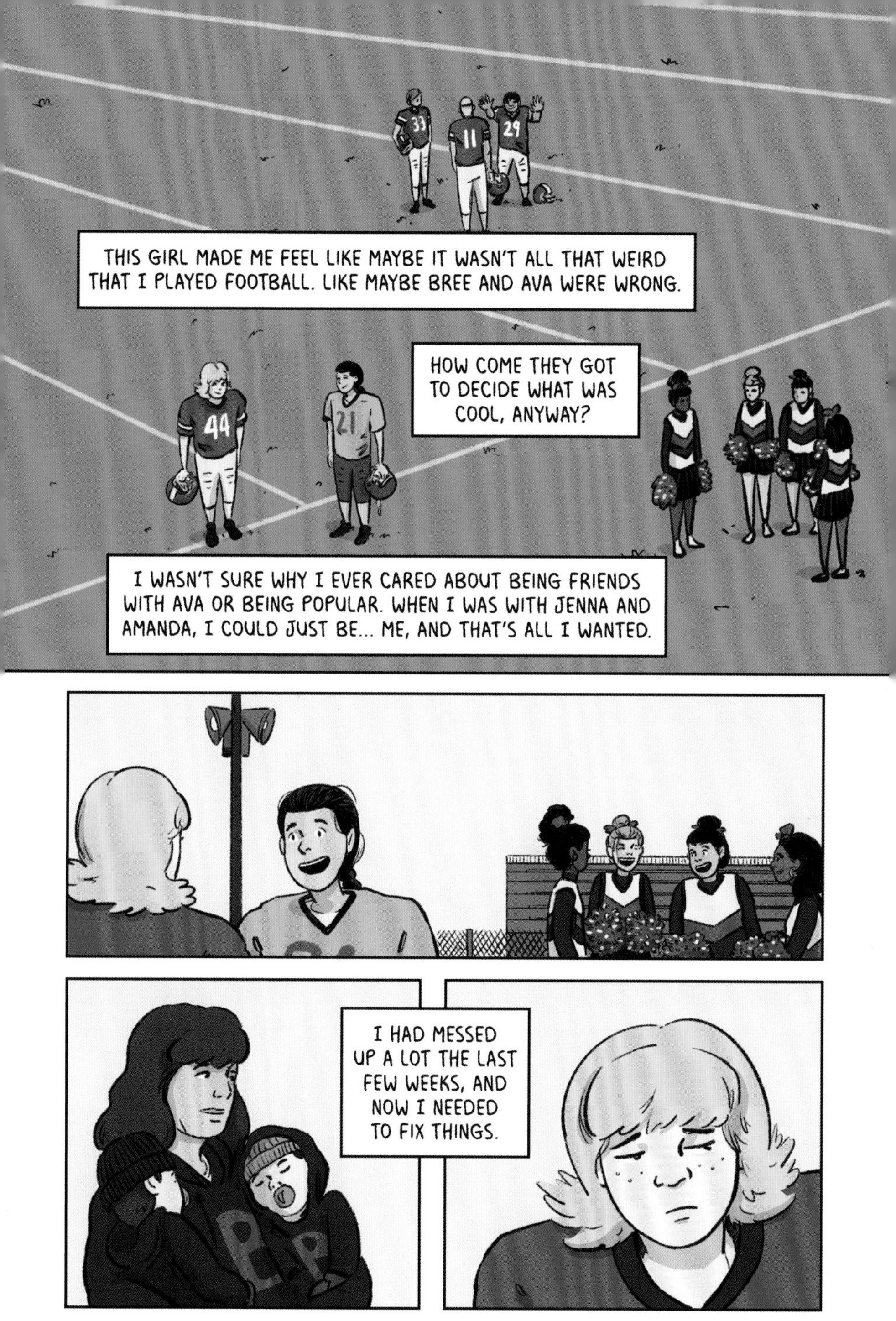
THIS GIRL MADE ME FEEL LIKE MAYBE IT WASN'T ALL THAT WEIRD THAT I PLAYED FOOTBALL. LIKE MAYBE BREE AND AVA WERE WRONG.
HOW COME THEY GOT TO DECIDE WHAT WAS COOL, ANYWAY?
I WASN'T SURE WHY I EVER CARED ABOUT BEING FRIENDS WITH AVA OR BEING POPULAR. WHEN I WAS WITH JENNA AND AMANDA, I COULD JUST BE... ME, AND THAT'S ALL I WANTED.
I HAD MESSED UP A LOT THE LAST FEW WEEKS, AND NOW I NEEDED TO FIX THINGS.

CHAPTER 10

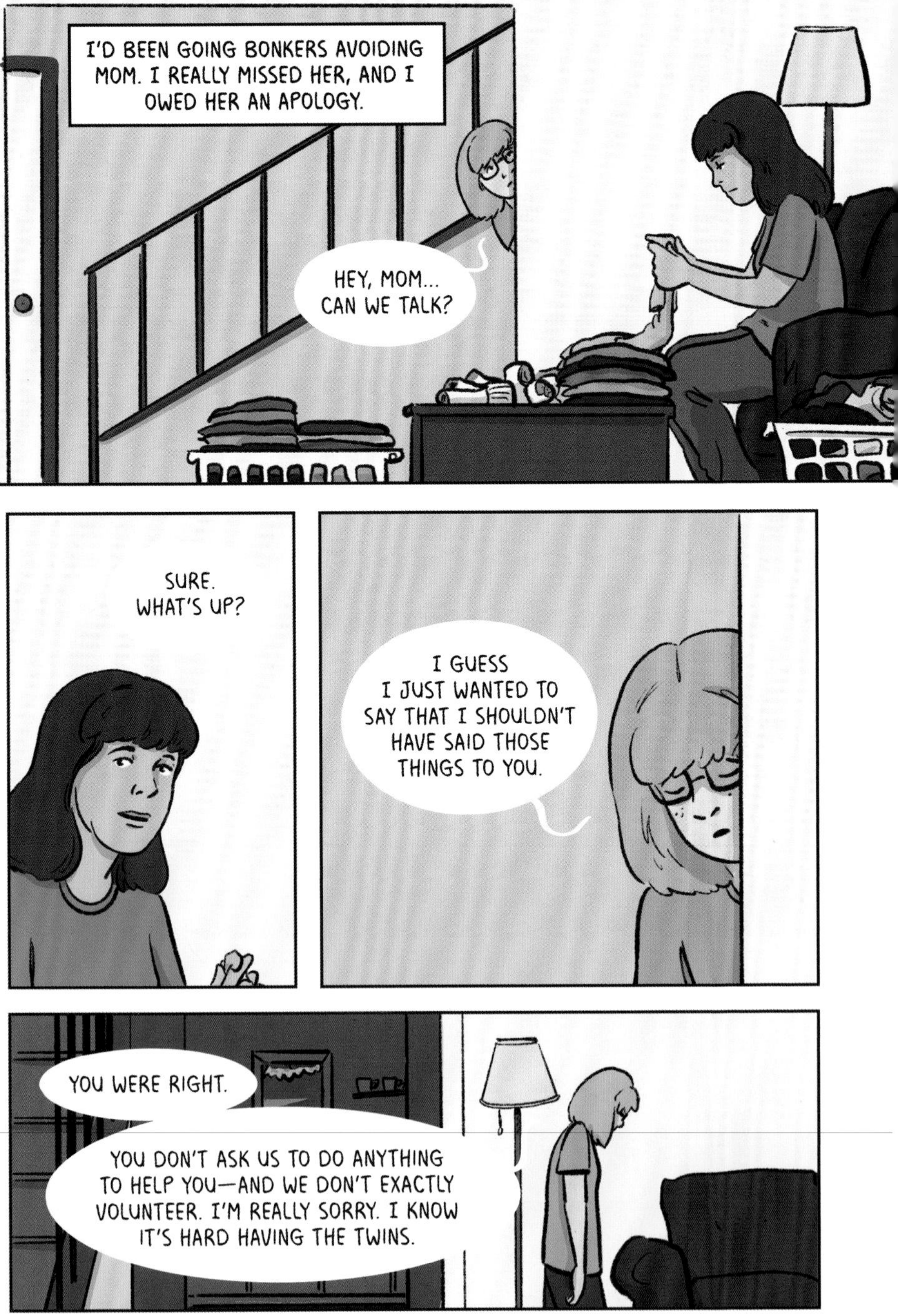
I'D BEEN GOING BONKERS AVOIDING MOM. I REALLY MISSED HER, AND I OWED HER AN APOLOGY.
HEY, MOM... CAN WE TALK?
SURE. WHAT'S UP?
I GUESS I JUST WANTED TO SAY THAT I SHOULDN'T HAVE SAID THOSE THINGS TO YOU.
YOU WERE RIGHT.
YOU DON'T ASK US TO DO ANYTHING TO HELP YOU—AND WE DON'T EXACTLY VOLUNTEER. I'M REALLY SORRY. I KNOW IT'S HARD HAVING THE TWINS.

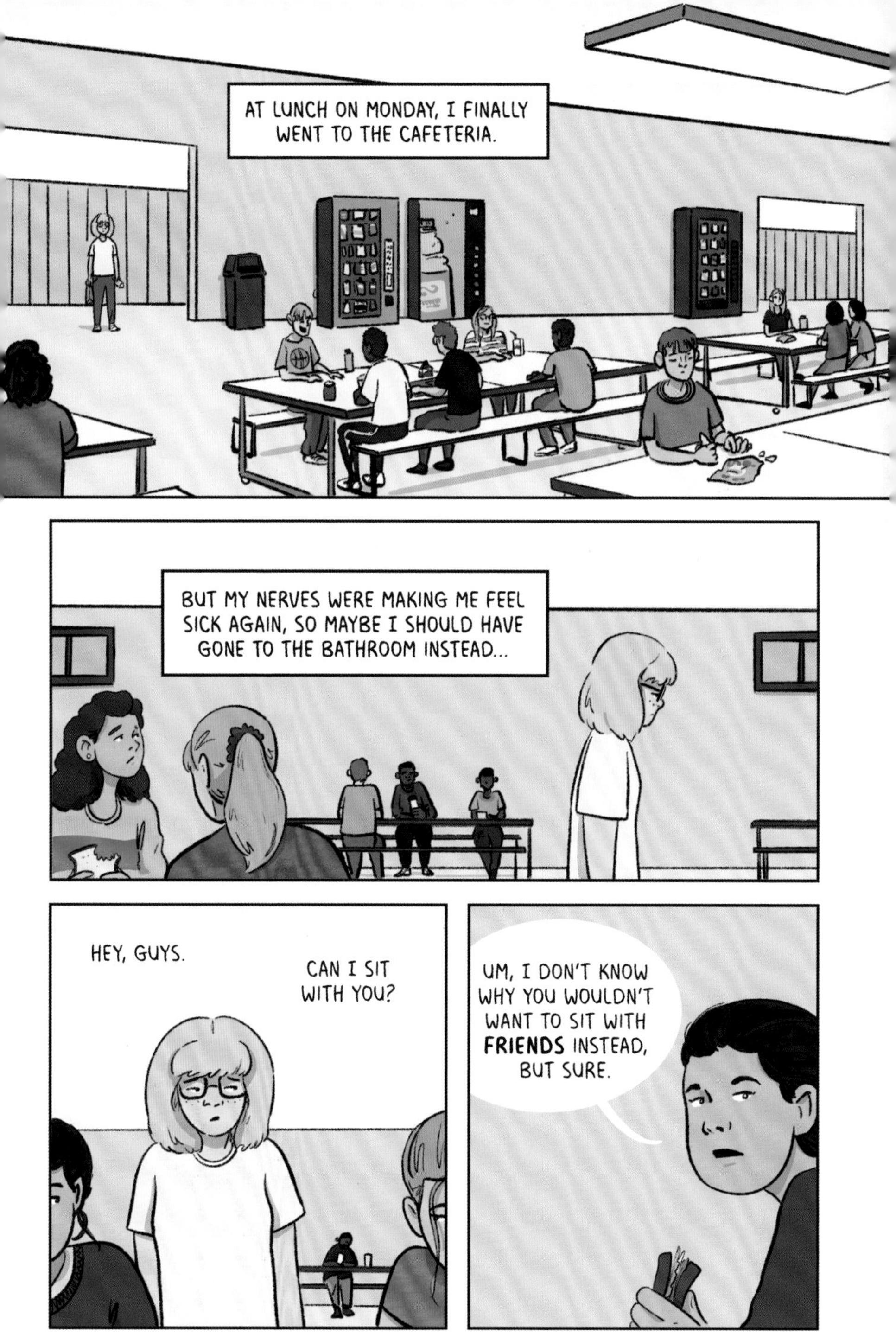
AT LUNCH ON MONDAY, I FINALLY WENT TO THE CAFETERIA.
BUT MY NERVES WERE MAKING ME FEEL SICK AGAIN, SO MAYBE I SHOULD HAVE GONE TO THE BATHROOM INSTEAD...
HEY, GUYS.
CAN I SIT WITH YOU?
UM, I DON'T KNOW WHY YOU WOULDN'T WANT TO SIT WITH **FRIENDS** INSTEAD, BUT SURE.

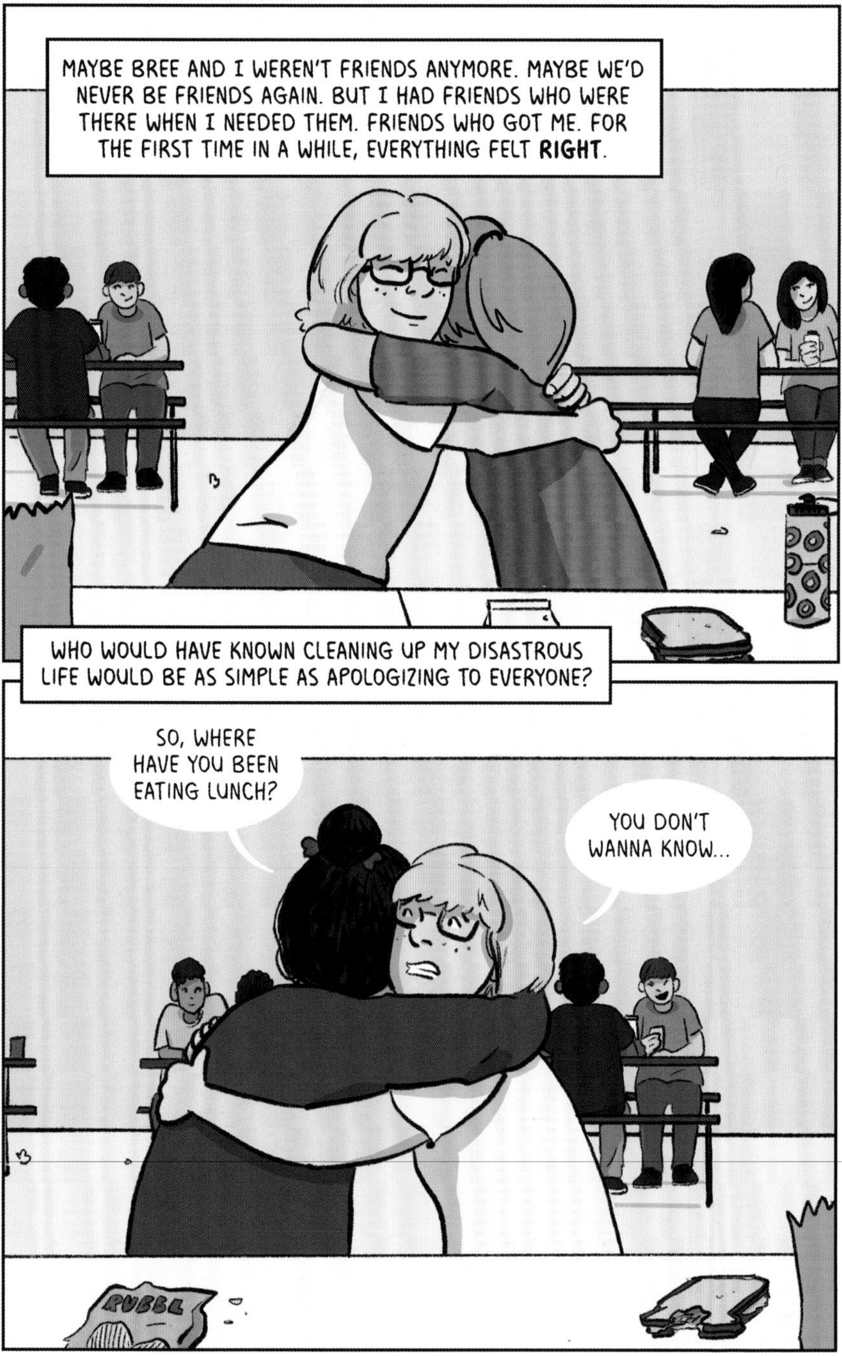
MAYBE BREE AND I WEREN'T FRIENDS ANYMORE. MAYBE WE'D NEVER BE FRIENDS AGAIN. BUT I HAD FRIENDS WHO WERE THERE WHEN I NEEDED THEM. FRIENDS WHO GOT ME. FOR THE FIRST TIME IN A WHILE, EVERYTHING FELT **RIGHT**.
WHO WOULD HAVE KNOWN CLEANING UP MY DISASTROUS LIFE WOULD BE AS SIMPLE AS APOLOGIZING TO EVERYONE?
SO, WHERE HAVE YOU BEEN EATING LUNCH?
YOU DON'T WANNA KNOW...
RUBBL

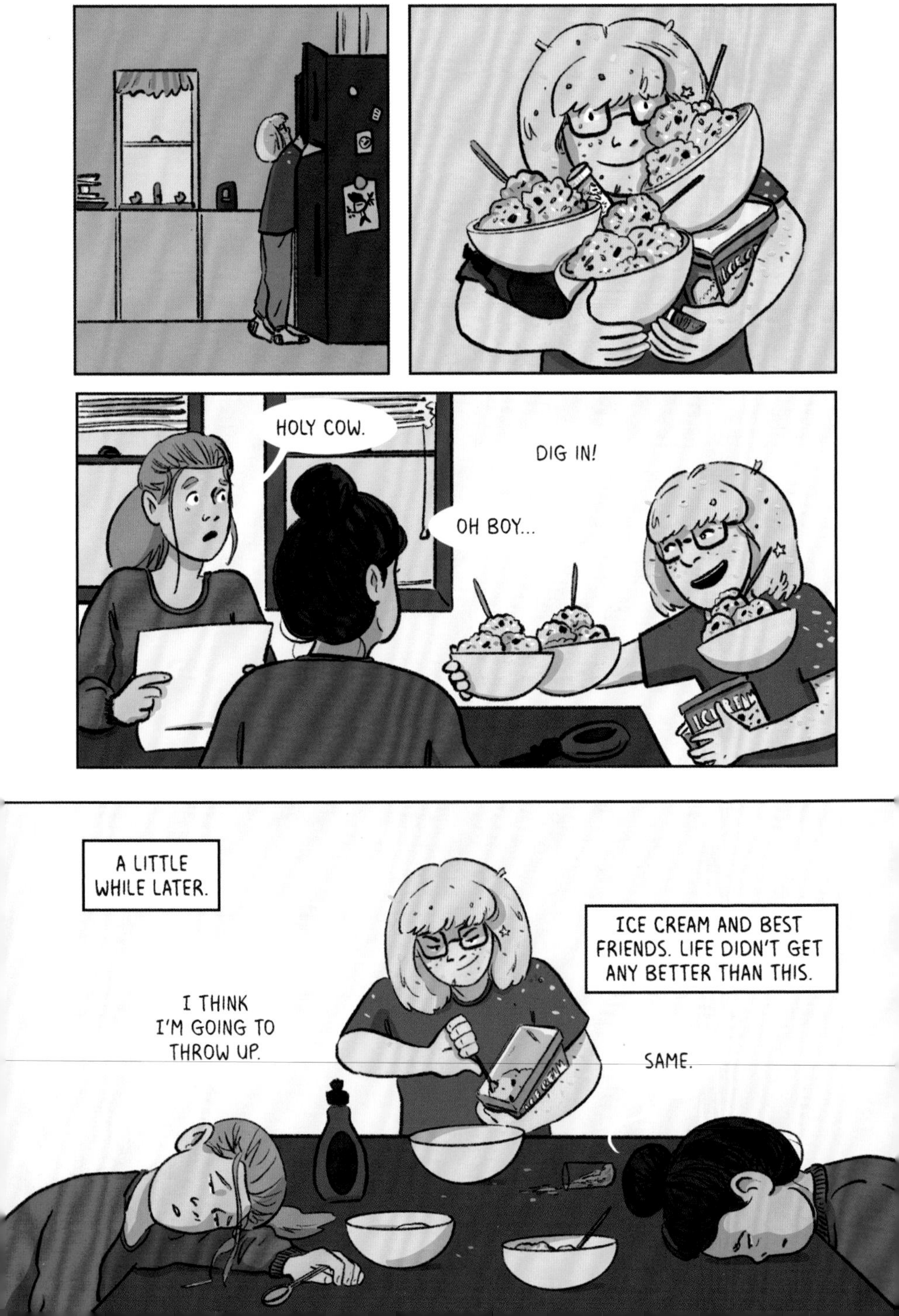
HOLY COW.
DIG IN!
OH BOY...
A LITTLE WHILE LATER.
ICE CREAM AND BEST FRIENDS. LIFE DIDN'T GET ANY BETTER THAN THIS.
I THINK I'M GOING TO THROW UP.
SAME.

231

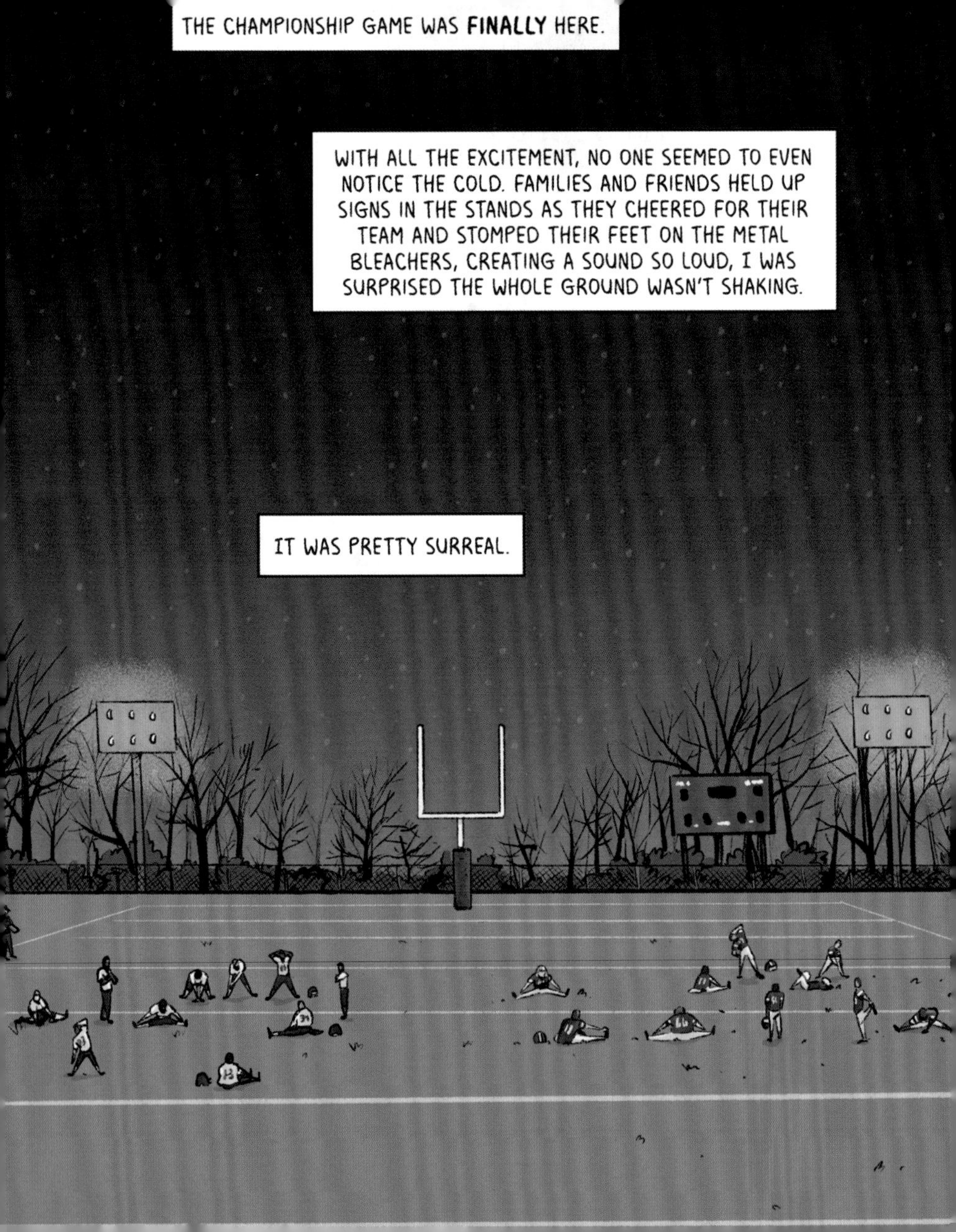
THE CHAMPIONSHIP GAME WAS **FINALLY** HERE.
WITH ALL THE EXCITEMENT, NO ONE SEEMED TO EVEN NOTICE THE COLD. FAMILIES AND FRIENDS HELD UP SIGNS IN THE STANDS AS THEY CHEERED FOR THEIR TEAM AND STOMPED THEIR FEET ON THE METAL BLEACHERS, CREATING A SOUND SO LOUD, I WAS SURPRISED THE WHOLE GROUND WASN'T SHAKING.
IT WAS PRETTY SURREAL.

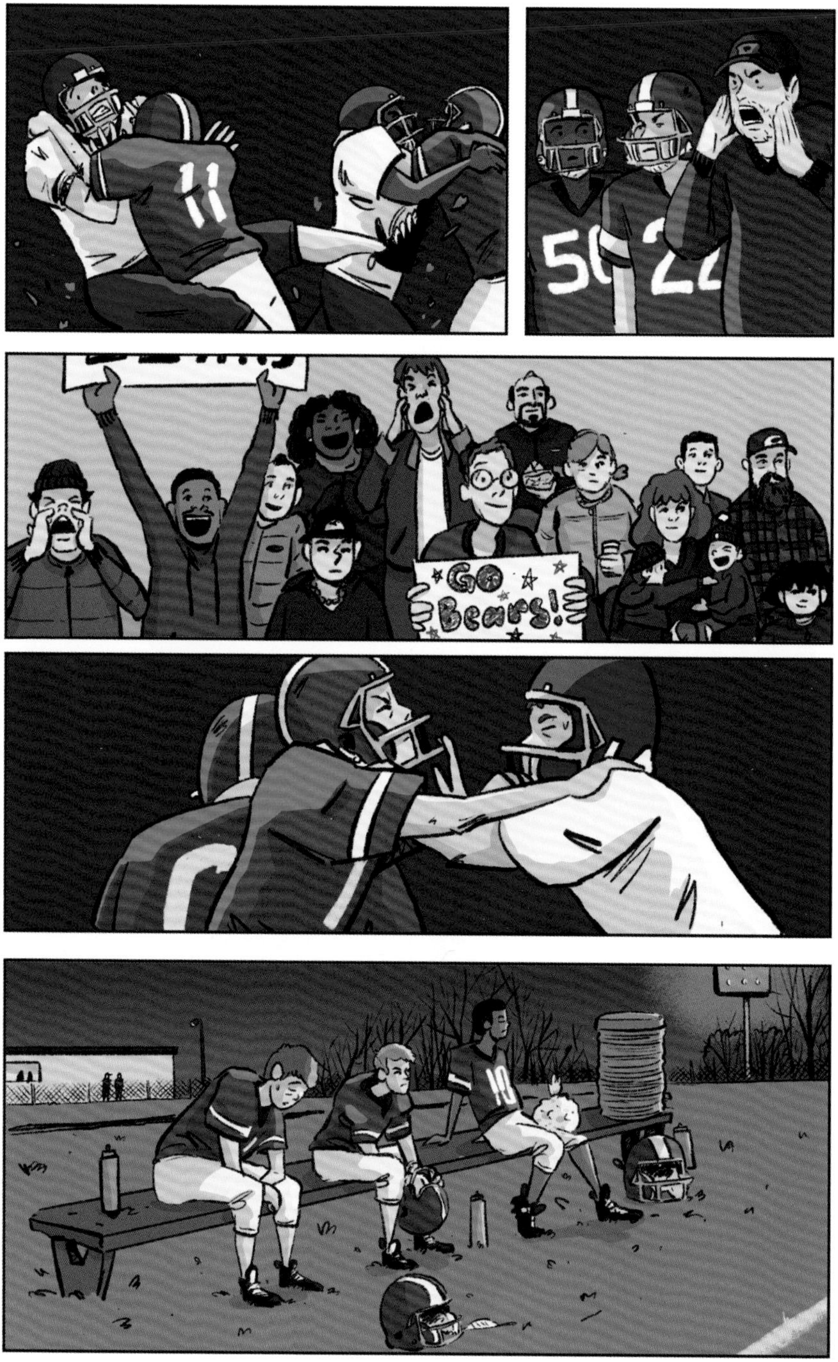
GO Bears!

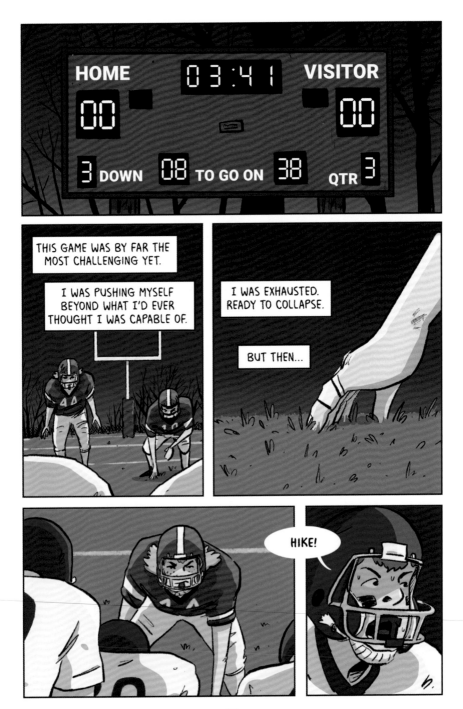

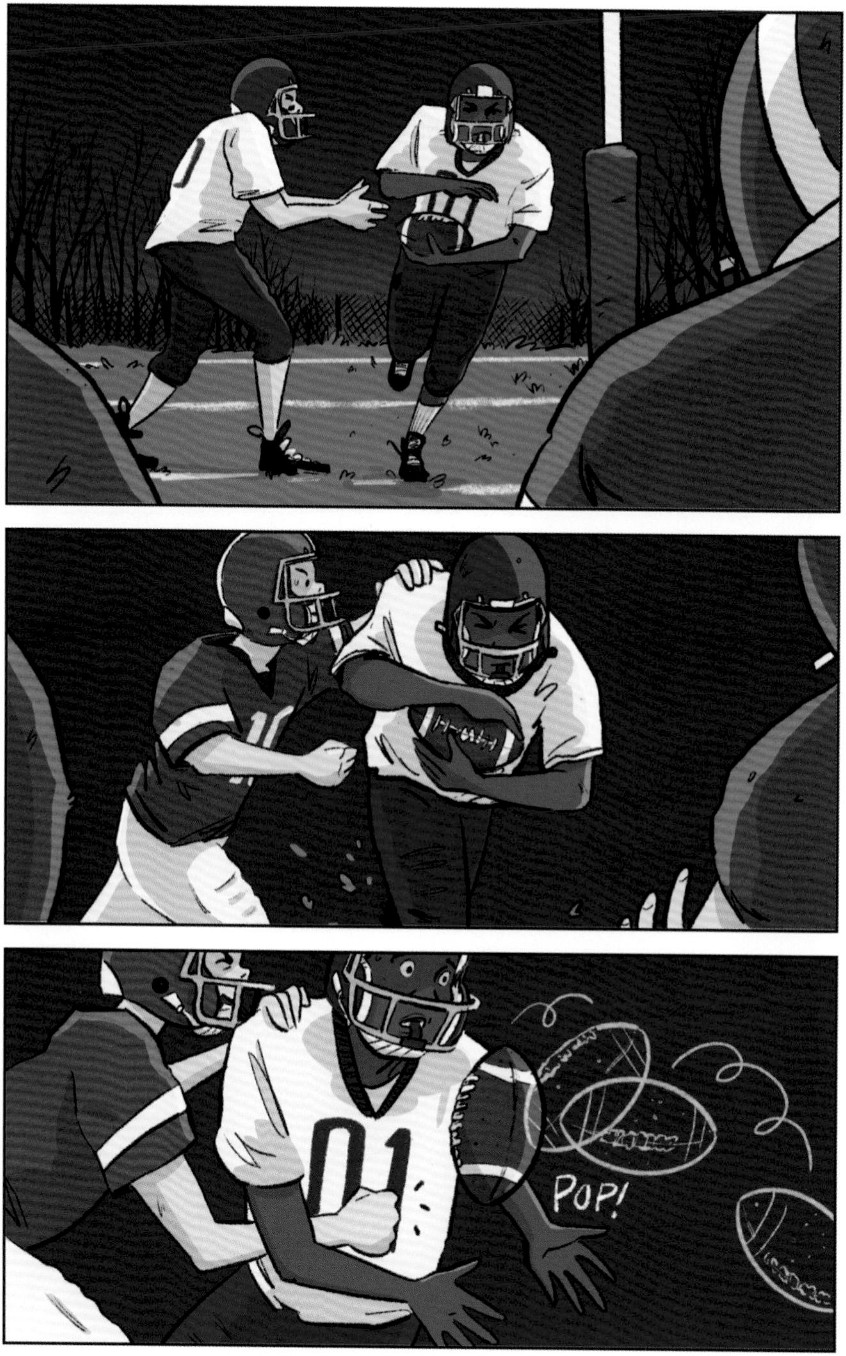
POP!

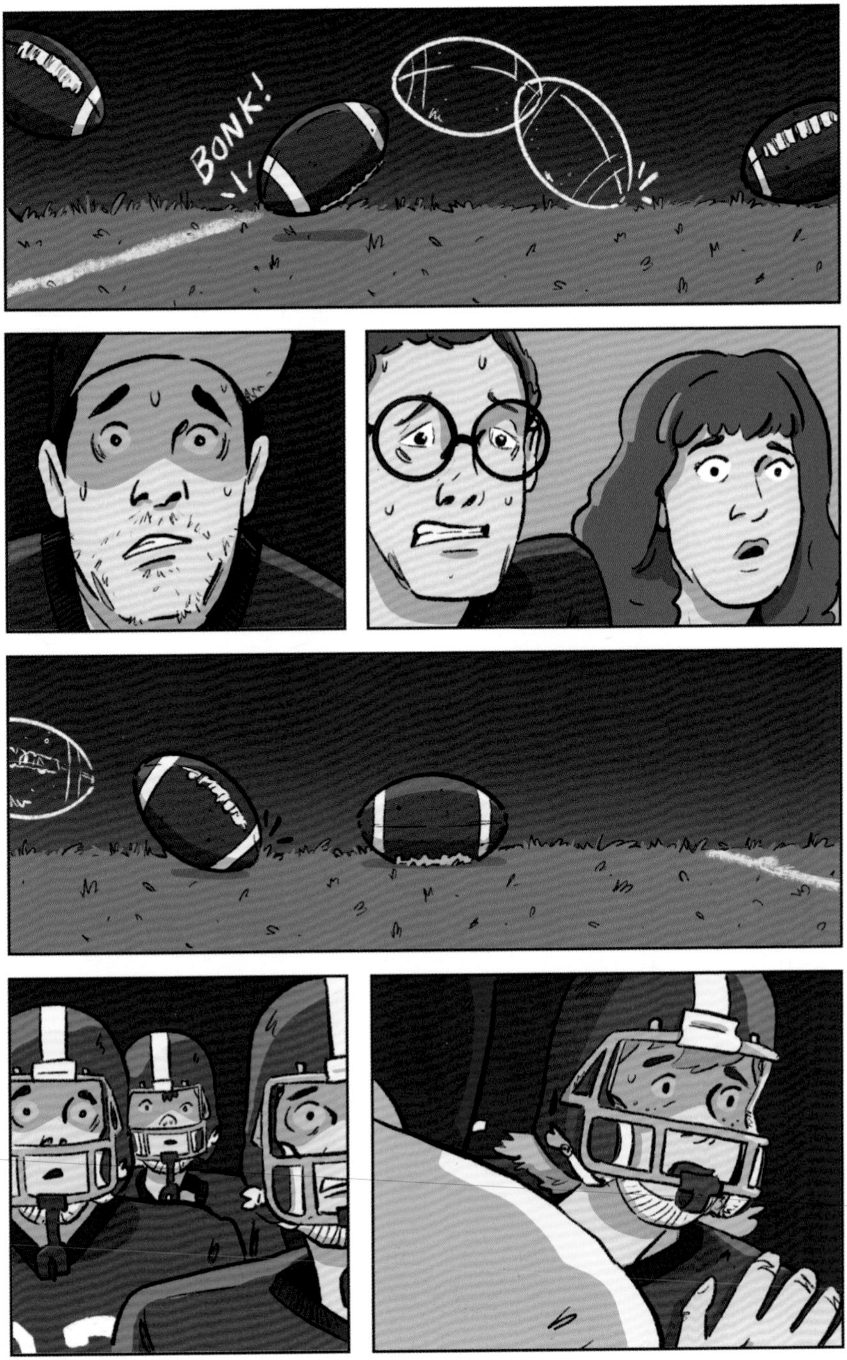
BONK!

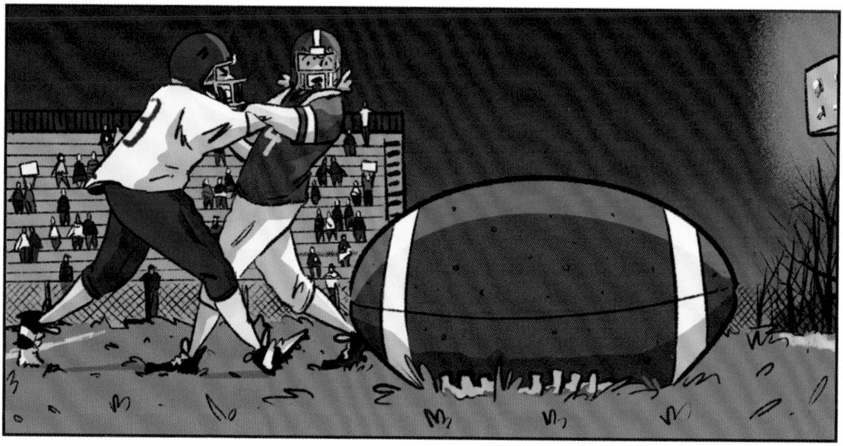

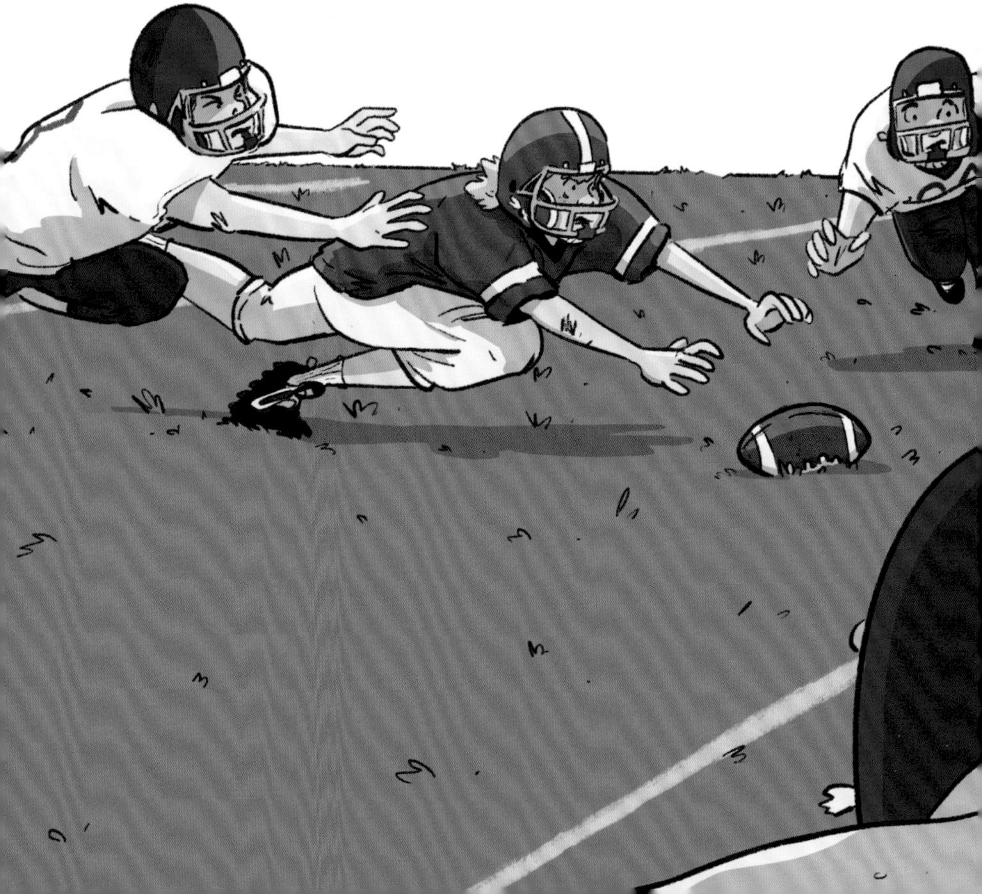

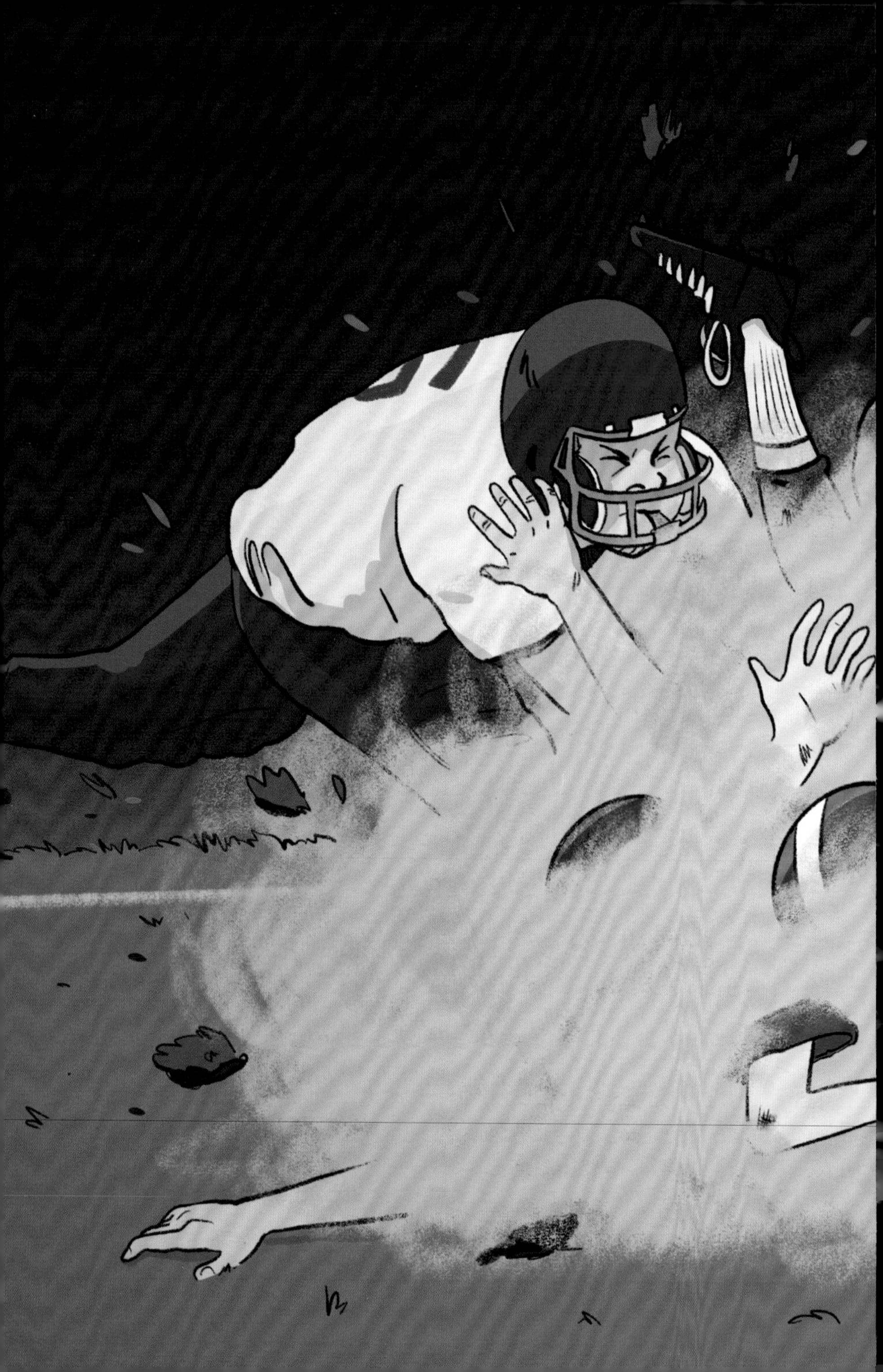

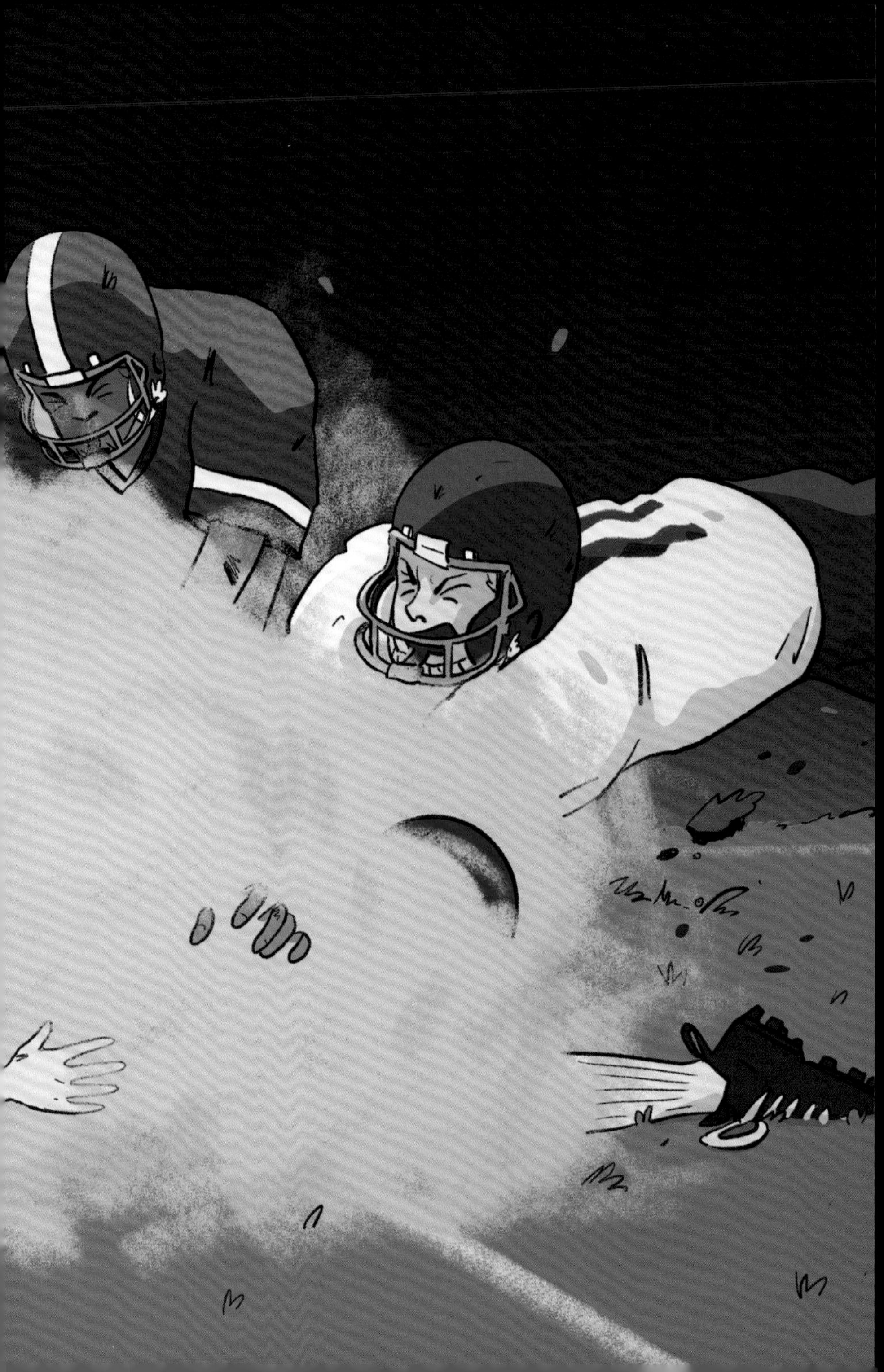

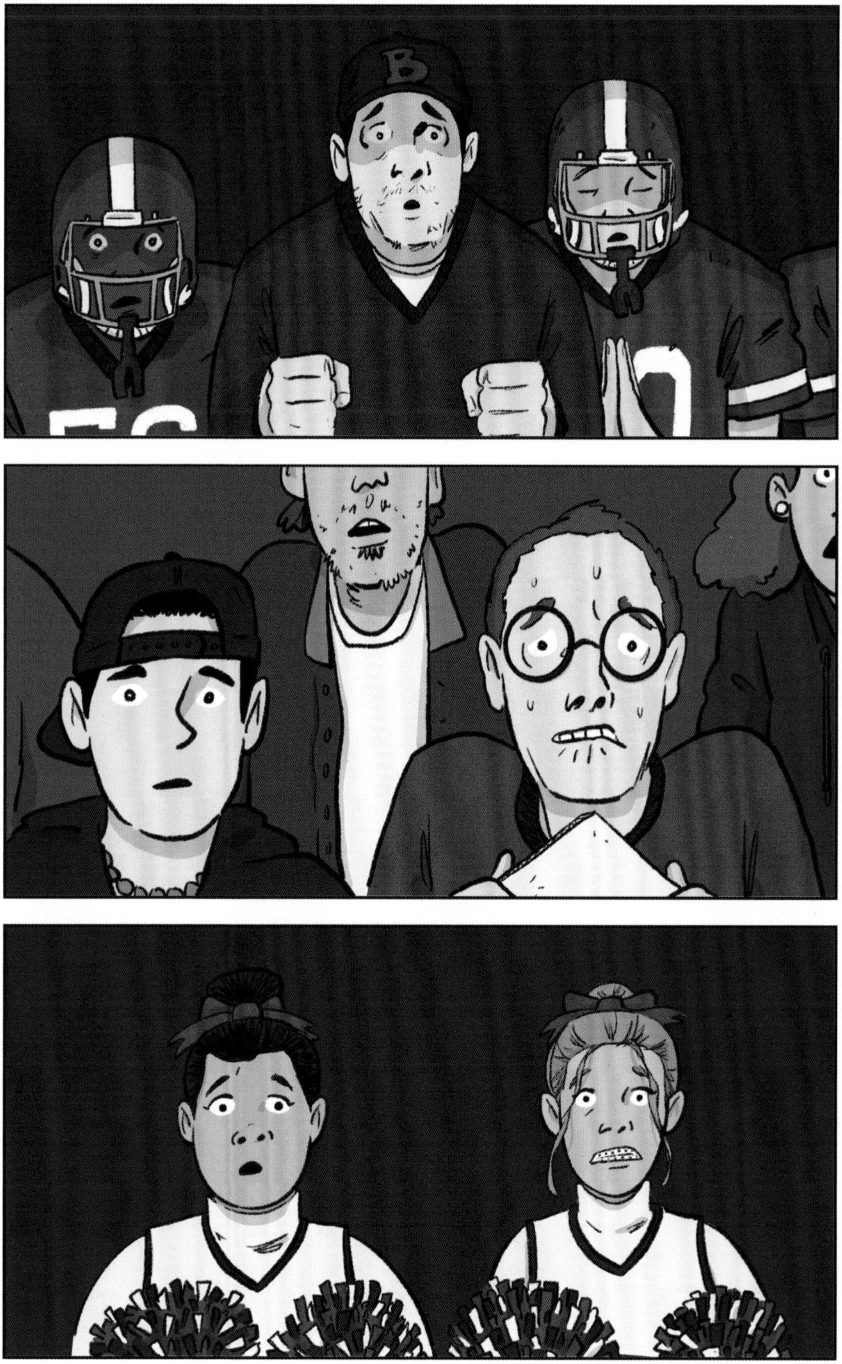
B

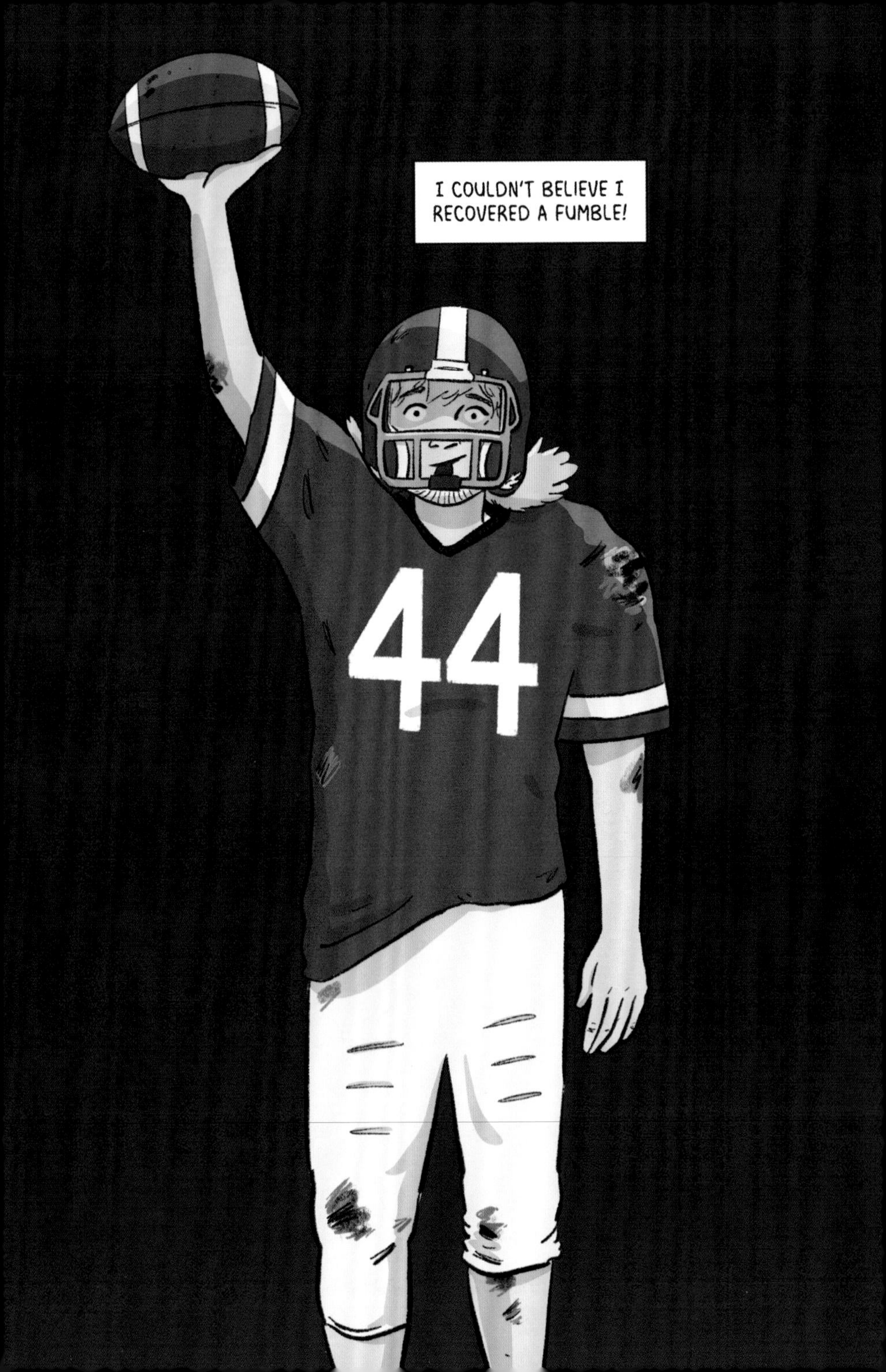
I COULDN'T BELIEVE I RECOVERED A FUMBLE!

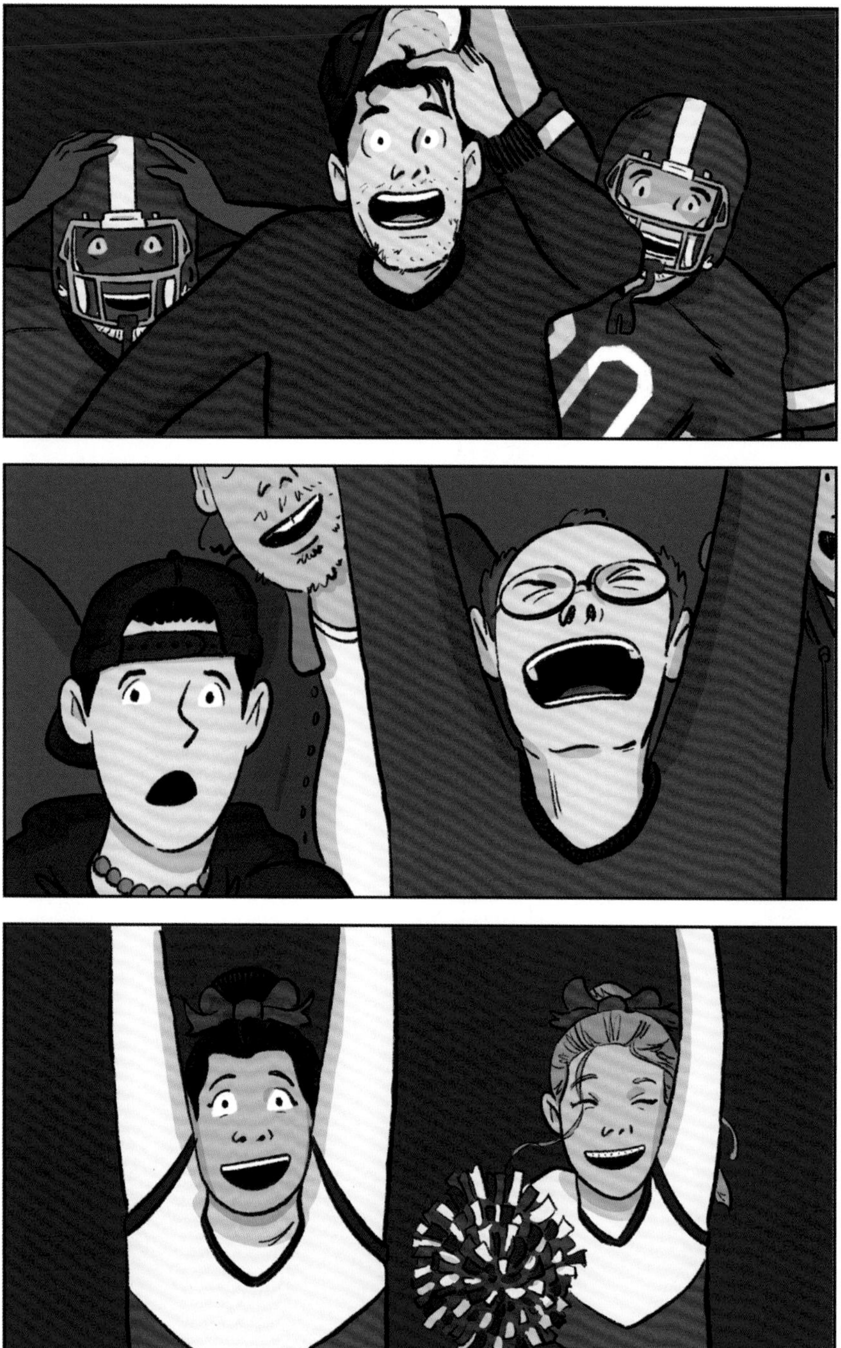

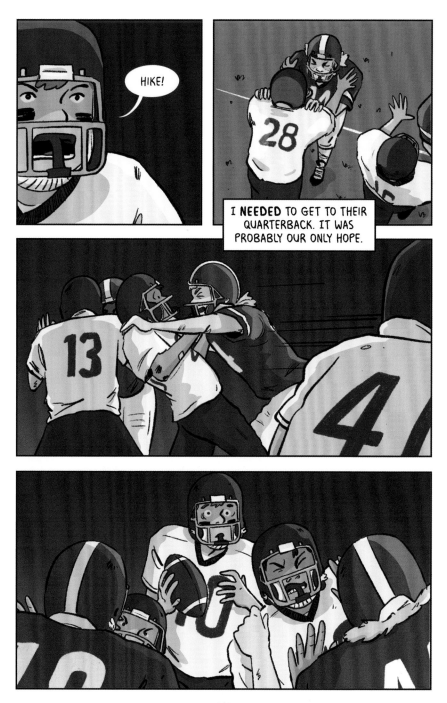

HIKE!

I **NEEDED** TO GET TO THEIR QUARTERBACK. IT WAS PROBABLY OUR ONLY HOPE.

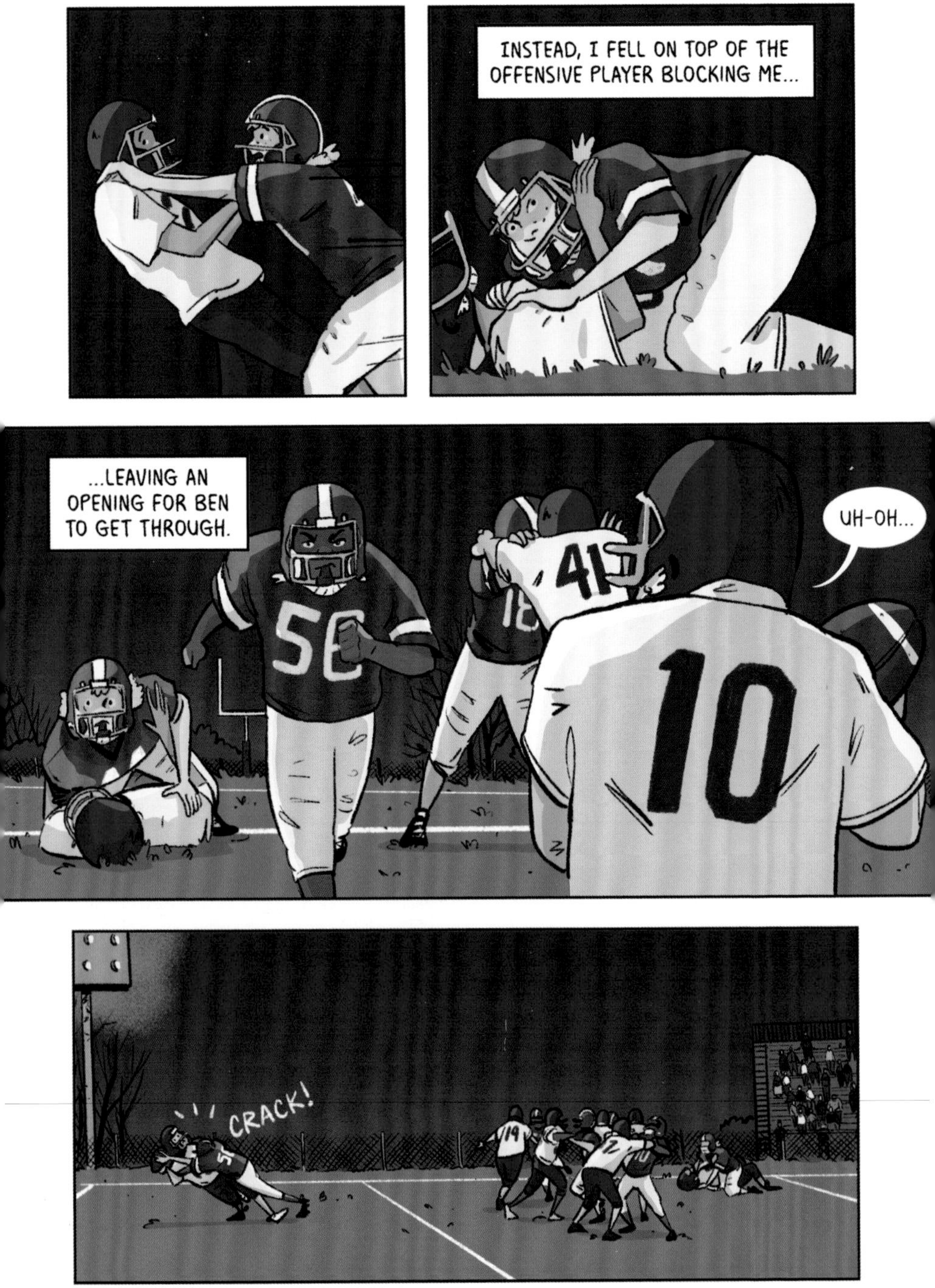
INSTEAD, I FELL ON TOP OF THE OFFENSIVE PLAYER BLOCKING ME...
...LEAVING AN OPENING FOR BEN TO GET THROUGH.
UH-OH...
CRACK!

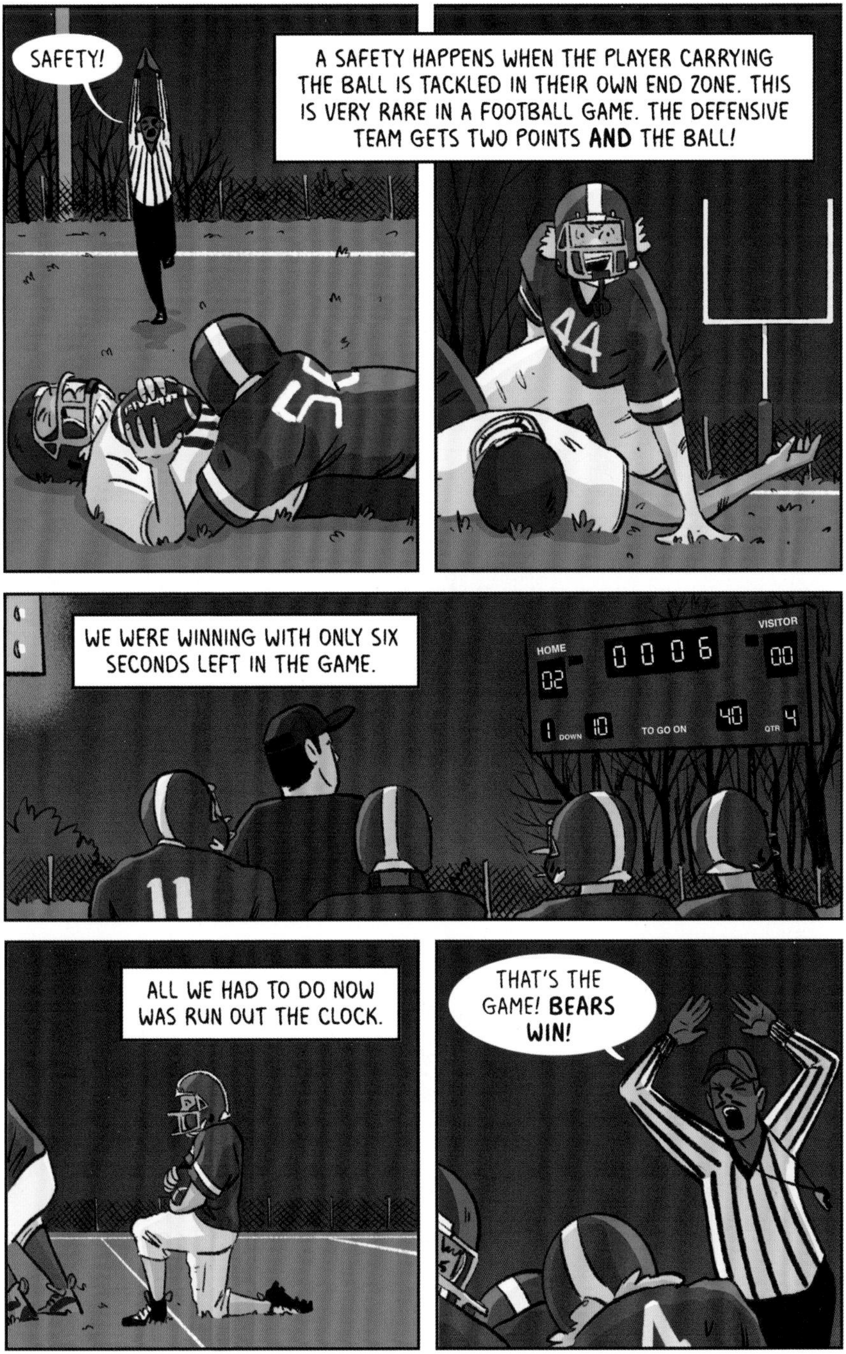
SAFETY!
A SAFETY HAPPENS WHEN THE PLAYER CARRYING THE BALL IS TACKLED IN THEIR OWN END ZONE. THIS IS VERY RARE IN A FOOTBALL GAME. THE DEFENSIVE TEAM GETS TWO POINTS **AND** THE BALL!
WE WERE WINNING WITH ONLY SIX SECONDS LEFT IN THE GAME.
HOME
VISITOR
0 0 0 6
02
00
1
DOWN
10
TO GO ON
40
QTR
4
ALL WE HAD TO DO NOW WAS RUN OUT THE CLOCK.
THAT'S THE GAME! **BEARS WIN!**

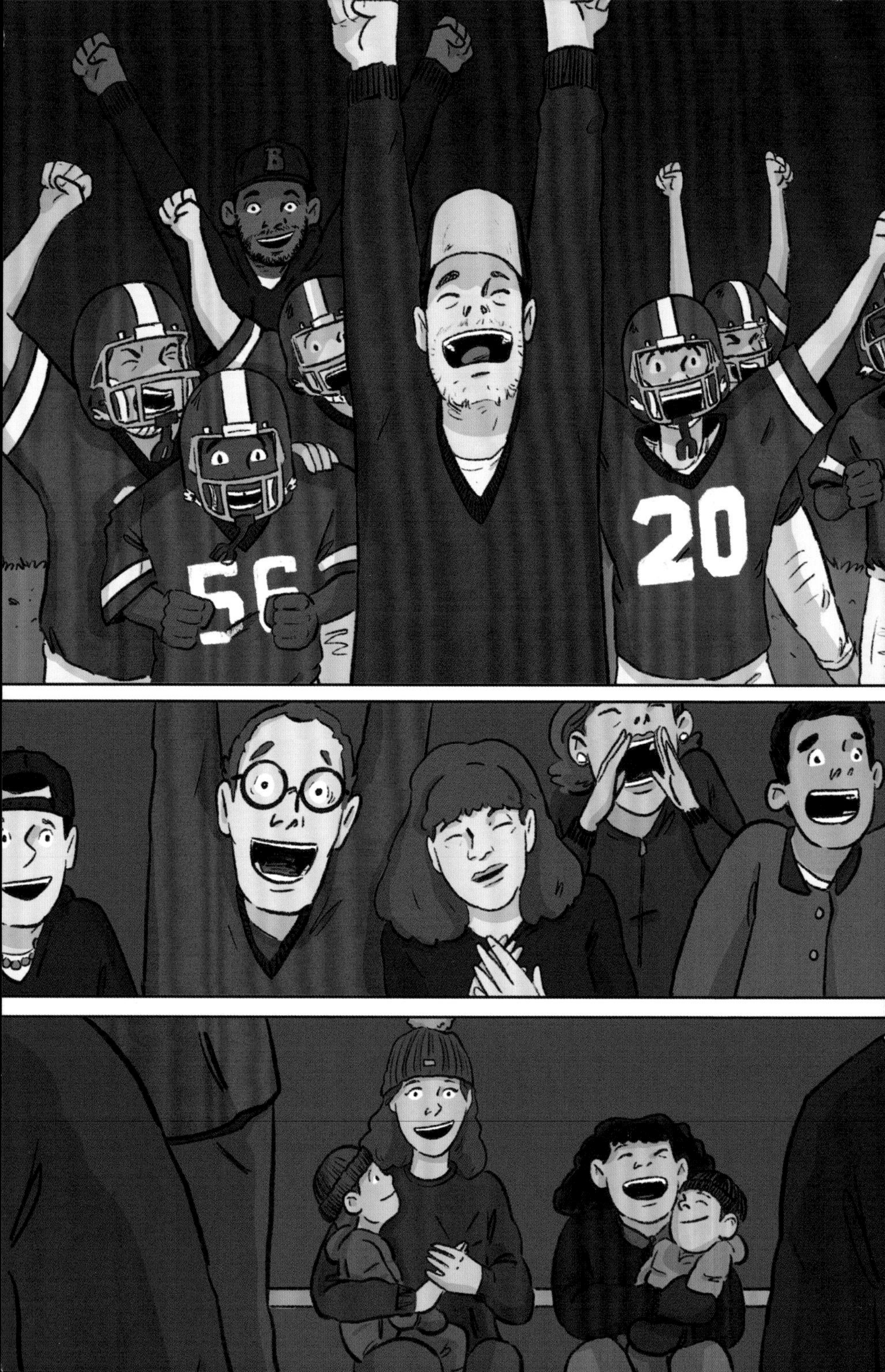
56
20

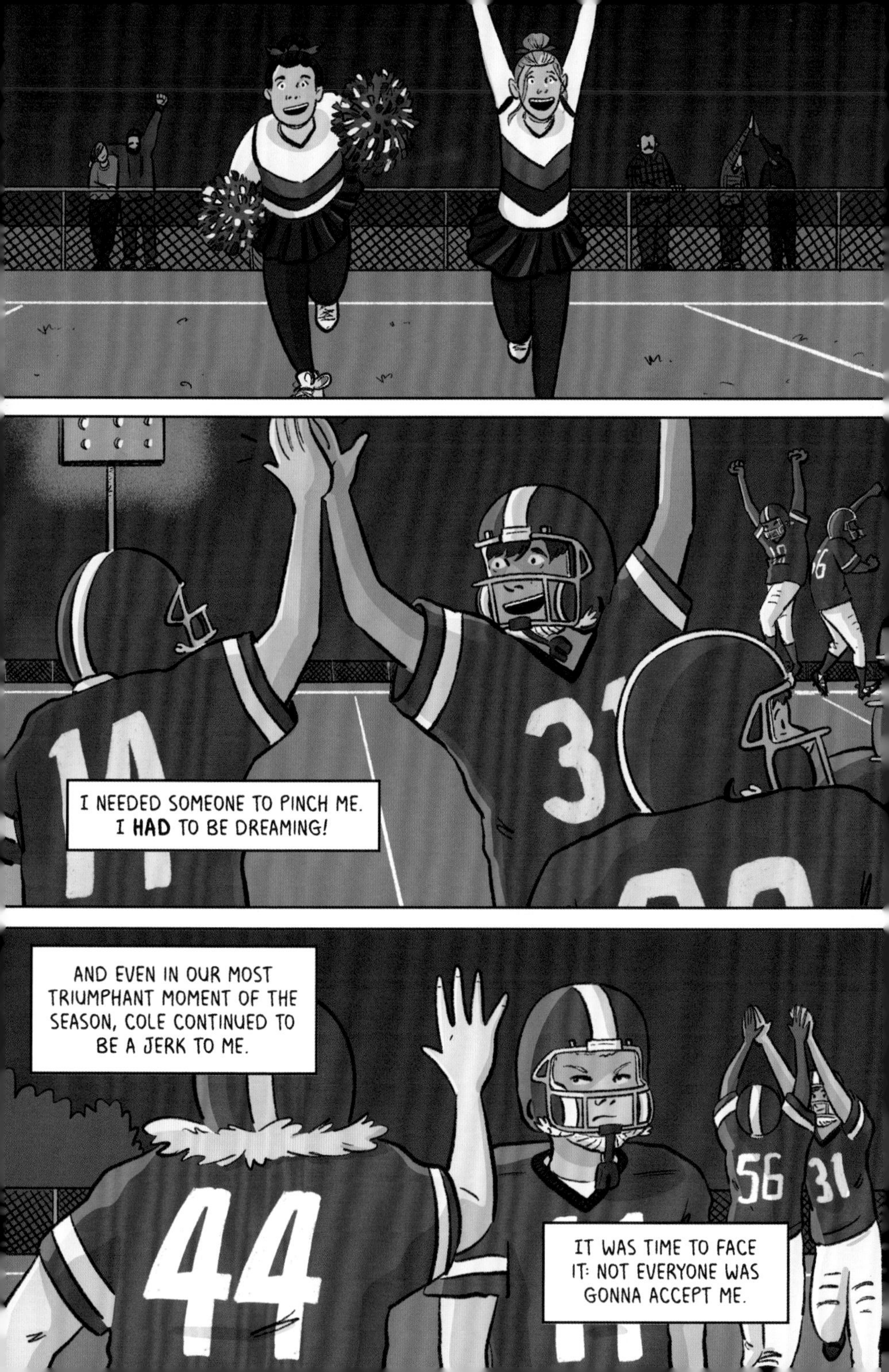
I NEEDED SOMEONE TO PINCH ME. I **HAD** TO BE DREAMING!
AND EVEN IN OUR MOST TRIUMPHANT MOMENT OF THE SEASON, COLE CONTINUED TO BE A JERK TO ME.
IT WAS TIME TO FACE IT: NOT EVERYONE WAS GONNA ACCEPT ME.

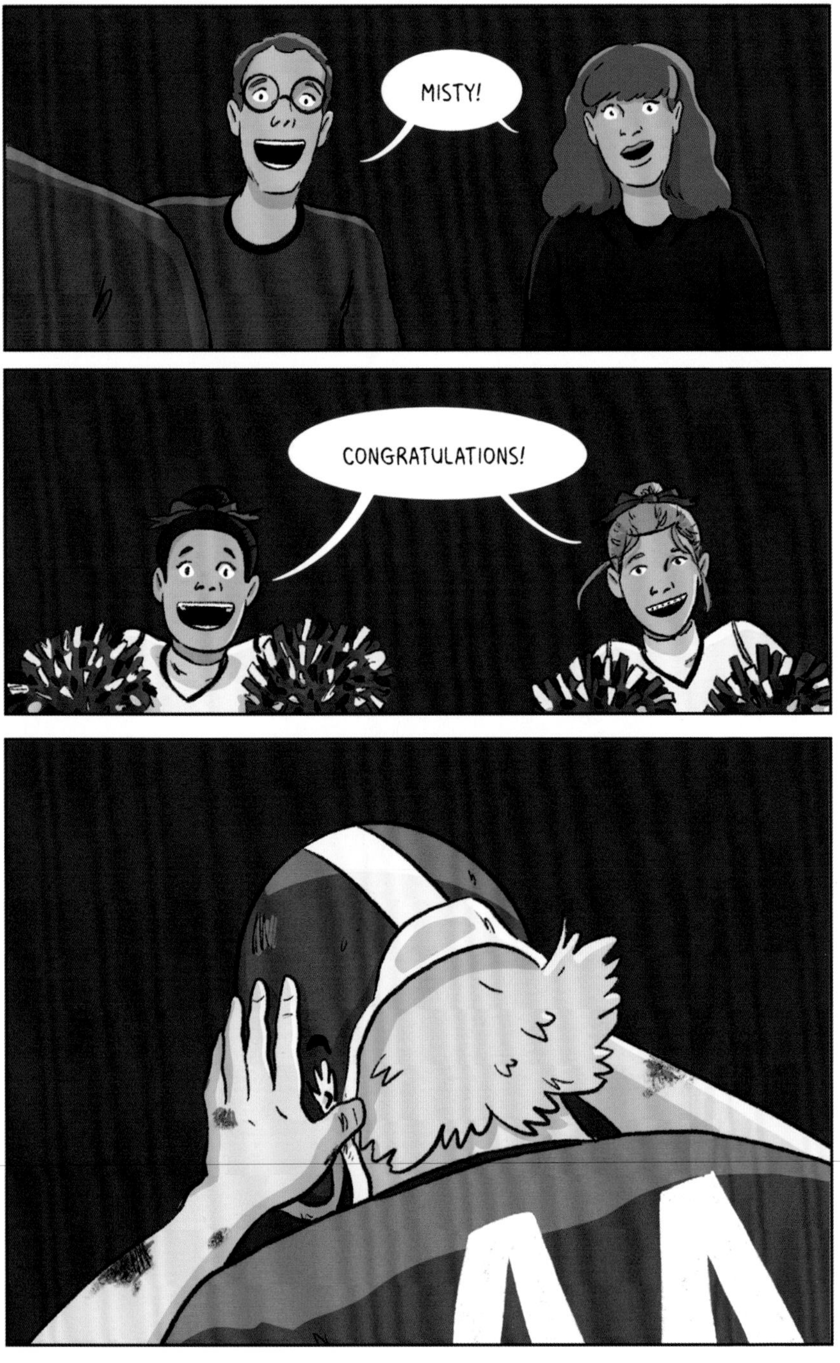
MISTY!
CONGRATULATIONS!

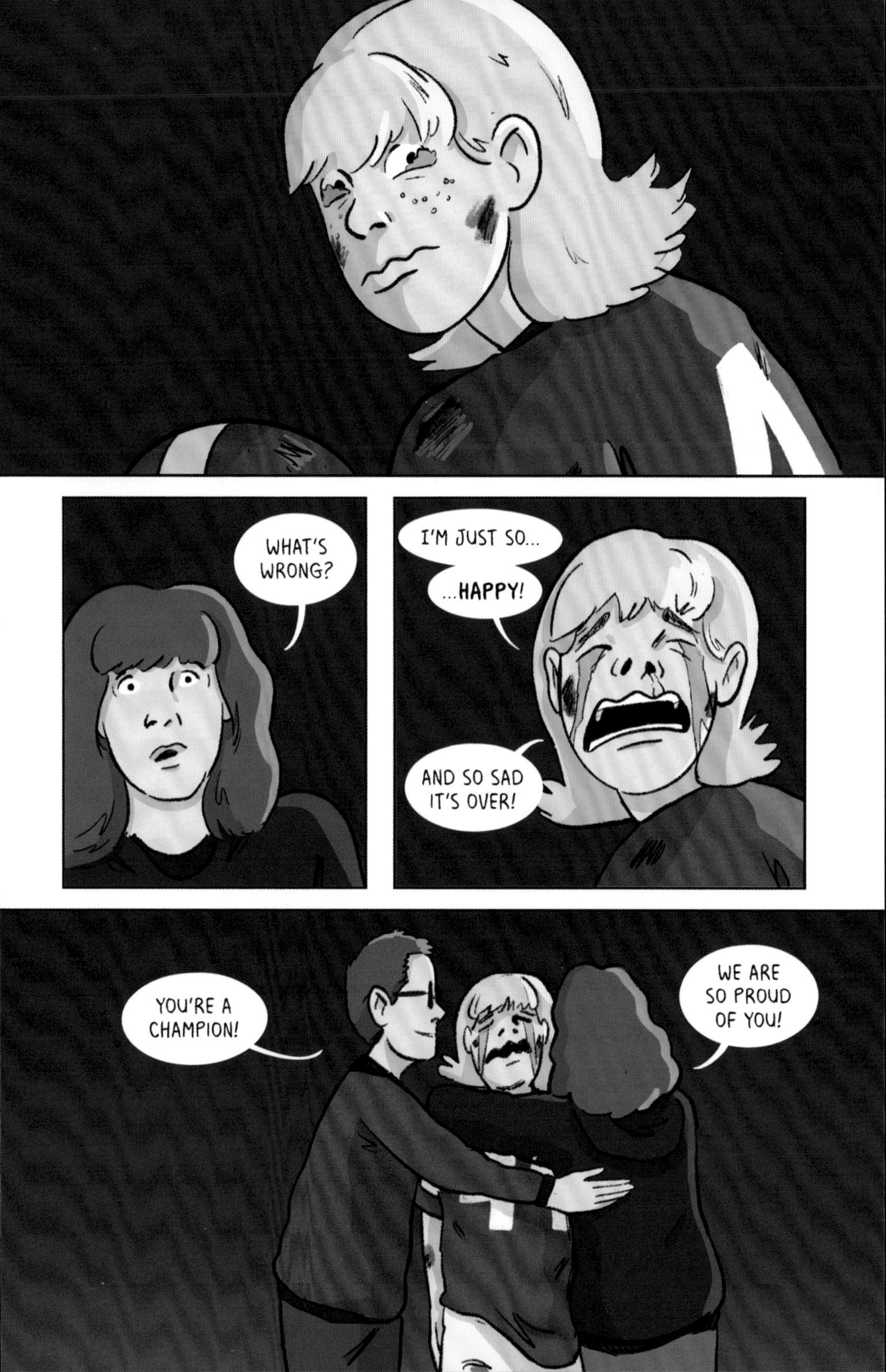
WHAT'S WRONG?
I'M JUST SO...
...HAPPY!
AND SO SAD IT'S OVER!
YOU'RE A CHAMPION!
WE ARE SO PROUD OF YOU!

AUTHOR'S NOTE

While this is the true story of my football season in seventh grade, recalling details from decades ago can be difficult. I did my best to faithfully depict what I remember about events and people at that time—especially myself. I used my diaries from middle school and interviewed family members as part of my research.

In most cases, names and likenesses were changed to protect the privacy of the real-life people represented in this book—most of whom I no longer have relationships with. In addition, certain characters and storylines were consolidated, and in a few cases, somewhat fictionalized for the purpose of streamlining the story.

SOME FUN FACTS:

• I NEVER TOLD "CHARLIE" I LIKED HIM. I WAS WAY TOO SHY! BY THE FOLLOWING SUMMER, THOUGH, I HAD A CRUSH ON HIS COUSIN.

• I DIDN'T PLAY FOOTBALL AGAIN AFTER SEVENTH GRADE. BY EIGHTH GRADE, THE BOYS WERE BIGGER THAN ME, AS CRAIG HAD PREDICTED, AND I WORRIED I WOULDN'T BE AS GOOD AS THEM ANYMORE. NOW I REALLY WISH I'D AT LEAST TRIED.

IMPORTANT NOTE: In 2019, the Surgeon General of the United States released a warning that tackle football is dangerous for children because of repeated hits to the head. If you are interested in playing, please talk with an adult and research the most up-to-date information. Note: Flag football is a fun alternative, and it's also super awesome!

ACKNOWLEDGMENTS

Thank you to my brilliant editor, Donna Bray, for believing in this book, for being patient through approximately one million revisions, and for helping me to shape it into what it is today. I don't even have the words to express how grateful I am to have you as an editor. Thank you to my agent, Daniel Lazar, for making all of this possible, for your guidance and support, and for helping me believe I can do this whole writing thing. Thank you to Torie Doherty-Munro for always answering our questions and for everything you do behind the scenes. Thank you to Dana Fritts, Laura Harshberger, and Tiara Kittrell, for working your magic to help bring this book into the world. Thank you to David Wilson—my husband, the illustrator of this book, and the most selfless person I know—for being able to read my mind and completely understand and capture twelve-year-old Misty, for cheering me on when I doubted myself, and for helping me write this book for nearly two whole years. Thank you for supporting me in everything I do—and for giving me the time to do it (aka watching the kids). Thank you to early readers Jay Wilson and Chad Lewis for

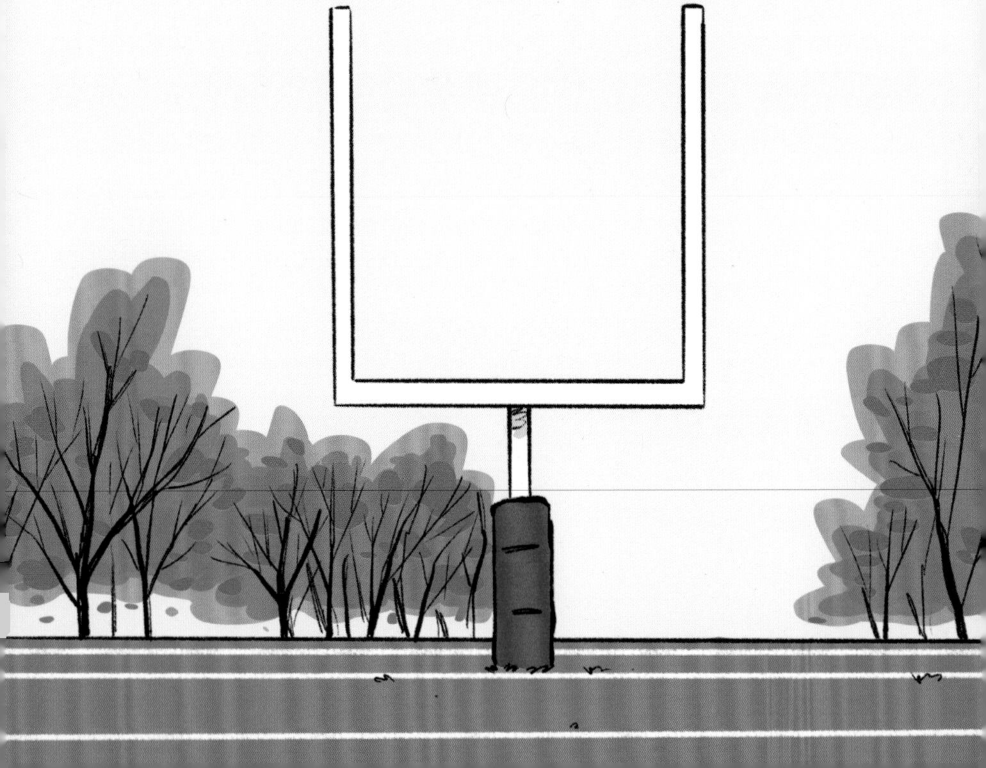

the feedback. Thank you to my family, especially my mom and stepdad, for always supporting me in my endeavors, no matter how wild they seem. Thank you to my writer friends for helping me navigate publishing, for answering my questions, giving feedback, listening to me vent, letting me bounce ideas off of you, and for being an all-around wonderful support system: Jess Burkhart, Jessica James, Jennifer Iacopelli, Erica Davis (especially for the jokes!), Isabel Sterling, Shelly Page, Vanessa Montalban, and the #22debuts Slack group. Thank you to all of my students at Walls and Crestwood Intermediate School for inspiring me to write my story and for your excitement throughout the publishing process. Thank you to my seventh-grade football coaches for never treating me any differently than the boys on the team. And lastly, thank you to *Julie and the Phantoms*, my comfort show that played on repeat when writing was just plain hard (and when it wasn't), and to AO3 for being a bright spot in a tough year and for making me a better writer.

—MISTY

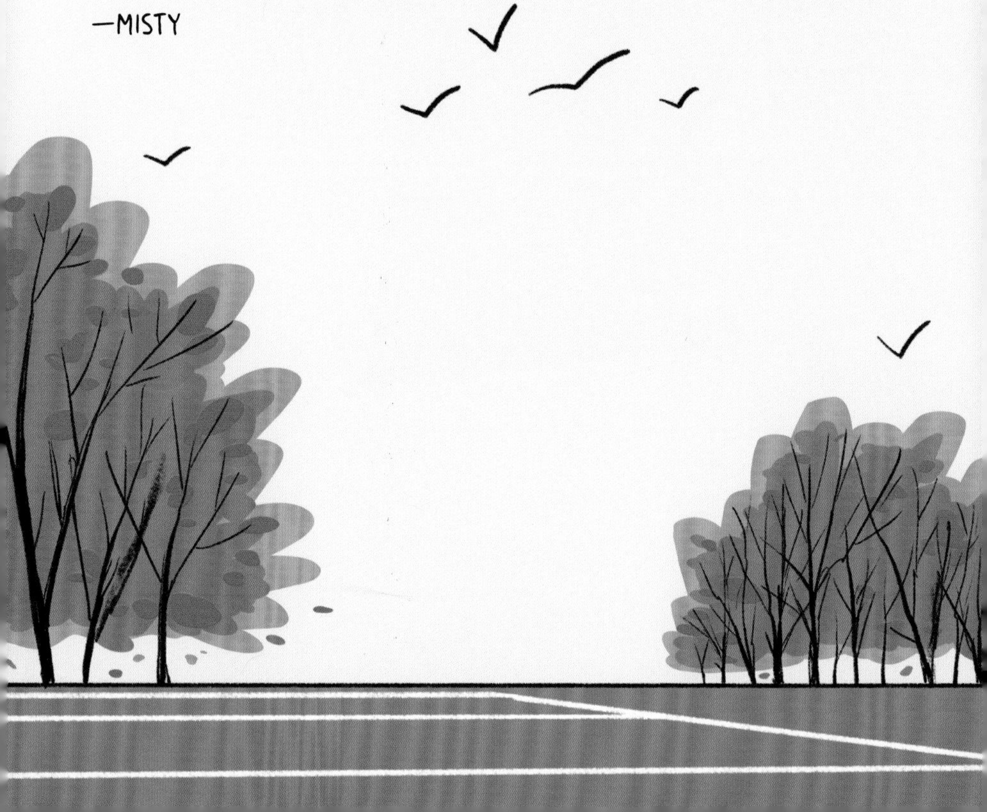

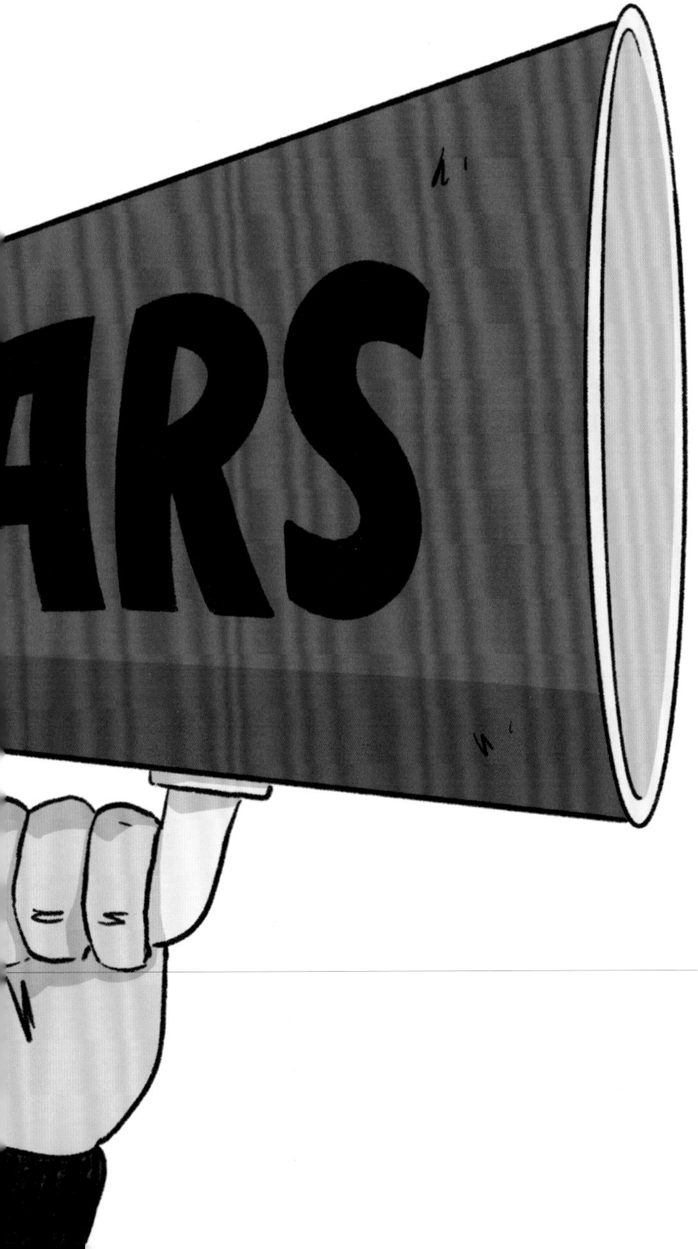
ARS

Thank you to editor extraordinaire, Donna Bray, for your confidence and insight. Daniel Lazar for all your hard work and guidance along the way. Dana Fritts for your expertise. Mom and Dad, for all the support. The Wilson brothers and the Air Dave Sunday football league. Matt Stansberry and Chad Lewis, my creative partners in crime. Dustin Dolerhie and Kevin Beers for being there when I needed to escape the creative side for a moment. Anne Trubek, for your wisdom and friendship. Ken Visocky O'Grady, for your enthusiasm and understanding. Jerry Kalback, for helping me become the illustrator I am today. Misty, you never cease to amaze me. And it seems as if you haven't changed much since middle school Misty—jumping into whatever your heart desires. Whether it's hospitality management, nursing, teaching, raising kids, playing football, or writing books. You are a great example of someone who proves that anything is possible if you put your mind to it. Thank you for sharing your journey with me.

—DAVID